D1375711

John Kampfner joined the BBC as political correspondent in 1998, having been chief political correspondent of the *Financial Times* for the previous three years. Before that he was a renowned foreign reporter for the *Daily Telegraph*, where as Berlin and Eastern Europe correspondent and bureau chief in Moscow he reported on the fall of the Berlin Wall, the collapse of Communism and the Soviet coup of 1991. He is the author of the acclaimed *Inside Yeltsin's Russia – Corruption, Conflict, Capitalism*. John Kampfner lives in Bloomsbury, London, with his wife and two daughters.

Robin Cook

JOHN KAMPFNER

PHŒNIX

A Phoenix Paperback
First published in Great Britain by Victor Gollancz in 1998
This paperback edition published in 1999 by Phoenix,
an imprint of Orion Books Ltd,
Orion House, 5 Upper St Martin's Lane,
London WC2H 9EA

A CIP catalogue record for this book is available from the British Library.

ISBN: 0 75380 847 1

Picture Credits
All pictures are reproduced courtesy of Robin Cook except:
Final-year class at Royal High: courtesy of Joan McLean
With Margaret, Peter and Christopher, and in the constituency (both pictures):
Scotsman Publ. Ltd, Edinburgh
At Kelso: Stuart Paterson/*Glasgow Herald*
With John McCririck, and with Gaynor at Mansion House: Sean Dempsey/PA
Launching a new era in foreign policy: Fiona Hanson/PA
With Madeleine Albright: Gill Allen/*The Times*/PA
At the Golden Temple of Amritsar: John Stillwell/PA
At the Patterson Arran Bakery: Mirror Syndication International
At Har Homa: Nati Harnik/Associated Press
On 2 May 1997: Rebecca Naden/PA

Typeset by Production Line, Minster Lovell, Oxford
Printed and bound in Great Britain by
The Guernsey Press Co. Ltd, Guernsey C.I.

Contents

To Lucy, Alex and Constance

Preface

Shortly before the 1997 general election I decided to write a book about the role of the radical left in the Labour party under Tony Blair, approached through its most controversial proponent, Robin Cook. My subject agreed to cooperate, but wanted it known from the outset that this was not to be an authorized biography. Events certainly took their course, but I have tried to remain true to my original intention. This is not, and never was, intended as a hagiography, or a justification of any particular action or course of events. It plays to the agenda of neither supporters nor detractors.

In nearly a year of research, and several hundred interviews, I have received assistance from an extraordinary range of Cabinet members, backbenchers, peers, political advisers, civil servants, journalists and contemporaries of Robin Cook. My thanks go to all of them. I do not intend to name any of the politicians who have given me their time, because much of that cooperation was on the basis of non-attribution. Those who were happy to be identified are named in the course of the narrative.

Thanks go first to Robin Cook himself, who has provided time in his busy schedule to meet me on several occasions to field my questions. Many officials in the Foreign Office and the constituency have been helpful in setting up meetings, answering factual questions and providing copies of speeches and other public documents. Among them are David Mathieson, Andrew Hood, David Clark, Jim Devine, Peter Hastie, Nigel Sheinwald and Lynn Rossiter.

I am also grateful to, among others, Gordon Best, John Brown, Bill Campbell, Duncan Campbell, the other Duncan Campbell, Christopher Cook, Peter Cook, George Dewar, Henry Drucker, Keith Geddes, Richard

Hogg, Mary Kaldor, John Kay, Gavin Kennedy, Brian Lang, John McCririck, Iain McLean, Harry Reid, Sandy Ross, Mary Southcott, Eddie Spiers, Nigel Stanley, John Whitworth and Alf Young.

The Royal High School in Edinburgh provided me with much useful material, thanks to its acting rector Dr John Murray. The *Scotsman* and the *New Statesman* gave me access to their libraries. Thanks also to David Scott and Lesley Dell for putting me up in Edinburgh. Among many journalists who have helped are Andrew Adonis, Robbie Dinwoodie, Peter Jones, John Lloyd, Catherine McLeod, John Penman, Philip Webster, Michael White and Ruth Wishart. At the *FT* I am most grateful to Andrew Gowers, Richard Lambert, Julia Cuthbertson, Robert Peston, Philip Stephens, Nick Timmins, David Wighton, George Parker and Liam Halligan. I am grateful to Ric Bailey and others at the BBC for giving me time to complete the book. Thanks to Leda Pitsillidou for transcribing interviews, and to Gillian Bromley for copy-editing.

Special thanks go to Steve Richards of the *New Statesman* and Ewen Macaskill of the *Guardian* for reading drafts of the book. Last, but by no means least, come Sean Magee, my editor at Victor Gollancz, and everyone at the Cassell Group for their help and encouragement for this, and for my previous book.

John Kampfner

Introduction

The opportunity was tailor-made. From the moment he set foot in the cavernous first-floor office, joining an illustrious line of Foreign Secretaries, Robin Cook had the world before him. In his first year in the job, Britain would be taking over the presidency of the European Union, presiding over the eight most powerful industrialized nations and hosting a Commonwealth summit. As a permanent member of the UN Security Council, Britain would have pivotal roles in all the world's trouble spots. Conflict continued in the former Yugoslavia; tension was growing on the Indian subcontinent; the search for peace in the Middle East was proving more arduous than ever. Cook would be at the heart of international diplomacy in a new government under Tony Blair which promised much and of which much was expected.

Foreign affairs was not the portfolio Cook had originally wanted. He was there largely at the insistence of Gordon Brown, who, resenting Cook's self-portrayal as leader of the intellectual left in the Labour leadership, had demanded that he be removed from any position of influence in domestic policy. So Cook set about putting his imprint on the Foreign Office, a department intrinsically hostile to change. In his mission statement issued shortly after taking over, he pronounced that things would be done differently. Ethics, he said, would play a greater role.

Nobody, not even Cook's most ardent enemies – and there were plenty of them – believed he would get into so much trouble, so quickly. At the time of the general election he was seen as Brown's main rival. After a year's vilification in the media, some in Blair's entourage were wondering whether he ought to be dropped. The apparent fall from grace was astounding for a man whose judgement had not previously been publicly questioned.

He was hoping for a quieter time in his second year, but that too was not to happen. On the personal front, he had to endure weeks of vilification following publication of the memoirs of his former wife, Margaret. Her accusations of serial adultery and alcoholism left both of them in the mire. He tried to retrench, but he and his team seemed unable to keep out of trouble. For months he was dogged by accusations of bungling and deception in the Sandline affair – in which arms were sold illegally to Sierra Leone. And just when it looked as if he would be able to ride out criticism from a parliamentary committee looking into the saga, his office was forced to admit that a copy of the report had been leaked to it by a pliant Labour MP.

This book traces the rise of Robin Cook – son of a schoolteacher, assiduous pupil, ambitious young politician – to become one of the great dispatch box orators of the modern generation. He humiliated the Conservative government over health cuts in the late 1980s and over illegal arms sales in the mid-1990s; but the more successful he became, the more he was resented by powerful cliques in the Labour party.

By the time he took over the Foreign Office, Cook had assembled an unenviable array of opponents. Members of the same government; Tories humiliated by his forensic skills in the Commons; figures in the media and the security services, seeking revenge for campaigns he had led in the 1970s and 1980s to make them more accountable – all these were soon to be joined by a small but influential set of civil servants resentful of his manner and his desire for change. Initially he kept them at bay, but the very public break-up of his marriage undermined his defences. He had always believed that the private lives of politicians should not be a matter of public discussion. He knew they were, but for years had tried to deny that reality. His public relations went from bad to worse. He toyed with the idea of trying his hand in Scotland, but was prevented from doing so. And yet, on the international stage he won wide respect. His relations with Madeleine Albright, US Secretary of State, and with most of his European counterparts were extremely good. Wherever he went, Blair would be asked by world leaders to pass on their gratitude for Cook's adept handling of a particular round of negotiations. Back home, however, nobody wanted to know. Cook's friends were convinced he was the object of a vendetta.

But for all the talk that he would be one of the first out, he was still there – whereas two of those who had helped to turn the screws against him – Peter Mandelson and Charlie Whelan (Gordon Brown's spin doctor) – had been forced to resign. By the start of 1999 Cook was hoping that he could put the in-fighting and the personal setbacks behind him, and concentrate on serious policy. Air strikes against Iraq had provided the first real foreign policy crisis. But nothing would match the tragedy that was about to unfold in Kosovo.

I

Dickens Made Simple

The smell of burning coal hung over the valley. He still remembers it – the smoke from the hearths of miners' homes. This was Bellshill, a coal and steel town in Lanarkshire, just to the east of Glasgow, in 1946: on 28 February that year Robert Finlayson Cook was born.

He spent his first years with his mother Christina, and her mother-in-law Bella, at 28 Beechwood Gardens, a semi-detached, pebbledashed bungalow provided by the council. Rationing was in full force. Those winters the snow never seemed to stop falling, the air was silent and the nights were interminably long. But it was a happy home. Cook remembers the narrow garden, which seemed vast to him at the time. His grandfather kept vegetables in the back and pansies in the front. His father, Peter, had found his first proper job, as a science teacher in Aberdeen, but he could not afford to rent a place large enough for all of them. So he lived in digs and would travel down whenever he could. Peter was the eldest of four sons of a miner who had been blacklisted for his part in the General Strike. He was the first in the family to gain a formal education, proud of his achievement and determined to give the same opportunity to his only son. It was an impeccably Old Labour start.

The family tree was far from conventional. Peter Cook had met Christina Lynch on a blind date just before war broke out. One of his friends said he was going to the pictures with a girl, who was bringing a girl friend, and persuaded Peter to make up a foursome. Being an impecunious student, he had to borrow one and ninepence off his father. He said it was the best investment he had ever made. In Christina's middle-class circle there was some scoffing at her choice of a miner's son; but her own family history had seen far greater disparities ignored. Cook's great-great-grandfather on his mother's side, a groom in the house of a Highland laird, ran off with the landowner's daughter, breaking all the conventions of class. The fugitive couple lived in hiding in Lanarkshire, where they changed their name to Lynch. They promised their two sons they would tell them what the real family name was; but, said the boys' father, 'It's of no use to you. Lynch has done for forty years and so it will for the next forty.' This was one of the more original ways of acquiring blue aristocratic blood. Cook's great-grandfather became a pipe major in the Argyll and Sutherland Regiment and spent seventeen years in India at the end of the nineteenth century, during which time he played in front of the Maharajah of Nepal, the man whose portrait adorned the wall of a succession of Foreign Secretaries – including, initially at least, Cook.

Peter and Christina married in 1941. Peter had gained a degree in chemistry in 1939, and took up his first permanent appointment as a teacher on 1 September that year, two days before war broke out. It lasted two months; then he was sent to ICI to make bombs at a vast ammunition factory on the Ayrshire coast. His main contribution to the war effort was to help cut down the fuse time of the British incendiary bomb. He and his team reduced it from 32 seconds to 19 – a vital improvement, because the 32-second fuse was giving the Germans time to stamp out Allied attacks. At the end of the war ICI asked him to pursue a career with the company, but he declined. He would have been much better-paid if he had stayed on, but he wanted to go back to education which had liberated him from a future down the pit.

Christina, a supervisor at the same factory, had first-hand experience of the dangers of munitions work. The managers had great difficulty persuading women not to take their rings into work, and one of the women, wanting to show her engagement ring to her friends, had smuggled it into the factory by hiding it under her tongue. Once inside, she placed it on the bench. Her job involved using hammers and cordite: she hit the ring and a terrible explosion occurred in which half a dozen women were killed.

Robin and his mother eventually moved up to Aberdeen when he was nearly four years old. His first memory was of disappearing down the street after losing his bearings. For the next few years they rented a couple of rooms from a doctor, the young child sleeping in a small bed next to his parents. By the mid-1950s Peter had earned enough to pay £2,700 for a semi-detached house in Rubislaw, a solid middle-class area of Aberdeen. What Robin remembers most vividly about the house is the cream distemper paint on the walls, which he hated; but he was happy at school and at home.

The small family was close-knit and inward-looking. They kept themselves to themselves; social life was seen as getting in the way of hard work. Peter was set on establishing himself as a good teacher, and his son looked up to him. As an only child, Robin spent a lot of time on his own. He read avidly, and by the time he was eleven he had devoured all of Dickens. He never thought twice about not having brothers or sisters.

'When you're an only child you're not thinking: "God, I'm an only child." It seems to be the natural state of existence. It's part of education to discover later that other families aren't made the same way as you. It is true that I'm perhaps unusually introverted for my profession and that probably reflects the fact that I did spend an awful lot of my time by myself. But I'm not asking for sympathy. I was very happy,' says Cook of those years. 'I had an excellent relationship with my parents and actually think that quite often only children do have better relations with their parents because they are thrown together much more. They gave me a good disciplined upbringing, but they weren't authoritarian. I wasn't spoilt, they brought me up with a very strong sense of duty, which had been drummed into me. I always felt totally secure in my childhood.'

He never lacked for anything, but luxuries were rare. Holidays were invariably taken in Scotland, in guesthouses – some fairly bleak and windswept – by the sea. Once, though, they went to London. Robin's parents left him on his own in Hamleys for the morning to rummage around the cornucopia of games and toys. When his mother came back and asked for him, the salesman replied: 'Is that the little lad who speaks with a Scots accent and asks the price of everything?'

Robin Cook had just turned seven when his first recorded written words were committed to paper at the primary school of Aberdeen Grammar. It was 5 March 1953, and his class had been given jotters to write down the news for the day. Robin's entry said: 'Today Joseph Stalin died. All the people of Russia will be very sad.' Alongside the words was a drawing of two men carrying a stretcher with Stalin on it. Cook early developed a taste for newspapers and current affairs, and made his first speech at the primary school debating society at the age of eleven. His first forays into the world of drama came at the same time, but he and other boys in his year resented being given female parts because their voices had not broken. It was at primary school, too, that his friends gave him the diminutive 'Robin': he liked it, and it stuck.

Leaving Aberdeen at the age of fourteen was a terrible wrench. Peter Cook had been appointed head of science at the Royal High, one of Edinburgh's most prestigious boys' schools. It was a good job, but Robin made it clear he did not want to go. 'I'm afraid I was a real pain to my father at that time because I was utterly miserable that he'd got promoted and we had to leave,' Cook recalls.

In those days the Royal High stood imperiously on Calton Hill, across from the castle, looking down towards the centre of the city and across to Arthur's Seat. It was an establishment proud of its traditions. Founded as the

Abbey of Holyrood in 1128 by King David I, it became a seat of learning, austere but with the odd touch of liberalism. It was now one of four schools run by Edinburgh Corporation that charged nominal fees. Entry was strictly by selection on academic criteria, so while its ethos was determinedly middle-class, some boys from poor families also got in. Its alumni include Sir Walter Scott, Alexander Graham Bell, Robert Adam and three former Chancellors of the Exchequer – Lords Brougham, Erskine and Wedderburn. At the other end of the scale, the school also produced in the mid-eighteenth century William 'Deacon' Brodie, the gambler and robber eventually hanged on gallows he had himself designed for the city of Edinburgh, and Dr Robert Knox, the surgeon who funded the 'bodysnatchers' Burke and Hare in the 1820s, although Knox himself was eventually exonerated of criminal involvement. Cook apart, the school's most famous recent former pupil is the comedian Ronnie Corbett. The rivalry among Edinburgh schools was intense. Edinburgh High disparaged the posher and more England-oriented boarding schools such as Fettes (where Tony Blair studied) and George Watson's (where Malcolm Rifkind was educated), and another private school, George Heriot's. The disdain was apparently mutual.

Cook entered the Royal High in the third year and instantly joined the top stream, 3X. Most of the other boys had been together since the age of five. Arriving at the same time as his father did not make it easy for him to assimilate, but bullying was rare and he soon settled in. Brian Lang, now chief executive of the British Library, became Cook's first pal. 'I made a point of befriending him in the first week. I felt sorry for him. We spent time together in breaks. Robin was charming when he made the effort.' Soon everyone was calling him by his nickname, although the school insisted on calling him Robert in official ceremonies and end-of-term reports. Cook cannot remember when the new name was conferred, or why he stuck with it. It just happened. Iain McLean, a friend known as 'the prof', says they all had nerdish tendencies. 'It was a pool of very smug people he was coming into. This was a full-time narrow-minded culture. There was no sex, no drugs, and precious little rock and roll.' It was also a particularly ambitious group of teenage boys. They all worked hard, and fed off each other's achievements. Cook was no slouch, but McLean was the brightest of the bunch. In his final year he was awarded the 'dux', which goes to the pupil with the highest grades; he was also head boy. He is now a professor of politics at Oxford. McLean's mother, Joan, remembers how Cook, a slightly built boy with neat red hair, would turn up at their home to seek Iain's help about homework. His attempts to disguise his shyness would sometimes grate. 'He used to knock on the door and mutter with a grunt – "Iain in?" He struck me as having few social graces, rarely said hello or goodbye, but for all that his heart seemed in the right place.'

Cook admits that, like most of his contemporaries, he was a bit of a swot. 'I wasn't unpopular, I had lots of friends and they were very happy times. But I was possibly rather singlemindedly intellectual in my image and pursuits.' With his parents living on the outskirts of town, he rarely took his friends home. As in Aberdeen, the Cooks did not mix much – even though Edinburgh had much more to offer. The household remained self-contained. Peter was methodical in helping his son in the evenings. Young Robin felt he had a certain standard to live up to. 'He was very anxious that I should do well, and so I always completed my homework,' says Cook now – with a hint of regret: 'I think if I've got a weakness in my working method, it is precisely that I will always do the homework thoroughly, however long it takes, which means that I find it, even after all these years, very difficult to sign something without having read it.'

Peter Cook stayed at the Royal High only three years, but he left his imprint. He shook up the science department, introducing more modern teaching methods. What was his secret? According to the school's annual report: 'First of all wide interests – literature, wine, pictures, radio and science. And in no sense were his interests those of a dilettante, even in science. Secondly, there was his unfailing interest in people; his pupils responded quickly to his teaching, realising his concern for their welfare and sympathy for their difficulties. And lastly, there is his wit, humour and power of repartee.'[1]

Out of school, Robin and his friends would dress fogeyishly: Edinburgh was many months behind the south in the fashion stakes. But they were not completely cut off from the new trends taking London, Liverpool and other British cities by storm. Like the other boys, Cook bought the Everly Brothers' single 'Cathy's Clown', the Christmas number one in 1960. Cook wanted to impress his new classmates with his acquisition; but he was banned by his father from playing it at home because, no sooner had he got back, hotfoot from the record shop, than he was told his aunt Cathy had died. The Royal High was traditional, but it was also quite liberal for its time. If sixth-formers were caught in the pub (they would wear long raincoats to hide their uniforms), they would be shooed away; punishment would usually be light. Most of the time, the boys would go to one of the new-style cafés that were springing up and drink an early Scottish version of cappuccino. They would all do charity work; Robin's year was seen as particularly vibrant and innovative, but occasionally their entrepreneurial spirit got the better of them. Cook recalls one school collection for Oxfam. 'The other kids set to selling crisps and cakes at break, doing odd jobs and selling raffle tickets. Our class decided we would go big, we looked at the market and realized the market wanted a disco. So we threw a spectacularly successful disco in the church hall, the whole of the High School, George Watson's

ladies, and we made four times the money. To our chagrin we were disqualified on the grounds that we hadn't really entered into the spirit of the thing.'

Culturally, there were two groups at the school: the aesthetes and the
athletes. Rugby was particularly strong, with the first team winning the
Scottish championships and spawning a future captain of the national side,
Colin Telfer. Brian Lang was the boy to be seen with at parties: a good rugby
player and a good scholar. Cook had little time for sport, although he did
make it to the 5th XV at rugby (there were only five competitive teams),
playing as prop forward. The team's best run was three weeks unbeaten –
made up of two draws and one postponement.

For the aesthetes, the kudos was to be had in one place alone – the literary
and debating society. Not quite as prestigious, but still fashionable, was the
drama society. Cook joined both, and made his way to the top of both. He
was, he says, 'all right as a straight actor. I've never been good as a mimic.'
He is most proud of a production of Jean Anouilh's *Antigone* in his fifth year,
in which the late Ian Charleson played the leading role. But his record was
mixed. Brian Lang remembers a Cook production of *The Fireraisers* by Max
Frisch: 'Everything that could go wrong did; people forgot their lines and
the record with the sound effects was warped.' Under their English literature teacher Hector MacIver, the boys were allowed to study contemporary
authors, such as Anouilh and Samuel Beckett, as well as the classics, and
would go to the Gateway theatre in Leith Walk on Saturday afternoons to
see how it should really be done. One of the more memorable such
occasions was a performance of *Waiting for Godot*, which was considered a
bit risqué at the time. Dylan Thomas, too, was particularly popular at
school, but for Cook one author takes pride of place: 'During that time I
read quite a lot of George Bernard Shaw and was highly influenced by his
thinking and style,' he says, and he has tried to incorporate some of Shaw's
mockery and urbane irony into his own parliamentary speeches.

Plays were performed in the round in the school assembly hall, an impressive amphitheatre with a central well, a First World War stained glass
window at one end and at the other a huge oak door opening majestically on
to the city. Debates were also held there, on Wednesday afternoons for the
school on its own, and on Friday evenings with other schools from the city.
For many of the boys, those Fridays were the only time they, as a school, had
any contact with girls, and even then each school had to sit separately in neat
rows. Four years after Cook left, the school moved to a purpose-built site in
the suburb of Barnton. It took the door with it, but the debates would not be
the same again. The original school building was for several years seen as
the prospective home of a future Scottish parliament, with the assembly
hall as its chamber; but that project fell into abeyance after the 1979 referendum, and it remained largely unoccupied.

Cook became president of debates in his final year, 1963–4. The battle for the top job was bitter, giving him the first taste of the personal rivalries that were to affect his later life in politics. Also vying for the position was John Whitworth, a close friend who became a poet – a somewhat eccentric one. 'I was always seen as a future head of debates until Cook came along,' says Whitworth. 'He was, and is as an MP, the best debater I have heard. So I had to make do with heading the drama society.' Cook won, according to Whitworth and others, by persuading first-years with little idea of what was going on to vote for him. 'That kind of ballot rigging went on all the time in our type of Scottish school,' says Whitworth. 'Everything was fair in love and war.'

Whitworth took the consolation prize, head of the dramatic society – but it took him some time to forgive Cook. A few years later they would share a flat, and the jealousies of old were laid to rest for a time. Then, more than a decade on, Whitworth's feelings of resentment were rekindled when he suddenly recognized a voice on Radio Four. This was 1981. The poem was entitled 'Scribble Scribble':

> Painting the house a month ago,
> And listening to the radio –
> The World at One, a dreadful play
> And Brian Johnston Down Your Way,
> I heard a studio debate
> On something rotten in the state,
> Increased police brutality,
> Buggers (both kinds) in Russian fee,
> Another England batting farce,
> The country at a pretty pass,
> When, jargoning across the air . . .
> I cried, 'That voice. It's him.' 'It's who?'
> Doreen asked. (She was painting too.)
> 'It's him. The Honourable Member.
> At school they took bets, I remember,
> Which was the pushier little snot
> Of us two.' 'And you've changed a lot?'
> Murmured Doreen.
> Of course he just
> Revealed his eloquence and thrust
> While still a bare-kneed treble, whence
> He soon eclipsed my eminence,
> Junior Assistant Secretary
> To the school Debating Society,

And fastest rising cleverdick,
Which, naturally, got on my wick.
(It still does, rather) . . . [2]

Another decade on, and the poem was reproduced by the *Mail on Sunday*, much to Whitworth's embarrassment. Eighteen months after that it was reprinted again in the *Independent on Sunday*, to which Whitworth complained, making clear the poem was meant primarily as a 'description of my vile and spotty self'. He wrote: 'What I should have celebrated was young Robin's leading role in the great boiled fish riot when the Red Flag was raised above the science block and the disgusting comestible removed for ever from the school's lunch menu.' (Neither Cook nor his friends can recall such a rebellion, but Whitworth insists it took place.) Whitworth wrote to Cook to say he had intended no offence by the poem. Cook replied, saying he had been perfectly relaxed about it, and invited him for lunch at the Commons. 'The food here is very definitely pre-nouvelle, but then it needs to be in keeping with the Edwardian ambience.' The style of his note was all too reminiscent of the Royal High.

Cook's predecessor as head of debates was Richard Hogg, now professor of English at Manchester University, and a good friend of Cook's in their undergraduate days; his successor was John Kay, today director of the Wafic Said Business School in Oxford. The society, says Kay, produced an overpoweringly self-confident type of debater, caustic, almost clinical in manner. The boys faced their biggest challenge on 'sealed hat nights', when subjects were pulled from a hat, and the two speakers on each side were given a minute to marshal their arguments. 'People would be forced to take positions for the sake of them,' says Kay. 'The system bred a certain character – acerbic wit and detached commentary. There was a particular brand of Edinburgh rationalism that was considerably sharper than anything I heard later at the Oxford Union or anywhere else.' Cook won several prizes. The required delivery, Hogg says, would border on the pompous. Cook's entry in the school's annual report, *Schola Regia*, for July 1964 was typical of its time: 'The most striking feature of this year's society has been a much increased unity within the society itself and the total lack of deeply-felt odium which would have put paid to any grandiose plans for a vigorous session of activities,' he wrote. 'Since a need exists for this society, and I believe there also exists a tacit will for it, all that can be said is that the future lies with every responsible member who must strive to fulfil his duty and privilege.'

With debating activity came a growing passion for politics. Cook is fond of telling the story of how he and his friends would stroll down the hill to Princes Street, Edinburgh's main shopping thoroughfare, to the John Menzies newsagent. 'They would all buy *New Musical Express*, I would buy the *New Statesman*. English people have always had a very strong anti-intellectual streak to their make-up, which is much more suppressed in Scotland where education has always been an acceptable ladder. There's always been a much greater respect for learning in Scotland. This meant that my streak was not held against me by my peers.' He preferred being just a little apart from the group.

The era of John Freeman's editorship of the *New Statesman*, and Cook's final terms at school, 1964, was a time of vibrant debate and optimism among the left. Harold Macmillan had gone in the wake of the Profumo affair; Harold Wilson, harbinger of a more radical Labour party, had taken over as leader of the opposition following the death of Hugh Gaitskell; a new form of direct action had begun with the Aldermaston marches; and Alec Douglas-Home's Conservative administration was entering its final months, with Labour forecast to return to power after thirteen years in the cold. Almost everyone in Cook's sixth form was on the left, far to the left of Wilson. Cook's own political hero was Aneurin Bevan, the great thinker and radical of the Attlee government, whose tortured attempts late in his career to reconcile idealism with the more mundane realities of day-to-day politics intrigued Cook.

The Royal High would from time to time hold mock elections, in which the best debaters would square up against each other as opposing candidates. Iain McLean recalls one contest in early 1964 in which he stood as the Communist contender and which, he said, convinced him that Cook was on his way to greater things. 'Robin was the Labour candidate. He not only marshalled his arguments, but he employed modern market methods, handing out little tags to all the boys. He won over the floating voters and cruised to victory. He did not appreciate anyone standing in his way, and was prickly when criticized. But he was like the Pied Piper then – he had swarms of boys running after him. He had dozens of camp followers. It showed me how driven he was.' Charisma was mixed with ruthlessness. 'He was very objective-oriented, almost cold in his pursuit of objectives. I admired that. He always wore two badges on his blazer, a black and white anti-apartheid one, and a CND one. He would concentrate on these causes. He had a very instrumentalist approach to his politics, very unemotional.'

The fusty side of school grated with Cook, and he was quick to pass judgement on his teachers. One in particular, George 'Jock' Dewar, his classics master, he dubbed a 'typical bourgeois'. Dewar, now retired, admits his tastes were old-fashioned. He describes Cook as 'not outstanding, but a good scholar', and has not forgotten that set of boys. 'There was a very high esprit de corps in that class. It still stands out after all these years. Cook enjoyed himself in the limelight. He did enjoy being self-important.' Dewar remembers Cook being more left-wing than most pupils, predicting during the 1964 US presidential election that if Barry Goldwater, the Republican candidate, came to power 'there will be World War Three'. Whitworth says Cook liked to call himself a Christian Marxist. 'What impressed me was that he would take principled positions and stick to them. He never tried to suck up to anybody.'

Cook passed his highers easily enough in 1963 – in English, Maths, Latin, Greek, physics, chemistry, history and applied maths. Modern languages were not pushed at the school, something he would regret in later years. The exams were taken in the boys' penultimate year, giving them a virtually free last nine months at school to apply for bursaries for university. Cook and all his friends were chosen as prefects. 'We swanned around, having a good time,' recalls Whitworth. Prefects were allowed to administer corporal punishment on the smaller boys, using gym shoes, but Whitworth says Cook set himself apart by taking a stand against it. Prize-giving on the final day of the last term was a spectacular event. The Provost of Edinburgh would make the first of several speeches, followed by the singing of the school song and the national anthem. As the singing drew to a close, the Memorial Door would open, excruciatingly slowly, to the accompaniment of a piper, and the boys who were leaving would file out one by one, shaking the hand of the headmaster as they ventured out into the world. Even the toughest would have tears in their eyes.

The boys continued to keep in touch long after they left. Cook took part in annual class reunions until he moved down to London a decade later. Most of them stayed together at university, although two – McLean, the head boy, and Whitworth, the debating chief manqué – went to Oxford. Cook would have liked to have gone with them, but the teachers did not encourage a move to English universities and his parents were also reluctant for him to leave Edinburgh. 'I had wanted to sit for Oxford and my father persuaded me that my mother would want me to stay at home, so I – perhaps ungraciously – agreed I'd stay at home,' he says. Then, in his final year, after the university places were settled, Peter Cook told his son that he had been promoted – to headmaster of the Kirkcudbright Academy, a good school in Galloway, near Dumfries. This inevitably meant a move from Edinburgh. 'You can imagine the immense power of my father in this position at this stage of life. I had made a sacrifice and now they were moving away from me. So I thoroughly enjoyed that period. He had to sell his house in Edinburgh and was given a tied house. He had a lot of money from the proceeds which he wanted to invest, so he bought this flat in Goldenacre, in the centre of town, just for my use.'

And so, in autumn 1964, Cook joined the ranks of Edinburgh university freshers, with four years ahead as a student of English literature.

2

Labour over God

Why English? He was good at it, devoured books and admired writers for their mastery of language. 'The second reason,' he recalls, 'is that at that point I was going to enter the church as a minister and in those days it was traditional to take an arts degree before proceeding to Divinity.'

While he was at primary school, Cook's parents took him to Craigiebutler church in Aberdeen every Sunday. He won a prize for the recitation of the shorter catechism – Question: 'What is the chief aim of man?' Answer: 'The chief aim of man is to glorify God.' His reward was to be allowed to plant nasturtiums all the way round the church on a wet and windy Sunday afternoon. 'A very presbyterian sense of reward that was.' The family dutifully continued the tradition at their local church in Edinburgh. Christina and Peter Cook 'were not mystical, they were not into spiritualism, but they were committed and diligent church-attenders,' Cook recalls. The Royal High held morning service, but was not particularly religious. The Christianity in which Cook was brought up was typical of Protestant Scotland at the time: ascetic, shorn of ritual but with a deeply embedded sense of community. His later loss of faith was neither sudden nor dramatic.

This is how he remembers it: 'There was no sort of Damascene non-conversion. It was just that doubts, metaphysical doubts grew and threw off abiding certainties. Don't forget that you are also dealing with somebody who is highly rationalist, who took physics, chemistry and mathematics as highers, and if I were locating myself in any kind of European tradition it would be very much in the tradition of the Edinburgh Enlightenment period of rationalism. I'm not by constitution a mystical or spiritual person and the world can be very satisfactorily explained without reference to Genesis. In the course of my first year I came to the view that there was no

God, and since then have been a signed up and conforming atheist. It was, of course, the swinging sixties and I think what finally put me off seeking to become a minister was that one or two people around were prepared to say: "Well of course these days not believing in God is not in itself an insuperable obstacle." What then happened psychologically inside me is that my commitment to the Church of Scotland as a minister of religion transferred itself into the Labour party and socialism.'

For any arts graduate in Scotland at the time, the choice was 'to become a doctor, church minister or lawyer', says Brian Lang, his old school friend. 'Robin believed in a well-organized Church of Scotland God who promoted social positions.' It was perhaps no coincidence that John Smith's father, like Cook's, was a teacher, while Gordon Brown's was a minister. The professions of their forebears exerted a strong influence on these young Scots.

Cook retains a strong respect for the Church of Scotland, especially for its campaigning against poverty. He regards the approach of the Scottish church as more in touch with the concerns of ordinary people, especially the downtrodden, than its English equivalent. On a political, intellectual level he retains a close link. Just before Christmas 1997 he invited representatives of the Council of Churches to his office. 'I'm not an evangelical atheist. In some senses I mildly envy those who've retained their faith and can still drop back quite easily into talking to them on level terms.'

Having lost his religious faith, a move into full-time politics seemed the most appropriate – indeed, the obvious – move for someone whose strongest skill was oratory and who saw his life's mission as to do whatever he could, on whatever scale, to tackle inequalities in wealth. Until that point Cook's politics was confined largely to intellectual debate; he had yet to put his skills and convictions into practice.

Shortly after freshers' week, Wilson scored a narrow victory over Douglas-Home in the 1964 general election and George Brown launched his national economic plan, with the ringing declaration: 'Brothers, we are on our way.' Cook had naturally joined the university Labour club and passed from the school debating club to the Union. But already he wanted to branch out beyond student politics and helped with leafleting during the national election campaign. He became friends and co-conspirators with a young activist, Martin O'Neill, whom he had met during a school debate in 1962 when O'Neill was opposing and Cook seconding the opposition to a motion stating that, as Macmillan appeared to think, the country had never had it so good. They remained in touch while O'Neill went to Edinburgh's other university, Heriot-Watt.

Their first taste of the less refined side of politics came in the 1966 general election. O'Neill and Cook turned up at the local Labour headquarters offering their services. The agent told them to go round to meetings held by the Tory candidate and disrupt them. The sitting member for Edinburgh North was not any old candidate but Walter Francis John Montagu Douglas Scott, also known as the Earl of Dalkeith (the title did not prevent him from going into the Commons). He first won the seat in a by-election in 1960, and to the young Labour Turks epitomized much that was complacent and unjust about politics in the city. These two 'disreputable-looking youths' had, according to Cook, 'a wonderful election', heckling from the back of the hall and asking difficult questions. The Earl was not one for thinking too hard about abstruse points of detail. At these meetings he carried around his answers on a set of index cards which he would glance at before responding to questioners. The key to success for the intruders was to think of issues on which there was no guidance hidden in the shoebox in front of him.

'It worked brilliantly for two weeks until the Earl's wife, the Countess of Dalkeith – who had been a celebrated model at the time, very beautiful, very poised – managed to stop us scampering for the door,' Cook recalls. 'She peeled her glove off, stretched out her hand, and said how terribly exciting it was to see such young people interested in politics. She did hope that when her sons grew up they would go to everybody's meetings so they'd hear all points of view. Martin and I were so shame-faced that we didn't go back to any future meeting. In subsequent years I realized that the agent had actually been trying to get rid of Martin and me. The sting in the tail is that during the 1979 election I was sitting in my own committee rooms and two students fell in – one with hair down to the back of his waist, the other with a beer belly that sort of fell on to the desk. They said they were here to help, could they go canvassing? I said: "Actually I've got something you could do that would be more important than canvassing. It would be really helpful if you go round the SNP candidate's meetings and disrupt them."'

By the end of the campaign, Cook and O'Neill had well and truly fallen out with the Labour agent. They were gaining a bit of a reputation. O'Neill recalls getting 'hell' from him after he found them fly-posting around George Street. 'He said he was prepared to testify to the police that the material had been stolen from the Labour party.'

During his four years at university Cook rose effortlessly in the party to become chairman of the university Labour club. He also became co-chair of the Scottish Association of Labour Student Organizations set up by Gavin Kennedy, a student at Strathclyde. Kennedy went on to stand against Cook, as a candidate of the Scottish National Party, in the 1979 general election. He is now a professor at Edinburgh business school. The other co-chairman was George Robertson, who was studying at Dundee and became MP for Hamilton in a by-election in 1978.

Cook started going to national and Scottish Labour party conferences in his third year. That was real politics. For him and his contemporaries in Scotland, student politics was strangely divorced from the radicalism prevalent elsewhere in Britain and Europe. They read about and discussed Daniel Cohn-Bendit and the Paris riots, the murder of Martin Luther King and the shooting of Rudi Dutschke. But they did not protest. Even the activism of the London School of Economics seemed a world apart. Cook the undergraduate had the obligatory poster of Che Guevara in his room and sympathized with the anti-Vietnam War protesters, but neither he nor his friends would be seen tramping the streets. The economist John Kay was secretary of the Labour club in 1967: 'We couldn't imagine in those days having arguments over issues. We never had the depth of emotional involvement. It was all about sparring. We didn't go and hold placards; people would have thought that a bit grubby. We were more intellectual. We would discuss issues such as prison reform, or welfare, not foreign affairs. If we had a political hero it would have been someone like Tony Crosland rather than Che. John P. Mackintosh came to talk to us once. We all had enormous respect for him.' The students also had 'teach-ins' – like sit-ins, where they decided to debate a subject of national importance instead of going to lectures.

The drama crowd was the most fashionable, according to Duncan Campbell, a contemporary of Cook's; students involved in debating and politics were seen as a trifle nerdy. Evenings revolved around heavy drinking, but virtually no drugs. The city was several years behind London in the liberation stakes. The pill was available only to married women. Abortion was still illegal, but could be procured for fifty pounds – the most used back street doctor was called 'the drunken doctor' – and if you made a girl pregnant you were expected to 'arrange things' or marry her. This atmosphere had an effect on Cook, who would later regard liberalizing laws on sex, especially in Scotland, as a priority. Although he did not hang around with the drama crowd, he went frequently to the Traverse, a theatre run in a room of a tenement block off the High Street by Jim Haynes, a charismatic American. Haynes also started the Paperback Bookshop, the town's first left-wing arts bookshop, which sold *Private Eye*, which was seen as dangerously subversive. Cook was often to be found there, browsing through the latest pamphlets, magazines and books.

In the Christmas term of his second year Cook became arts editor of *Student*, the weekly university newspaper. The editor was Campbell, whom he would come across again a decade later running the news desk at *Time Out*. The offices were in a basement room in Buccleuch Place. Press night was Tuesday, when every week they would scramble the paper together by dawn, often making the deadline by a whisker. 'It was terribly seedy and full of ink on the floor, but somehow or other we got the paper out,' recalls Cook. To make some money on the side, particularly juicy stories would be sold on to the *Edinburgh Evening News*. Cook himself did quite a few pieces on the theatre. Richard Hogg, his old school and university friend, became a film critic. 'He sent me to see a Swedish film, *Dear John*, a sub-Bergmanesque effort. When I gave him my copy he told me to rewrite it in no uncertain terms.'

Cook began to grow a beard, and soon took to it. 'He looked much the same then as he does now,' says Hogg, who particularly remembers his narrow flowery ties and short white raincoat. 'We all thought we owned Edinburgh, going from pub to pub.' When the pubs shut at ten, the gang would go back to someone's house, cans of McEwan's in hand, to play cards – poker, rummy, whist, canasta or whatever they came up with. Hogg remembers several of these sessions taking place in Cook's parents' flat in Bangholm Terrace, Goldenacre, looking out on to George Heriot's sports ground. 'We got through large amounts of alcohol,' says Hogg. 'Robin didn't play as much as the others and didn't drink as much either, although he was always happy to help supply the booze and crisps. He had a more puritan streak and didn't like to gamble. Some of us would risk what for us at the time was a lot of money.' They were too level-headed to risk their academic futures, though: by 'honours', the third and fourth years, evenings would see Cook and his crowd less often in the pub and more often in the faculty library, where about twenty of them established a routine of having a coffee break around eight-thirty, then going back to their books until the library closed at ten. They would then drink more coffee in someone's digs or get carry-outs of beer.

As at the Royal High, the debating society of Edinburgh University was the focal point of Cook's life. The Union membership was all-male, but debate nights were open to all. Debates were terribly grand affairs, with men in black tie and sometimes gowns. They would be preceded by dinner at the Beehive restaurant in Grassmarket (the committee had a conspicuously large budget), and would usually be followed by a dance. Here members of the debates committee, the elite, would retire to their own room where a crate of beer would be waiting for them and their guests. The room was beyond the ticket barrier for the dance, adding to the cachet for the girls invited by committee members. Contemporaries remember Cook as a good dancer, although he is embarrassed to admit it. He was the leading Labour light on the debates committee, following in the footsteps of another student politician with a future, George Foulkes. The Tories had the svelte and aristocratic Lord James Douglas-Hamilton, the second son of the 14th Duke of Hamilton, just arrived as a postgraduate having been president of the Oxford Union. With him – younger and very much in his shadow – was

Malcolm Rifkind. The president of the committee was another Tory: Eddie Spiers, a politics and history student two years below Cook who became a close friend, notwithstanding their political differences. Spiers is now professor of strategic studies at Leeds University.

It was through the debates committee that Robin Cook first met Margaret Whitmore. At first glance they seemed an unlikely match. Whitmore, a medical student, was a sensible and cheery west country girl, already two years ahead of him: having arrived in 1963 from an English school with A-levels, which were more advanced than highers, she went straight into the second year. Her background was markedly different from Cook's. She had been born in South Africa, the daughter of Louis Arthur Whitmore, an RAF squadron leader who himself had been born in India, and Joyce Winterbottom. On being decommissioned from the services in 1953, Louis had gone to work as an aeronautical engineer in Somerset.

At Edinburgh, Margaret Whitmore quickly fell in with a crowd of girls from Kirkcaldy High, sharing digs with four of them. She joined the Nationalist club, which was very much in vogue: that she was English did not seem to bother her or them. She put together a health policy for them in her second year and helped the nationalists on the debates committee. She was impressed by the dinners with evening dress in the union hall. Margaret had heard about Cook well before they met, and when they did was instantly struck by his 'excellent company, brilliant wit and charm'. He was equally impressed, and within a fortnight of their beginning to go out together asked her to marry him; but Margaret urged him to hold off. They looked to outsiders like a charmed couple, but those who knew the pair had their doubts. 'Some of us were surprised when he took up with her,' recalls Hogg. 'We thought all medics were raving mindless Tories. For someone like Robin who took his politics so seriously, and who was so ardently anti-nationalist, it was all a bit strange.'

There were personal as well as political reasons for scepticism about the new romance. Cook had been going out with another student, Maureen Clarke: indeed, Mo, as she was known, was his first real love, and on the surface they seemed more compatible: she too was doing English; her father was also a teacher. But theirs was a volatile on–off relationship. When Margaret started to go out with Robin, she suspected he was still close to Mo. She recalls that her suspicions were heightened when one morning, having been told not to come round the night before because he had important work to do, she found two coffee mugs on the draining board. She confronted him, and he said he would give Mo up – which he did, in the summer of 1967; but she was extremely upset when he dropped her and persuaded him that they should get back together. His friends would say of that period that he was 'running two'. Eventually Margaret had had enough, and left him around the time of his finals. He took it badly, but they got together again soon after, and Mo left the scene. Margaret herself had been quite smitten by George Foulkes, who was president of the student representative council and was seen as quite a catch.

Whitmore lived with Cook in his flat much of the time, although they both led busy separate lives. He was increasingly engrossed in politics, and would have countless friends and acquaintances around the flat, discussing issues over copious amounts of whisky. They had both completed finals in 1968 and Margaret was embarking on her houseman's year. Kennedy and Whitworth stayed as lodgers during that year and remember that she had little time for these somewhat effete lounge lizards. 'She didn't like Robin's friends. She saw her role as keeping people away from him. She had a way of putting you in your place,' remembers Kennedy. He remembers her as being very protective, coaxing him into improving his diet, dress and tidiness. 'She looked apart from the rest of us. She was always well turned out in among all us would-be hippies.'

They married on 15 September 1969, after a roller-coaster courtship of three years. Margaret had two weeks' holiday before starting work at the Western General Hospital in Edinburgh. Their wedding was a close-knit affair, at St Alban's church in Westbury Park, Bristol, with a small reception in a hotel overlooking the gorge for around fifty family members and friends. Eddie Spiers was best man. Another Tory, Raymond Fraser, was usher. Few of the Edinburgh Labour crowd were invited by the Whitmores. The couple were seen off to Bristol station on their way to honeymoon in Innsbruck and Lake Maggiore. They had, it seemed, everything going for them.

3

Sanitation, Slums and Seats

Theory and practice collided early in 1969. To his chagrin, Cook had failed to gain a first in his finals the previous summer, even though he had won the class prize of the year, out of sixty students. His paper on eighteenth-century authors had let him down. Nevertheless, he was accepted as a postgraduate student and set about his Ph.D. At the same time he had become more deeply involved in city politics and broader community affairs: he had been appointed chairman of the Scottish branch of the Child Poverty Action Group and a member of the Scottish Advisory Council of Shelter.

These commitments sat uneasily with academia. In the day Cook worked on his doctoral thesis, provisionally entitled 'Serialization and the Victorian novel' – a study of the weekly or monthly magazine serializations that heavily influenced writers such as Dickens and are arguably the ancestors of late twentieth-century television soap operas. In the evenings he would campaign, visit slums – housing was becoming his main interest – and take part in Labour party meetings. Cook can pinpoint precisely the moment at which he decided to give up the life of a scholar. 'I was crossing the old quadrangle and I met a Canadian who was doing an M.Litt. beside me. Nice guy, very genuine, very into his literature and the perfect academic, and, bless him, he had had a breakthrough in that he'd discovered half a dozen articles published anonymously by Dickens, which he attributed to Dickens. His thesis was "Sanitation and the Victorian novel". There isn't actually much reference to sanitation in the Victorian novel. There's quite a bit of smallpox in *Bleak House*, and cemeteries. But he'd written half a dozen quite satisfying chapters on why sanitation does not appear more often in the Victorian novel. I met him coming the other way with the latest copy of *Victorian Studies* under his arm. It contained the last of his articles. All previous forewords had been attributed first to his professor and then to him. But on this occasion some benighted typographer had reversed it, so it was attributed in reverse order, giving the student pride of place. He was jubilant. I remember thinking then: if this is what it's about, you know, it's not for me. I can't achieve this degree of intensity about the ordering of names on a minor magazine about sanitation in the Victorian times.'

His first priority now was a full-time job and proper income. 'I was newly married, had no visible means of support and no obvious profession, having not gone into the church and not gone into academia.' He went into supply teaching. This was a time of a shortage of teachers. Within minutes of turning up at the department of education at Linlithgow, which ran schooling in West Lothian, he was ushered into the director's office. The director was straight on to the phone, and the following Monday Cook began as a form teacher at Bo'ness Academy. It was a rough ride. The class, 4D, was the sink class for early school leavers and had not had an English teacher for two months. 'I can still vividly remember the moment when I was sitting at my desk, the door swung open and in came a chanting, singing and cheerful 4D who stood rooted in horror and consternation that there was now a master in the room. The thing of which I'm most proud is the fact that I actually did achieve a civilized relationship with that class. I'm not sure I'm satisfied with what I did for them, because they required skills that I was not trained to provide. They were literally illiterate – they couldn't read or write. The first two months we had a terrible tussle in which I belted them and they fought me.' His use of corporal punishment was brought up during the 1997 general election campaign. 'I was described as being an inadequate or something. But everybody in the school did use it at the time. I think it was a good idea that it was banned but it would have been impossible unilaterally to opt out of it.'

Cook stayed at Bo'ness for a few months but rapidly realized that teaching was not for him. By the time he had graduated he had built up a number of political contacts, and his political commitments were taking up virtually all his time out of the classroom. He was already secretary of Edinburgh City Labour party and, together with his old friend Martin O'Neill, had manufactured a little local coup. He and Martin had kept in touch throughout their university days, and on graduating they plotted their course. The Labour party in Edinburgh was a fairly sleepy body: machine politicians ruled the roost internally, but the city had long been run by the Conservatives, and in the nadir of the first Wilson government, in the late 1960s, Labour had lost a number of council seats to the SNP. One of the most moribund constituencies was Edinburgh North, and it was here that Cook and O'Neill – who had already made themselves known at Scottish party conferences and other meetings – joined forces in early 1970 with two other young activists, Bob Cairns and Sandy Ross, to force out the old guard.

O'Neill became constituency chairman, and the business of the first meeting he presided at was to select a candidate for the general election Wilson had called for June 1970. This was the point at which Cook decided to take the plunge. He faced a straight choice: he could either opt for activism on the periphery of another job, or give it a go on the national stage. It was not a difficult decision. Through a process of elimination he had tried, and discarded, religion and education. If he was going to get involved in politics, he wanted to go the whole way. He felt he had the brain for it. He had proved to himself that he could speak in public, and knew what it took to garner support. Sandy Ross, who is now head of regional programmes at Scottish Television, was the local agent and had got to know Cook in their final year at university. 'Even then it was obvious that he was the sharpest of all of us. I rarely came across anyone with such a clear idea of where he was going,' recalls Ross.

Cook won the nomination without much of a fight. The team fought a colourful and controversial campaign, his opponent the very same Earl of Dalkeith whose campaign appearances he had tried to disrupt four years earlier. Cook was now twenty-four, twenty-two years younger than the incumbent. Just before the election, Parliament had passed legislation lowering the voting age from twenty-one to eighteen. In his personal election address to constituents, Cook informed them that not only was he standing for Parliament for the first time, but that 'the last time I was too young to vote.'

Apart from a brief interlude after the 1945 landslide, Edinburgh North was not Labour territory. A compact constituency, it incorporated the affluent Georgian houses of the New Town. Cook and his friends knew what they were up against, but were nevertheless determined to make a splash. The Earl's pet subject was forestry, about which he had spoken in the Commons thirty-three times; the Cook team's strategy was to present him as an out-of-touch rural aristocrat. They sent a volunteer to the *Scotsman* newspaper, pretending that she was from the gentrified *Scottish Field* magazine, to request a photograph from the archives of Dalkeith in hunting fig, and reproduced the picture for a leaflet with the caption: 'Does this man really represent you?' As soon as it was printed, they set off around town fly-posting, with a bucket of paste on the back seat of Cook's rickety red Rover. They were spotted by police and, having tried unsuccessfully to give them the slip, were finally stopped and given a stern telling-off. Not only did the poster campaign come to an abrupt end, the leaflet itself backfired. 'It was the sort of ironic, intelligent and too smart thing that naïve people do campaigning for the first time,' Cook recalls. Traditional Tories failed to catch the irony and thought it was a wonderful photo of their man. To launch the leaflet, Labour organized a photo-call. Star of the show was Liz Foulkes, wife of George and the only person they knew who could ride. Cook was supposed to pat the horse in front of the cameras. Instead, he did what the photographers asked him to do and had George give him a leg-up to join Liz on the back of the horse. The *Scotsman* duly obliged on the eve of the election with the picture printed above the caption: 'Down among the also rans.' Among those campaigning for the Earl was Cook's best man Eddie Spiers. 'Margaret found it odd that I was working for the enemy camp; Robin took it in his stride,' he says. So safe was the seat that the Earl himself only began campaigning in the last week – he had been away before that having an ear operation. He irritated Cook by growing a red beard while he was away. Spiers says this was purely a coincidence: 'I had never seen him before.'

Election day could not have been worse. Mr and Mrs Cook, in the car they had acquired only the previous week, had a collision with a dustcart outside the polling station on Broughton Street. 'It was an unbelievably undignified scene, with Robin emerging from his red Rover arguing furiously with the driver from the council,' recalls Ross. The crash even made it on to the Scottish evening television news. Cook was, according to his friends, an 'excruciatingly bad driver'. John Whitworth, the poet, has no difficulty in recalling where he was on 22 November 1963, the night John F. Kennedy was assassinated: 'I was in Robin's car when he crashed it trying to park on the way to a debate at a girls' school. You didn't go in Robin's car if you could help it.'

As expected, the Earl of Dalkeith won the seat with a comfortable majority of 3,878. The following year tragedy struck in the form of a riding accident that confined him to a wheelchair. He stood down from the Commons on the death of his father in 1973 when he assumed the title of 9th Duke of Buccleuch and 11th Duke of Queensberry. His and Cook's paths have not crossed since; the closest they came was perhaps shortly before the general election of 1997, when, visiting his father's grave, Cook and his mother were driving through the Ayrshire hills when they decided to stop off at Thornhill, one of the Duke's estates. The proprietor was not there, but his house manager showed them around and served them tea in the tea room of the great house. In September of that year, the Duke hit back at Cook's repudiation of the role of hereditary peers. 'It is all very well for Robin Cook to rail against hereditary peers, but I might remind him how I defeated him decisively at the 1970 general election,' he said. 'Does this mean that I am less qualified than he is to have a voice in parliament, simply because I subsequently inherited a peerage? And what about the scores of hereditary peers who are far more dedicated and assiduous parliamentarians than I am, but did not have the opportunity of defeating the sharpest brain in the Labour party?'[1]

Even though everyone had expected Cook to lose in 1970, he took it badly. Sandy Ross remembers: 'He wanted to give it up and go to London to train as a barrister. He said he'd had it and was never going to get a seat in parliament. We had a long conversation in the Abbotsford pub. I told him to be patient. It was a strange moment of self-doubt.' It was the first of several such moments in his career, all of which he hid from public view.

It did not take long, however, for him to recover his resolve. Those same SNP *arrivistes* who stormed to prominence on the Edinburgh Corporation in 1967 and 1968 lost their places in 1971. The first fraught year of Edward Heath's Conservative government had seen a Labour revival in Scotland. In Edinburgh, a revolution was taking place. Labour was in charge for the first time. A new, younger and more dynamic generation of councillors was emerging, Labour and Tory alike. Cook was elected for the Holyrood ward. Of the other new council members, five more would become MPs a few years later. George Foulkes, who had been president of the Scottish union of students and regional organizer of the pro–Common Market European Movement, had won a seat a year earlier. He was seen as at least a match for Cook in terms of electability and political weight. They were joined by John McWilliam, who was treasurer of the local Labour party and went on to become MP for Blaydon, a seat he has held since 1979, as well as Ron Brown, who became MP for Edinburgh Leith from 1979 until his ignominious ejection from the party in 1992. The two Tories were Cook's old adversaries at the university debating society – Lord James Douglas-Hamilton and Malcolm Rifkind.

After leaving his teaching job, Cook had moved to the Workers' Educational Association, a state-funded organization aimed at providing new skills and educational courses across the community. In 1971 he was appointed regional tutor-organizer for Lothian. The WEA was a good place to be, a useful vehicle for political advancement: Neil Kinnock had gone down the same road in Wales. It provided Cook with a small income and was tolerant of its tutors' commitments elsewhere. Notwithstanding those commitments, Cook was highly assiduous in his approach to the job. Henry Drucker, now managing director of Oxford Philanthropic, a development consultancy, was a lecturer in politics at Edinburgh from 1968 and a prominent figure in the city Labour party. He describes the WEA at the time as 'so old it was incredible. It was totally run down. All the people on it had personally known Keir Hardie. Robin introduced new courses and lectures and tried to modernize its practices.'

Cook ran conferences on poverty and housing in the Lothian region. He also organized weekend schools for trade unionists. During the role-playing exercises the shop stewards were asked to become managers and, to his amazement, took with alacrity to locking out the workers. The bulk of the evening classes attracted a more middle-class Edinburgh crowd. To broaden the appeal, Cook and his colleagues decided to offer metalwork art as a new course. 'Of course, what this overlooked is that people who spend all day working with molten metal don't want to spend the evening working with molten metal. But the middle classes loved it; we had an all-graduate intake for that class.'

At the same time he made his way rapidly on the corporation. Taking over as convenor of its housing committee in 1973, he became responsible for 52,000 tenants, with another 5,000 on the waiting list, and construction plans for over 2,000 new homes. 'It was a very exciting, innovative and rewarding year,' he recalls. 'We had no housing department when I took over. The whole house-letting operation was done by a man who was a junior figure in the hierarchy.' Cook and his committee reorganized the corporation's entire approach to housing, setting up a new housing department, introducing a points system for allocations, and changing the slum clearance programme. At that time the demolition of large areas, and exporting of communities to the suburbs, was accepted practice. 'I was part of the movement to save the inner city, and Edinburgh remains unusual among big cities in that it has a very large residential city centre population.'

Tam Dalyell, who was MP for West Lothian at the time, remembers Cook as a 'very young, thrusting and an extremely competent convenor of housing'. Of the 5,000 units, most of them tenement flats, earmarked for clearance, Cook's committee ordered that 3,000 be preserved and modernized, by putting in internal bathrooms and proper plumbing. Cook is proud of his achievement: 'I remember celebrating with the deputy director of housing, who'd done the revised plans with me, and after the second round of whiskies he said he'd been going back through the list. "You know, councillor," he said, "I noticed that all the ones we recommended for retention were the ones where the sun had been shining when we visited them, and with all the ones we recommended for demolition it had been raining that day." That injected a note of objectivity into our study. But I can still now go round Edinburgh and see streets that would have been demolished and they are bloody fine housing, most of them in owner occupation. You can get a buzz out of what you do at a local level that you can't always get at national level.'

Cook worked differently from most of his colleagues on the corporation. Drucker remembers that while other councillors would go down to the pub at lunchtime, the housing convenor would invariably be in the council chamber or library preparing a speech. He would then release pre-delivery texts to the *Edinburgh Evening News* to ensure maximum coverage.

'Eventually the paper was told by other members of the council that they had to go easy – there was too much Cook in it and not enough of them,' Drucker says. Ambition was driving him to become more than just another local councillor. Each speech had to be flawless, each decision had to be meticulously worked out. If it took time, so be it. The tone was being set: he would rather work long hours alone than socialize.

Cook stood down from the city party secretaryship in 1972 to give himself more time for his work as housing convenor and at the WEA; but still the pressures were not easily reconciled. 'I did find that year extremely frustrating because when you were up at the council you were constantly thinking what you ought to be doing back at the office; when you were in the office you were constantly thinking what you ought to be doing at the council.'

The juggling with home life was even more complicated. Margaret Cook had trained in haematology and pathology, and was working all hours at the Western General. Shift work was part of the routine. While expecting their first child she had begun a brief stint as a consultant lecturer, giving up work a fortnight before Christopher was born, on 7 February 1973, and going back two months after the birth. Their second son, Peter, was born not long after, on 17 May 1974, and this time she worked right up to the delivery date. The happy couple were interviewed by the local paper: Margaret said she was planning to return to her hospital job as soon as she could, and eight weeks later, as after Christopher's arrival, she went back, now employing a nanny they called 'nurse'. Once a week, when Margaret was on call, Robin's mother Christina would stay over to look after the boys. Like many two-career young couples with children, they were cutting it fine. Exhaustion took its toll and money was tight: but here were two intelligent, independent-minded but compatible people starting out on their respective vocations full of enthusiasm.

Harry Reid, a local education reporter at the time, remembers his first meeting with Cook. It was at a pub in Leith, the Great Junction Bar, late in 1971. 'He organized a party meeting about crime and punishment. I remember thinking: "This guy, there's something about him." He had a great sense of fun and seemed to be orchestrating the whole meeting.' A while later, Reid remembers interviewing Cook in the new home that the couple had bought, 22 East Mayfield, by Edinburgh's Commonwealth Pool. Cook the city councillor and up-and-coming politician was changing Christopher's nappy as he gave the reporter his considered responses on the burning issues of the day.

This kind of life took a lot of effort, but the effort was beginning to pay dividends. It was in those same months that his first big break came.

4

Proud to Rebel

Not long after Cook despaired of his parliamentary prospects, he received a piece of news he had been hoping for but had not dared to expect. Tom Oswald announced he was retiring as MP for Edinburgh Central at the next general election.

Since arriving in the Commons in 1951, Oswald had made precious few speeches in the chamber. He was very much a stalwart of a bygone generation, responding to each letter from a constituent by hand – for him campaigning and policy-making were alien concepts. The highest he rose was parliamentary private secretary to the Scottish secretary. Yet the constituency was one of the most prestigious in central Scotland and there was no shortage of aspirants. Cook emerged as a front runner. So did George Foulkes. Foulkes was the senior of the two in local politics, popular and well-known on the circuit. On paper, he should have won.

The short-list came down to four. The two protagonists, Foulkes and Cook, were joined by Stephen Haseler, a young activist, and John Henderson, who had been Oswald's agent. Haseler, an academic, had stood unsuccessfully for Labour in English seats in the previous two elections and later became a member of the ill-fated Greater London Council. From there he went on to become one of the founders of the SDP. Drucker was constituency chairman, but when the regional party found out that he was a naturalized American it barred him from running the selection. A little-known regulation adopted during the war by the National Executive Committee stipulated that aliens could not be party members. That rule was soon changed.

Foulkes takes up the story: 'There were three candidates of the right, against Cook on the left. I tried hard to persuade Henderson not to stand, as

I would clearly have beaten Haseler into the final round. But Cook and others talked Henderson into it. Even then I was confident. It seemed likely that Haseler would be the first to be knocked out. Drucker had promised me that he would lobby for me to get those votes. Instead he played a double game.' In the second round Henderson confounded the odds to score better than Foulkes. He was never going to be a match for Cook, who prevailed easily in the run-off. 'I was shocked when the result came through,' says Foulkes. Had he won the seat he would have been a good bet for a junior position in the Callaghan government, as he was on friendly terms with Roy Jenkins.

Cook is convinced that Foulkes' views did for him. 'It was broadly perceived that he was a candidate of the right and I was from the left. I think it's probably fair to say that he was seen as the favourite son. I always had a lot of respect for him and the people who backed him, even though they were of the right. But when he went out, rather than back Henderson, a man of no particular opinion who in conventional terms would have been a loyalist and followed the leadership line, they backed me as somebody who at least had conviction and was running because I believed in something.' Still, it had taken cunning tactics by Cook and his friends to keep his main opponent out, and it was only when Foulkes won the nomination for South Ayrshire in 1979 that the wound completely healed. From that point Foulkes brushed off any lingering sense of grievance, although the hard lesson in Machiavellian politics did knock some of the stuffing out of him. Now one of the older members on the government benches, he has had to make do with a junior ministerial post in Clare Short's Department for International Development.

Cook had laid the groundwork before the selection meeting. Sandy Ross, his agent for both general elections in 1974, remembers how Cook assiduously courted party members, turning up to humdrum ward meetings in the middle of winter to show his face week after week. Keith Geddes, now head of Edinburgh City Council, recalls meeting Cook for the first time that year and how impressive he was on the student grant issue. 'He'd make a point of turning up to committee meetings even if there were only twenty people there. He would give a twenty-minute speech that he'd written out obviously with a lot of care as each one made specific references to particular ward issues.' Cook carried with him lists of local members, and all relevant facts and figures such as diary events and social gatherings. He also had other young members of the city party spreading the word for him. These included Gordon Brown and Nigel Griffiths.

His government paralysed by the striking miners, Ted Heath called a general election for 28 February 1974. Voters were asked to determine 'who runs Britain'. The election had been a long time coming for Cook since winning the nomination. But the time had been used well. By now Ross had amassed a highly professional campaign outfit; there would be no more larking around with horses and fly-posting. 'There was a cachet to working for Robin,' Ross recalls. He remembers a local trade union organizer bringing a succession of Edinburgh debutantes into campaign headquarters to help canvass. Judges and senior lawyers sent money, with notes apologizing for not being able to declare their allegiance in public. Gordon Brown was a member of Ross's team and had been put in charge of one of the wards. He was a prodigious academic talent, having entered university via a fast track scheme at the age of sixteen. But he was more than that. In November 1972, aged twenty-one, he beat several Establishment figures to become rector of Edinburgh University. Only the second student to hold this post, for the next few years he took on the elderly, stuffy members of the university court – and usually won. Cook would later help him in some of his battles.

'Gordon and I saw each other regularly – more than once a week,' remembers Cook. They would go as a group to the Abbotsford pub in Rose Street, the place to be seen for the young radicals. 'He was a phenomenon. Because he went up to university so young, one was aware of this prodigy who had become a leading student activist.' Cook did not see him as a threat at that point and they got on well enough, although they did not inhabit the same world. Younger than Cook and considerably more outgoing, Brown was a raffish figure at the centre of a fashionable socialite set. Not only Brown himself but his girlfriend, Princess Margarita of Romania, campaigned hard for the candidate, and the impression was not lost on Cook: 'Her canvass returns were always spectacularly good because the good citizens of Edinburgh Central would open their tenement doors and find this strikingly beautiful woman with long, dark hair, who was always dressed either in brown velvet or corduroy, standing at the door.'

Cook's majority in February 1974 was extremely small, only 961. But this time there was no self-doubt: he had made it, and on his twenty-eighth birthday, to boot. Ross organized a victory party at his girlfriend Vivien's George Street flat. Shortly after arriving at the party, the new MP for Edinburgh Central and his chairman, Henry Drucker, became engrossed in conversation. 'Robin and I talked in the kitchen for about an hour and a half, discussing politics. He apparently forgot about the other guests,' Drucker recalls. 'Robin was pre-eminent at political meetings but there was something about him that was not very comfortable with people. He seemed self-conscious in ordinary day-to-day social contact.'

Malcolm Rifkind had also just been elected for the first time, in Edinburgh Pentlands, giving the city two new MPs. With remarkable prescience, the *Edinburgh Evening News* carried an article on 4 March 1974 predicting that Cook and Rifkind would both go far and would track each other throughout their Commons careers. Headlined 'Neck and neck in the race to the Commons', the piece pointed out that they had attended Edinburgh University at the same time. Cook had studied English, Rifkind law. Rifkind had been president of the university's Conservative club, Cook had done the same for Labour; Rifkind was president of debates, with Cook later becoming secretary. Rifkind was first on to the council, taking the Newington ward, followed a few months later by Cook. In 1970 Rifkind had also been unsuccessful in his first bid for a seat, failing ironically against the Labour candidate, Oswald, in Edinburgh Central. Both had now been elected at the same age, becoming the youngest Scottish MPs at Westminster. Both had working wives – Edith Rifkind was a lecturer at Napier College. Cook's first child, Christopher, was one year old, Rifkind's was on its way. It concluded: 'Like the Joneses, you've got to hand it to the city's two new MPs in keeping up with each other. Even when it comes to families . . .' That connection lasted until Rifkind lost his seat in 1997. Cook shadowed him in the early 1980s when he was minister with responsibility for European affairs, and then during his tenure as Foreign Secretary in the mid-1990s. They also paired with each other for voting in the Commons. In spite of these common threads they did not become close.

Cook did not hang around when he got to Westminster. Nor did he go out of his way to endear himself to traditionalists. Within weeks of arriving he wrote to Admiral Sir Gordon Lennox, the Serjeant-at-Arms, the top behind-the-scenes official at the Palace of Westminster, complaining that he and some other members of the new intake had neither telephones nor desks. New MPs were supposed to be patient and tough it out. Cook, not one to take orders from any old official, threatened to buy his own cabinet and send in the bill.

Still, he was intensely proud of being there. One of the first things he did was to find out where the library was. From the outset he would spend many a long day and night there, buried in his books, impervious to the comings and goings. 'I still can't believe I'm being paid to be here,' he would say to his new colleagues. He was particularly chuffed when invited by Harold Wilson for drinks in Downing Street that summer. His was the first group of new Labour members to be asked. He told Brian Lang, his old school and university friend, that he thought he had been invited by Wilson to share with the Prime Minister his knowledge of the housing crisis. It was only later that he found out that he was near the top of the list because his surname began with C.

His parliamentary career was nearly cut short at the start. Early on the morning of 17 June 1974 the IRA exploded a 20lb bomb in Westminster Hall, the oldest part of the Palace of Westminster. Cook's office, just above where the policemen's café is now situated, was badly damaged. During his first few months in parliament he had taken the sleeper from Edinburgh each Sunday night – he had never been on an aeroplane before becoming an MP – and on arrival in London would go to his office to catch up on paperwork at the crack of dawn before going home to rest. This time he had decided at the last moment to change his plans, stay an extra night at home and fly down first thing Monday morning. By the time he got to Westminster the place was sealed off. The first thing he saw among the rubble was a calling card from his pile of stationery: 'Robin Cook MP called, sorry you weren't in.' He had been meaning to clear up his messy office.

By October, Wilson's minority administration had become virtually paralysed and he went to the country again. This time he fared marginally better, securing a majority of three. Cook's own majority rose considerably, to 3,953. This time his personal election address was more radical. Of the North Sea oil bonanza, he wrote: 'The profits should benefit the people and we would take a share in the ownership up to about 50 per cent. Taxation on profits would be increased to 82.5 per cent and a major proportion of this revenue would be allocated to a Scottish development agency, which would be set up to regenerate the economy and improve the environment.' On inflation: 'The main point in getting on top of our economic problems is to get a general agreement among us all – between the government and the ordinary working people. Already with the social contract we have given agreements on better pensions, decent housing and subsidies on food. A voluntary agreement is the only way.' On Britain's continued membership of the EEC, he said: 'There should be a referendum and I think people would be well advised to vote to come out. I do not think any of the four main points such as the agricultural policy, common currency, regional development and the system of control will be affected by renegotiation.'

After only eight months in the Commons, Cook had already made a name for himself. On 29 October 1974, as Parliament reassembled, he was given the rare honour of being asked to second the Queen's Speech. (It is usually proposed by an elder statesman on the government side and seconded by a younger member.) After the briefest of light-hearted banter that is required on such occasions, he went straight into his pet subject: housing. His constituency, he said, contained some of Edinburgh's worst council houses, 'stone-built tenements, each stairs containing sixteen to twenty-four flats, each flat comprising only one room and a kitchen, flats in which I am ashamed to say that whole families are still brought up today.' He moved on to welcome the Labour party's commitment to devolution for Scotland and Wales, but struck a note of caution:

I hope that those who have ravished the Scottish electorate with the prospect of future prosperity will not rat on their commitments. I hope that when we introduce Labour's plans for an assembly, plans we have been told will not work, North Sea oil will still curdle and eggs still crack, and I hope that those who have said this will vote against us in principle, and that we shall not find those who believe in separatism taking part in debates on devolution. For my part, I remember the words of one of our older poets, and I am sure that anything said more than 300 years ago cannot be controversial. I remember the words of William Drummond of Hawthornden, who said: 'Brethren, take a view of the map of the earth, there ye shall find that Scotland is not all the earth; and that England and it together make but one not immense isle.'

Referring to the twenty-six bills in the speech, Cook said: 'I suspect that when we meet a year hence we shall have done very well indeed to have finished with them all. I hope, however, that we have a very good try.'[1]

One of Cook's first decisions was to join Tribune, the broad alliance of left-wing Labour MPs. It did not take long for the goodwill between the left and the government to dissipate, and Cook was one of the thirty-eight Labour members who rebelled over the public expenditure white paper of 1975. His first big campaign, however, was divorce reform. His backbench Divorce Law Reform (Scotland) Bill, introduced in May 1975, sought to introduce the concept of marital breakdown, bringing Scotland into line with England. It failed to get a second reading nine times, as the government refused to give it parliamentary time. Cook felt particularly bitter towards Willie Ross, the veteran Scottish secretary, an old-fashioned sort who had nothing but disdain for social radicals. He was by no means deterred from pursuing objectives dear to his heart, however, and this was just the first of many attempts by Cook to liberalize legislation on family and other social issues.

The first crisis facing Wilson's fragile government concerned Britain's membership of the EEC. As a student Cook had started out as a member of the university Europe society, together with Rifkind, and a supporter of the Common Market. Two years later, in 1966, he changed tack when Wilson announced his bid to get in where Harold Macmillan had failed. Labour went into the February 1974 election with a promise to 'immediately seek a fundamental renegotiation of the terms of entry' under which Heath had taken Britain into the EEC in January 1973. If that negotiation proved successful, 'the people should have the right to decide the issue through a general election or a consultative referendum.' Eight months later, that pledge was firmed up, making it clear that the people would have their say within twelve months. When the promised fundamental renegotiation turned out to be cosmetic, the uneasy compromise within Labour collapsed. The split running through both Cabinet and the parliamentary party, which had first opened up in 1972, could no longer be papered over. Wilson, in a desperate attempt to keep his government intact, took the unusual step of giving his MPs free rein. Most members of the cabinet (16 to 7) joined the Conservatives and Liberals in calling for a 'yes' vote; the National Executive Committee and a special party conference called for April 1975 decided to oppose the government. Cook was firmly on the side of the majority in the PLP in calling for withdrawal. That campaign was led predominantly by senior figures of the left, among them Michael Foot, Tony Benn and Peter Shore. They saw the emerging institutions in Brussels as little more than a device to strip the Labour government of real economic power. The referendum that June gave the pro-Market lobby a majority of two to one.

Cook concluded from the result that the prospect of Britain's ever being able to leave the EEC would diminish with each year that passed. He and others argued that the next best option was reform of its institutions. However, on the issue of principle he was happy to sign up to any move to harry the government into challenging Brussels. In 1977 he joined sixty other Labour MPs in putting his name to an appeal in *Tribune* magazine, declaring: 'Membership of the Common Market has been an unmitigated disaster for the British people. The Labour movement should commit itself to taking Britain out of the EEC.'

A deep scepticism towards the EEC was one of several characteristics Cook had in common with another young, left-wing rising star, who had entered the Commons in 1970: Neil Kinnock, with whom he instantly became good friends. 'I looked around the new intake and picked up the fact that there was a smart new Scots lad who had also worked at the WEA,' Kinnock says. 'It was natural that we should strike up a friendship. He had the perfect combination of common sense with a little dose of humour and humanity.' Their views were perfectly in harmony with Tribune – anti-EEC, in favour of radical economic redistribution and intervention, and anti-nuclear. 'We were both religiously internationalist, but like so many in the party saw the Common Market as a capitalist club,' Kinnock recalls.

For a time, the anti-nuclear campaign looked like going the same way as the anti-EEC movement. Since its heyday in the early 1960s, with the Aldermaston marches and other mass protests, the Campaign for Nuclear Disarmament had almost disappeared without trace. By the mid-1970s, with the tensions of the Cold War apparently subsiding through detente, its membership had dwindled to little over four thousand. Nevertheless, the issue of Britain's nuclear stance was far from settled. Both Labour's 1974 manifestos promised a reduction in UK defence spending to the European

NATO average, and the October document explicitly pledged not to replace Polaris, Britain's ageing independent submarine-launched nuclear deterrent. Within months, however, as US–Soviet relations deteriorated, Wilson decided without public debate to upgrade it. Two years later, James Callaghan, his successor, agreed to a request by US President Ford to deploy US nuclear-armed F-111 bombers in the UK. By now the NEC and the Cabinet were at loggerheads on defence policy.

A CND supporter since his early teens, as an MP Cook threw himself eagerly into campaigning for unilateral nuclear disarmament. He joined a working party set up by the NEC to consider defence spending. The group was led by Ian Mikardo and included a number of academics, such as Mary Kaldor, then a researcher at Sussex University. 'We wanted to reopen the defence debate, an area the party was not supposed to discuss,' Kaldor says. 'I was impressed at how clever Cook was, how good he was at setting out the arguments – and telling jokes at others' expense.' Later in 1977 the group published *Sense About Defence*, outlining detailed plans for radical cuts in defence expenditure. The government promptly ignored it.

Many of Cook's activities got under the skin of a jittery party establishment. He went out of his way to create waves on the most sensitive aspects of defence and foreign policy and the role of the intelligence services. He became a darling of human rights and civil liberties campaigners. In April 1976 he was one of a group of Labour MPs who petitioned for the Commons defence select committee to investigate arms sales. 'It is never made clear how decisions are made,' he complained. 'Why are arms sold to Brazil but South Africa is supposed to be beyond the pale? Who decides that electronic equipment does not constitute weaponry even though it can be used by the armed forces?' He was a leading figure in SCRAM, the Scottish Campaign to Resist the Atomic Menace, which was set up in 1975 to fight against the proposed nuclear station in Torness. He argued that the project was based on an unrealistic and unreliable forecast of electricity demand, that the economic justification of its costs was dubious and that no one had demonstrated how the nuclear waste would be disposed of.

He made his debut as defence correspondent of the *New Statesman* on 23 July 1976. 'Into the Tornado' was a well-argued piece comparing the expenditure cuts facing many Whitehall departments with Roy Mason's burgeoning defence budget. A new generation of fighter aircraft was planned. 'Mason's achievement is no mean feat given the stunning expense of the plane, the Tornado, which will cost at least £6m per unit. The price of a pair of wings approximates to the amount which my local authority, a city of half a million, has just been instructed by the government to cut out of its budget,' Cook wrote. His columns for the newspaper were invariably well researched. They expressed a deep disappointment felt by many in the party that both Wilson and Callaghan had squandered an opportunity to break the mould. Both leaders had, Cook felt, allowed themselves to be boxed in by the Establishment at home and by international institutions abroad. In July 1978 Cook co-wrote a Fabian pamphlet with Dan Smith, a leader of CND and a member of the NEC defence study group, entitled *What Future in Nato?* The organization, they said, had failed to make use of the opportunities presented by detente, was over-reliant on the doctrine of nuclear deterrence, and – unless it could be seen to change – was redundant to the needs of Britain.

Cook's other hobby-horse was the activities of MI5, MI6 and the Special Branch. Many in the left were speculating about the possible involvement of the intelligence organizations in Wilson's sudden decision in March 1976 to step down as Labour leader and Prime Minister. At the same time, radical journalists and politicians in the United States were trying to highlight the role of the CIA in 'dirty wars' in developing countries, where a string of leftist leaders had been overthrown. In 1977 Philip Agee, a former CIA operative living in London, revealed a number of plots to destabilize governments in Latin America and the Middle East. He and Mark Hosenball, an American journalist working for the London magazine *Time Out*, named the entire corps of CIA agents in London and revealed the existence of GCHQ, the British surveillance centre in Cheltenham. Their pieces were commissioned by Duncan Campbell, Cook's old friend from Edinburgh, who was news editor at *Time Out*. Merlyn Rees, the Labour defence secretary, responded by ordering the two Americans to leave the UK. Cook was the most prominent MP to support their cause. Their expulsion coincided with the so-called 'ABC case', after the initials of the protagonists. Again at Campbell's behest, John Berry, a former signals officer, agreed to an interview with two other *Time Out* journalists, Crispin Aubrey and Duncan Campbell (no relation). The three were arrested and sent to Brixton prison. Cook drew attention to the fate of Agee and Hosenball and the ABC case in several articles for the *New Statesman*. He also raised the issue in an adjournment debate in the Commons, calling for an investigation into a series of thefts by Special Branch officers from the cars and homes of the accused and their friends. On 30 July 1978, Cook introduced a private member's bill to give the public greater access to official information. That, unsurprisingly, got nowhere. But he became close friends with the second Duncan Campbell, with whom he would work on a number of future projects.

Another *cause célèbre* of this period was Iran under the dictatorship of the Shah, aided by the Savak, his secret police. In November 1978 Cook was one of thirty Labour MPs who tabled an early day motion calling on the government to cancel a visit to Iran planned by the Queen the following spring. Nearly two years earlier he had castigated the West in the *New Statesman* for 'slavishly court[ing] this latter-day Caligula by pouring out a thorough cornucopia of arms before his throne'. The article went on: 'As a result of current orders from the US and UK alone, by the early eighties Iran will have more tanks, warplanes and helicopters than any state in the world excepting the two superpowers,' and concluded: 'Socialists can only hope that despite all the efforts of our arms exporters a more democratic regime will somehow succeed in sweeping aside Reza Shah and reopen the contracts for hospitals, roads and housing that are now being sacrificed to maintain the momentum of arms purchases.'[2]

Cook did not mark his first parliamentary term by winning his way on to the front bench. It nearly happened, and he believes he was fortunate that it did not. In his first set of appointments in 1976, Callaghan had a vacancy for a parliamentary under-secretary – the lowest-ranking minister – in the department of industry. He was trying to balance his government, and had earmarked that slot for a left-winger. He first sounded out Kinnock, who promptly turned it down. The job eventually went to Bob Cryer, although Cook was told later that government whips had been looking for him and could not find him. He had been in a cottage in the Cotswolds that weekend, without a phone. Kinnock told Callaghan later that he had 'obviously wanted a ginger-haired member of the Tribune group' for the post. In the event, Cryer lasted only two years in the job before resigning in protest over government economic and defence policy.

Tam Dalyell believes Cook did himself no favours, in the long run, by getting on the wrong side of most of the party grandees, notably Willie Ross. A stern traditionalist of presbyterian stock, Ross believed all young MPs had to keep quiet, work their passage and enjoy the patronage the older members could confer. Cook, for his part, did not try to ingratiate himself, did not bother with small talk and even at that early stage found it hard to hide his disdain for the less well-informed. 'Robin irritated a lot of the elderly in the parliamentary party,' said a fellow Scottish MP. 'They thought him a bit of a know-all. They would have felt uncomfortable with him as their junior minister. They felt threatened by him. Your face had to fit. Robin's fitted with none of them.'

Cook was by no means a lone voice speaking against an otherwise united party. The question of devolution for Scotland and Wales proved not only as difficult for Cook, but also as divisive for the Labour Party as a whole, as the Europe question. The long-dormant constitutional debate had been reawakened by the oil boom and Lord Kilbrandon's royal commission, reporting a few months before the February 1974 election, had outlined several options for change. Labour's Scottish executive was split down the middle. Wilson's new Cabinet was lukewarm about the prospect of giving away powers. However, some of them saw merits in a plan of limited devolution within the Union, which they believed would put an end to demands for home rule. As Andrew Marr noted in his history of the 1970s devolution battle, 'because it was born of weakness, mainly the weakness of the 74–79 Labour government, devolution was a slippery concept.'[3] Wilson was alarmed by the SNP's taking seven seats in the February election under the banner 'It's Scotland's oil'. By the time of the second election in 1974, the Prime Minister had cajoled the Scottish party into agreeing to 'a directly elected assembly with legislative powers within the context of the political and economic unity of the UK'; yet this time the SNP performed better still, taking 30 per cent of the vote and eleven seats in Scotland. In Wilson's view, there could be no backtracking on giving the Scots more power.

In his personal election address for October 1974, Cook expressed support for the devolution plan. 'This is necessary to let the people decide, and anything less is totally unacceptable. The assembly should have full powers to legislate on all domestic matters.' Shortly after he became an MP, he switched sides. Nearly a decade later, he would revert to his original view. His shifts on the issue were not comfortable, but neither were they unique. On the Conservative benches, Rifkind was in the course of that parliament to resign from Margaret Thatcher's first shadow Cabinet in protest at her positioning the Tories as hostile to devolution, but was later on to line up firmly with the anti-devolution camp. On the Labour left, Jim Sillars was another who agonized over the constitutional issue – to the detriment of his career, having been seen on his entry into Parliament in 1970, along with Kinnock, as a possible future leader. Sillars turned from an opponent to a supporter of home rule, eventually breaking away in 1977 to form the ill-fated separate Scottish Labour party. Critics of Cook saw in his conversion to ardent opposition to devolution an attempt to mark new ground, away from Sillars. Cook now acknowledges the 'error' of his position then, but ascribes it to a disarmingly personal motive. He had arrived at Westminster with two main interests – housing and social policy – which, had a Scottish parliament come into being, would have largely ended up being devolved. 'I suppose if I am frank, I possibly allowed subconsciously my own reluctance to let these things go to colour and complicate what should have been a more hard-nosed approach to what was the right thing for Scotland.'

Some in Scotland saw the prospect of devolution as contributing to an attempt to forge a new and more radical politics; others, as a hindrance to that cause. A few months after the October 1974 election Cook contributed a chapter to *The Red Paper on Scotland*, a collection of essays by thinkers and activists, edited by Gordon Brown. It was seen as a seminal text for the left at the time, diagnosing and attempting to solve the problems of poverty and inequality north of the border. The cover photographs were of the Upper Clyde shipbuilders' sit-in of 1971 on the front, and the Leith dockers' strike of 1913 on the back. Cook's ten-page contribution was on housing. It was a curious mix of detailed practical proposals on dealing with slums, drawn from his council experience, left-wing idealism and fervent anti-nationalism. 'Engels long ago described how the English middle-class instinctively designed their thoroughfares so that they need not be distressed by the sight of working-class housing,' he wrote. 'It is insane to blame this legacy of sub-standard housing on English domination. All our slum tenements were erected in the last century by Scottish builders on behalf of Scottish landlords.' He concluded:

> Universal provision of good housing is just as much an impetus to an egalitarian society as [is] universal education. If however we are genuine in our repeated demands for universal access to good housing then we must be prepared to make the necessary resources available. I will not pretend that these resources can be made available painlessly. They can only be found if we cut the resources we devote to other items of government expenditure, or if we are all prepared to cut our personal expenditure by accepting higher taxation or greater housing expenditure. But it is not a decision which will become any less painful by the simple expedient of transferring it to a Scottish parliament. Nationalism is only a romantic escape from the blunt truth that only a major re-ordering of the priorities of our society will provide a decent environment for every citizen within the foreseeable future.[4]

Opposition to devolution within the Labour party tended to be concentrated among northern English Labour MPs and younger left-wingers, like Kinnock and Cook, who saw any dabbling with nationalism as a betrayal of the working class. However, Wilson had seen his tiny parliamentary majority disappear and had been forced to enter into a pact with the Liberals. In Scotland, the nationalists made huge gains in district council elections in May 1977, leaving the party of government without control of a single important Scottish district council. Business managers in the Commons were desperate to push through the Scotland Bill, which under the stewardship of John Smith, a junior minister, received its second reading in November of that year. On the way the government was forced to concede an amendment stipulating that a majority for or against devolution in the forthcoming referendum must exceed 40 per cent of the Scottish electorate to have force. Cook backed the erection of the new barrier, although he preferred the figure of a third of the electorate. 'I want to kill not the bill but this issue,' he said, with remarkable prescience. 'If we are to kill the issue, it can be done only in the referendum to follow the bill. I have a lively expectation that it will be done. If I am right in reading the mood of my constituents, it will be defeated, not by the majority vote against it, but by the fact that we shall have such an unimpressive proportion voting that no government in their senses will be able to claim that they have a mandate for such major constitutional change.'[5]

The February 1979 campaign took place in foul weather and against a backdrop of strikes in schools, hospitals, among refuse collectors and other public sector workers – the so-called Winter of Discontent. Cook was one of the most prominent figures in the Labour 'Vote No' campaign. Others were Brian Wilson, now a Scottish minister, Adam Ingram, now Northern Ireland security minister, and Tam Dalyell. Gordon Brown was one of the leading figures in the 'Yes' camp, which suffered from receiving less financial support from Scottish business. Cook and his colleagues argued vociferously that the assembly, with 150 more politicians, would add an unnecessary layer of government, and would lead to a loss of Scottish influence at Westminster. No fewer than forty-seven days had been spent on the floor of the Commons – the equivalent of nearly a third of a year's worth of legislative time – considering a topic seen by many in the party as entirely beside the point in the economic crisis facing the country. Cook dismissed devolution as 'irrelevant to the real problems we face. Given the present economic situation, to go ahead with devolution seems to be like fiddling while Rome burns.'

So despondent and divided was the mood that about a third of Labour constituency parties declined to campaign at all. The Labour anti-devolutionists refused publicly to join forces with like-minded campaigners from other parties. On polling night, however, Cook formed the unlikeliest of alliances with James Douglas-Hamilton. The two former council colleagues mounted a protest when the presiding officer insisted that two thousand ballot papers on which the word 'no' had been written in the 'no' box would not be counted. 'Robin and I thought this was outrageous. We threatened to have the man removed, and summoned journalists to an impromptu press conference inside the Scottish Office. We were ordered out of the room but the officer eventually backed down,' recalls Lord James. Their protest did not affect the outcome. The result was broadly as Cook had predicted. Some 1.23 million Scots had voted for devolution, with 1.15 million against. The turnout, 63.8 per cent, meant the 'yes' vote represented only 32.9 per cent of eligible voters. The issue was dead in the water. The campaign had been messy, and on the Labour side there were no real winners. In any case, the result was overtaken by events. Within a couple of months Callaghan had ceded Downing Street to Margaret Thatcher and the Conservatives.

In spite of his devolution troubles, Cook looks back fondly on his backbench years under Wilson and Callaghan, saying he had never regretted not getting into the government. 'There was never any great ambition, and they were a gloriously happy six years for me. It was a far sight more rewarding being a left thorn in a Labour government than being in the futile position of opposition to a Tory government.' Yet for him, and for others on the left, those years were wasted years, epitomized by Denis Healey going cap in hand to the IMF in 1976. Wilson and Callaghan had been able to ignore the express wishes of the rank and file and substitute for reflation and redistribution a stringency dictated by foreign institutions. Many on the left of the party resolved that future leaders would not be allowed to get away with that.

5

Left Out

'Edinburgh's left-wing Wonder Boy, Robin Cook, MP, leapt right into big time politics this week – as one of the shadow cabinet's front bench treasury team.' It had been some time coming, but Cook had finally made it to the front bench, in the Treasury team led by Peter Shore and under the new party leadership of Michael Foot. The *Edinburgh Evening News* profile, published on 19 December 1980, was entitled 'Labour's Shooting Star' and accompanied by a cartoon of the MP, clad in the donkey jacket ubiquitous as a symbol of left-wing sympathies, emblazoned with his CND badge and carrying a placard that read: 'No Nuke Is A Good Nuke'. Since entering Parliament, the paper said,

> Mr Cook has been especially active in defence and housing affairs. He has been one of the leading figures to support the Scottish Campaign to Resist the Atomic Menace in their fight against the proposed nuclear station at Torness. And only a few months ago he was the main speaker at a major rally in Glasgow demonstrating against nuclear weapons, and the government's recent decision to go ahead with the cruise and Trident missile programme. At the march, 'Welfare not Warfare', Mr Cook said that the only way to survive a nuclear war was to prevent one, and the only way to prevent it was disarmament.

Cook admitted to the interviewer that he had been 'slightly surprised' at his appointment to a financial job: 'My own interest has been in housing and defence.' But he noted that he had served on two finance bill committees and spoken in many economic debates. He added, in two further remarks that would come back to haunt him: 'I am confident Labour will defeat the Tories at the next election, and I hope Michael will give me the chance to work on the Treasury in power, as I do in opposition.' As for his own numeracy: 'I don't know if I should tell you, but my wife thinks I'm so bad with the house-keeping that she said she'd emigrate if I was ever made chancellor.'

Cook's first two years at the dispatch box, during Thatcher's rocky pre-Falklands first term, provided him with the first real chance to demonstrate the debating skills he had learnt at the Royal High and university. His speeches were often witty and invariably thorough. He would relish any opportunity to put down opponents, especially those who had not assembled their facts as well as he. One such opening came in February 1982, as unemployment had reached three million for the first time and redundancies from old industries were occurring at an average of forty thousand a month. Speaking just before the budget, Mrs Thatcher sought to dampen expectations of any reflationary action to kick-start the economy by pointing out that Ulysses had 'resisted the siren voices and came safely home to harbour'. Cook, keen to demonstrate his classical education, sent a copy of Homer in translation to her at Downing Street. He then put down a Commons motion, making clear that 'Ulysses did not come home, but lost his ship with all hands. The original version of what happened to his ship may prove only too accurate a prediction of the future of British industry under monetarist policies.' The motion concluded by wondering 'whether the Prime Minister's novel version of Homer anticipates the forthcoming wreck of British industry under Conservative steering or merely reflects the depressing decline in education standards following the cuts in public expenditure.'

Callaghan had staggered on for a while as leader of the opposition, in a forlorn attempt to stave off civil war in the Labour party, and his first shadow Cabinet had no place for the likes of Cook or other members of the awkward squad. Yet party activists had already begun to clip the wings of the leadership. They were in a hurry, with less than five years to change party structures before the inevitable return of the next Labour government; as yet nobody doubted the validity of the revolving door theory which had seen Labour and Tory administrations make way for each other in rapid succession since the early 1960s. The 1979 party conference voted for mandatory reselection of MPs. That was just the start.

In October the following year the Labour conference voted for a non-nuclear defence policy. The decision was a direct response to NATO's announcement of 12 December 1979 that new American medium-range nuclear missiles – cruise and Pershing – would be stationed in Europe to counter the deployment of Soviet SS-20s. The first cruise missiles arrived at Greenham Common air base, near Newbury in Berkshire, in June 1980; their presence would be a focal point for the left for the next decade. CND had been revived into a significant force, and Cook was one of the movement's most prominent figures, often appearing as the main speaker in anti-nuclear demonstrations. The left was not only campaigning for a change in government policy, but was seeking to ensure that any future Labour administration would not be able to renege on defence commitments. It emerged after the election that a few months before leaving Downing Street, Callaghan had discussed with President Carter the possibility of replacing Polaris with a new US submarine-launched missile system, Trident.

Cook believed the anti-nuclear movement should be locked into a broader internationalist strategy. He was influenced by Professor E. P. Thompson, the veteran left-wing historian, who argued that nothing would change in Europe unless voters in NATO and Warsaw Pact countries became more active in lobbying against nuclear weapons. Cook joined forces with Stuart Holland, then MP for Vauxhall, Ken Coates, an academic who went on to become an MEP, and Mary Kaldor of Sussex University in helping Thompson promote the Appeal for European Nuclear Disarmament, which became an internationalist version of CND. More than sixty Labour MPs signed the END appeal. 'We were very clearly anti-Communist, linking peace with human rights. Gorbachev later took up a lot of this language. Robin was always a member of CND but he was excited by END and its emphasis on political change undermining oligarchies,' says Kaldor. She introduced Cook to the actress Susannah York, who invited them both to dinner at her house in Battersea to discuss the nuclear-free movement. Cook also recalls joining forces with Julie Christie at a rally in Glasgow, and claims that she was more nervous of speaking in front of large crowds than he was. He would frequently take part in protests at nuclear bases along the River Clyde. One colleague said of him at the time: 'He has a huge capacity to sway local people to his line of thinking, even people with a lot to lose economically from a military pull-out from the area.' But Kaldor believes that, for all his idealism, Cook was always more conscious than other activists in the movement of political realities at Westminster. 'In 1983 I wanted to turn an anti-nuclear demonstration in London into an anti-Falklands one. Robin refused, realizing the politics of it all, that the anti-war message would hijack the main message and that it would put the Labour leadership in a desperately difficult position.'

In essence, notwithstanding the change of government, Cook set about continuing where he had left off before the general election. In December 1979, he tried again to reform the security services. His private member's bill proposed the appointment of a director-general from outside, who would oversee MI5 and MI6 and be accountable to Parliament. The pretext for this latest move was the revelation that Anthony Blunt was the 'fourth man' in the Soviet spy ring. Cook told the Commons that the impression given by the security services that they were dedicated to catching foreign spies was so far from the truth as to be 'pure myth'. He insisted that the greater part of their activity was domestic surveillance of the British population. Naturally enough, given Thatcher's large majority and Callaghan's reluctance to become involved, the legislation flopped at the first hurdle.

However, Cook scored a triumph – indeed, one of his biggest triumphs – in July the following year when, after repeated attempts over three years, he successfully pioneered legislation to bring Scottish law on gay sex into line with the law in England and Wales, twelve years after similar reforms had been enacted south of the border. He persuaded the Conservatives not to stand in the way of a clause amending the Criminal Justice Bill to legalize private acts between consenting homosexual adults over the age of twenty-one, having elicited from the Solicitor-General confirmation that no prosecutions had been brought against consenting adults for ten years. Cook, honorary vice-president of the Scottish homosexual rights group, told MPs on 22 July that earlier that week British photographers had been arrested in Moscow for filming a demonstration in support of gays. He added: 'The state of the law in Scotland is no better than the state of the law in the Soviet Union and it would be better to put our own house in order rather than lecturing anyone else.'[1] In a free vote, the clause was carried by 203 to 80.

By this stage, Cook's work as an assiduous opposition MP and a champion of difficult causes was winning wide respect. Allan Stewart, an MP from 1979 to 1997 and a former Conservative minister, wrote that Cook was the Labour politician most feared among his colleagues. One early demonstration of his qualities was provided by the Housing Bill, one of the first pieces of legislation of the Tory government, which allowed council tenants to buy their own homes. Cook was described by several commentators as a 'one-man opposition' in the committee scrutinizing the legislation for Scotland. Stewart traced the secret of his success to the Commons library, for many a good place to sleep. 'I have seen Robin Cook in there many times. He was never having a quiet doze.' Stewart picked as another illustration the committee stage of the first Finance Bill of the Thatcher years. 'The issue was a complex one about the taxation of Scottish whisky. Yet he tended to be the one who would say something like: "Minister I am a little unclear as to how paragraph 21 (b) of the circular your department issued two weeks ago on this subject relates to the circular of 18 months ago."'[2] One colleague of Cook remembers meeting him at two o'clock one morning outside his office. 'Robin nonchalantly said "hi" as he passed by, as if there was nothing untoward about working at that time of the morning.'

Cook remembers being locked in the library twice because the security staff had presumed everyone had left. 'I've always enjoyed working there, yet it is rather curious that this is sometimes held as a half-criticism of me. I've never thought actually working in a library a freakish thing. I never really sought to make my way forward by networking and socialising. So maybe that was where the germ of this criticism originates.'[3]

Little more than a year after the general election, Callaghan gave up the ghost, fed up with the sniping and in-fighting that had beset the party since its defeat. Michael Foot's narrow victory over Denis Healey in the subsequent leadership election was to hasten the split within Labour and the formation of the SDP by the Gang of Four. Cook, however, saw Foot's victory not as a retrograde step, but as the start of a shift of the party towards purer left-wing platforms, which would allow it to campaign more vigorously against Thatcher as her government's legislative programme was getting into full swing.

'When Callaghan resigned, I immediately phoned Michael and said he must run. I suppose if you were pinpointing something that I've done politically which I bitterly regret it was persuading Michael – well, Neil was also among others to do so – to run for the leadership. Not because I think he was the wrong choice, but because we miscalculated how utterly ruthless the press and public opinion would be to somebody who was probably the finest and most honest and most decent political leader we have seen since the war. But he was savaged and travestied, and it's a measure of Michael's own stature that he hasn't let it scar him.' Cook, who was on Foot's campaign committee, remembers their victory party in November 1980: 'We went off to the Gay Hussar [a restaurant on Greek Street in Soho that was fashionable at the time]. We hired the upper room and had dinner; and at one o'clock in the morning, having been celebrating since six, we sang the Red Flag and went home. I remember the next day I had a monstrous hangover and I was sitting in my office, having crept in at ten-thirty, and rang for my secretary. She came in, the door slammed behind her and I thought, "Oh God, Catherine, please don't, I've got an awful headache." She looked at me with withering contempt and said: "Robin, you've got to face the fact that you can't go along drinking as if you're a young man," to which I said: "What do you mean, Catherine, I've been out celebrating with a man twice my age."'

Yet for all the promise of policy radicalism held out by this change at the top, Cook and others on the mainstream left of the party were soon becoming disturbed at the way Foot was being dragged along by events. Militant was in the ascendant. For moderates in the party, the situation became untenable when Labour's special conference at Wembley in January 1981 decided on an electoral college to choose the party leader and deputy, giving the trade unions the largest share of the votes in the college (40 per cent, against 30 per cent each for the PLP and the constituency parties). Policy pronouncements included returning to a call for Britain to leave the EEC. The Scottish party had been even more radical, voting for complete withdrawal from NATO. Days after Wembley, Roy Jenkins, David Owen, Bill Rodgers and Shirley Williams issued their Limehouse declaration; and on 26 March 1981 the SDP was formally launched. To Cook and others close to Foot this was an alarming development, an act of betrayal; yet even then they were convinced that the revolving door would see Labour back in power at the next election.

Cook was proud of his uncompromising views on Europe and disarmament. Like many others on the left especially in Scotland, he saw preservation of sovereignty for Westminster as key to advancing socialist policies. But some were sceptical of his motives. One particularly stern critic was Dr Dickson Mabon, a former Labour minister who had resigned briefly in the mid-1970s in protest at the party's anti-EEC stand. He accused Cook of tailoring his views for the sake of winning the nomination for Edinburgh Central. Cook responded: 'I am accused of an opportunistic conversion to unilateralism. I first joined CND when I was fifteen, and to suggest that I did this in order to facilitate future selection as a Labour MP is to credit my youth with a precociousness which I am afraid it did not merit. I am even more bewildered by the accusation that my "conversion from being pro-EEC to anti-EEC came just at the right time before his original selection conference for his present seat". At no time in my life have I been in favour of British membership of the Common Market. On the contrary, in the late 1960s I addressed a number of public meetings and debates in Edinburgh arguing against the application to join by the Wilson government – a full five years before my adoption for central Edinburgh.'[4]

Tony Benn, who had turned down a shadow Cabinet job since leaving government in 1979, decided to test the new electoral college by announcing, on 2 April 1981, his intention to stand against Healey for the deputy leadership, despite attempts by Cook and others on the left to dissuade him from rocking the boat. Benn had failed in his bid for the leadership against Callaghan in 1976 and many on the left felt that a defeat for the right this time would be just deserts; yet the presence of Healey as Foot's number two was widely seen in the party as a stabilizing compromise. The contest dominated the news for six months. Tribune, which had been founded in 1966 as the single left caucus in parliament, split over Benn's challenge. The Labour Coordinating Committee, an umbrella group of party members established in 1978 to push for changes within the party, voted to back Benn. Cook came under considerable pressure in his constituency to do the same, although he made clear that in the first ballot he would vote for a third candidate, John Silkin.

This was a pivotal moment for Cook. He was moving into a nebulous centre ground straddling the parliamentary leadership and the hard-line left. The policies by which these movements defined themselves would change over the years, but Cook's dilemmas did not. In 1981 he fell in behind his leader. He was to make the same decision several times thereafter. Now he rounded on Benn, describing his campaign as 'extravagantly diversionary' and defending Foot against attacks from the 'sectarian Left'. Writing in the *Tribune* newspaper, he said: 'The claim that if you are not with Tony you are against the Left is not only false but dangerous. The Left is now divided against itself to an extent that is without parallel.'[5] On 27 September Healey narrowly staved off Benn's challenge. Foot responded by setting in train plans to expel Militant from the Labour party. To the fury of Cook and others on the left, Benn and his friends in the Commons quit Tribune and formed the Campaign group.

Turbulence in the party at large coincided with upheaval for Cook. The boundary commission, which was redrawing many of the parliamentary constituencies, turned Edinburgh Central from a comparatively safe Labour seat into a marginal. Two inquiries were held, but the final appeal was lost in January 1983. Cook was in a desperate dilemma – could he, with such ambitions and expectations of high office, risk defeat and a term in the wilderness? At the same time, could he face the brickbats of running when times got hard? He decided, after some soul-searching, to look for another seat. (A similar choice was faced by dozens of Conservatives at the 1997 election; almost all of them opted for safer seats, exposing themselves to a wave of derision from Labour over what became known as the 'chicken run'.) In the course of the boundary changes, a new seat was created close by – Livingston, representing the new town and outlying villages along the M8 between Glasgow and Edinburgh. It was a much more working-class and left-wing constituency, and the area it represented was aesthetically a million miles away. But it was a safe haven and close to where he lived. The constituency's first agent was Jim Devine. A community psychiatric nurse, Devine was head of the Glasgow region of COHSE, the health union, and vice-chair of the party in West Lothian, from which much of the new constituency was being drawn. 'The choice was simple,' Devine says. 'We couldn't as a party in Scotland afford to lose Robin as an MP. And nothing was going to be easy in 1983.' One senior Labour MP says that Cook, for all his professions of doubt, had decided early on to switch seats. 'You could say I was not best pleased when he asked me and other constituency members late one evening what we thought he should do, only for us to read his announcement in the next morning's paper.' They were not the only ones to take a somewhat jaundiced view of Cook's decision. Many in the local party in Edinburgh, who had worked so hard for his nomination a decade earlier, felt extremely sour. His departure made the constituency virtually a lost cause in 1983. However, even some Scottish politicians who would not naturally be well disposed to Cook acknowledge that he probably had no choice and that he would have lost the poll himself that time around. It was won again in 1987 by Alistair Darling, a lawyer who consolidated the seat and made a meteoric rise into Tony Blair's first Cabinet as Treasury chief secretary.

No sooner was his decision made than Cook ran into new trouble. Another prominent victim of the boundary commissioners' deliberations was Tony Benn, about to see his Bristol South East constituency, which he had held for thirty years, disappear. He looked around for vacancies in other seats in the city, but none became available. He was encouraged by Tam Dalyell, who was moving from West Lothian to take the new adjacent Linlithgow seat, and others in Scotland to opt for Livingston. The chance of getting his own back at Cook was an added bonus. In an increasingly bitter contest in 1982 Cook and Benn canvassed activists in what would become the new seat. By the middle of the year Cook was home and dry. He asked Devine, a stocky, charismatic figure, to become his agent, a post he has continued to hold for sixteen years, becoming one of Cook's closest friends. Benn had to wait another year before securing Chesterfield in a by-election.

Cook became Livingston's first MP on 9 June 1983, with a majority of 4,951. For him, it was the only good news that night. Thatcher had been returned in triumph with a hugely enhanced majority of 144, on the back of the disintegration of the opposition and her military victory over General Galtieri. The Labour leadership was left licking its wounds after, in Gerald Kaufman's resounding phrase, committing itself to 'the longest suicide note in history'. Among the policies set out in that manifesto, *New Hope for Britain*, was a promise to cancel the Trident programme. It added: 'We will propose that Britain's Polaris force be included in the nuclear disarmament negotiations in which Britain must take a part. We will, after consultation, carry through in the lifetime of the next parliament our non-nuclear defence policy.' The policy fell apart at the hustings when Foot said this meant Polaris would be scrapped, and Healey said it would be retained. The economic section of the manifesto, 'Labour's Programme for Recovery', said withdrawal from the EEC was pivotal and promised a 'massive programme of expansion' including a 'huge programme of construction', a 'five year national plan in consultation with unions and employers' and a repeal of all Tory privatization and trade union legislation. The Treasury team that wrote it consisted of Peter Shore, Robert Sheldon, Jack Straw – and Cook.

Labour took 27.6 per cent of the vote, its lowest share since 1918. Its number of MPs, which had already fallen by 50 at the previous election, had now dropped by another 60 to 209, the lowest figure for either main party since the war. The immediate question was whether Labour could survive as the official opposition. The SDP/Liberal Alliance had received only 2 per cent fewer votes.

In the last few days of the campaign, as Labour's credibility ebbed further and further, Cook was at the centre of secret moves to promote Kinnock as the next party leader. Kinnock, who was shadow education secretary at the time, was visiting Cook's constituency as part of a sweep through Scotland's central belt. With Jim Devine in the agent's car, they stopped to plan out the vital first few days after the election. Cook asked Kinnock if he was going to stand. Kinnock said he would, and that he had already informed Foot, who was privately resigned to defeat. They agreed that Cook would run his national campaign, and Devine would be Scotland coordinator. Kinnock had been Foot's campaign manager two years earlier, and had been impressed by the way Cook, as a member of the team, had 'never massaged the figures for the boss. Unlike others, he talked straight and was never guilty of wishful thinking.'

The results north and south of the border revealed an even bigger discrepancy in allegiances than ever before. In England the Tories had taken 46 per cent of the vote, against Labour's 26.9 per cent; in Scotland the figures were 35.1 per cent for Labour and only 28.4 per cent for the Conservatives. Scotland had 41 Labour MPs, compared to 21 Tories. Cook, ever eager to appear on election night television, was asked for his reaction to the disparity. 'I'm beginning to think that if the Conservatives have this kind of majority we ought to have a Scottish assembly,' he responded.

Cook had given no public hint at a shift towards devolution. Indeed, in the 1979 election he had to be persuaded by his campaign team to include a party pledge to revive plans for a Scottish parliament. However, in the course of the 1983 campaign, as the scale of the likely Tory victory and Labour meltdown became apparent, he came gradually to believe that Scotland under the existing system had no means of fighting Thatcherism in full flight. 'It was something that had been growing on me throughout the election, but it would be wrong to say that I went into the studio in order to say it,' he recalls. His conversion took many in the party by surprise, and he tried over the next few months to explain it. He told the Scottish Socialist Society in July 1983: 'I have not been an extravagant supporter of the Scottish dimension, but I have changed my mind. I don't give a bugger if Thatcher has a mandate or not – I will simply do all I can to stop her. I do not think there is going to be any satisfactory stopping point for us short of some kind of federalism which will give that Scottish assembly or parliament an autonomy and independent source of revenue which it would have been denied under previous devolution packages.' There was a modest dose of *mea culpa* in his conversion. Cook now subscribed to the 'no mandate' argument. Thatcher's law did not apply north of the border – or so the theory went.

Foot resigned as party leader three days after the election. The following morning Kinnock phoned Cook. By then they were close friends. Robin and Margaret would sometimes stay at the Kinnocks' house in west London if they were on their way to the airport. 'I see myself, as Roy Hattersley once put it, as a convivial loner,' Kinnock says. 'Robin was the same. He wasn't one for exchanging dinner dates, which is maybe one of the reasons I got on with him.' They could joke at each other's expense – at one of his first shadow Cabinet meetings Kinnock dubbed Cook his 'hair bank'.

Cook had turned down a similar request by Hattersley to run his campaign. But he met with the rival camp throughout those weeks to ensure that the tussle remained as friendly as possible. With Kinnock expected to romp home, the two camps agreed that Kinnock's supporters should back Hattersley for the number two job, for which he had been nominated by Healey, who was standing down as deputy. In the end, Kinnock made it easily, with the hard left's Eric Heffer trailing badly in third, and yet further behind Peter Shore, standing on an anti-EEC platform. Hattersley easily staved off Michael Meacher for the deputy position.

But Kinnock's support base did not extend to the shadow Cabinet he inherited. The first time he addressed his senior colleagues, he found himself surrounded by ten who had voted for Hattersley as leader, against five who had voted for him. Cook was rewarded for his efforts by gaining a place in the shadow Cabinet for the first time, coming in tenth in the elections. This annual beauty contest was to many leading Labour politicians the most important event of the year, determining their status within the party. The summer months would be spent garnering support, making promises of patronage, and doing deals.

With European elections looming the following June, Cook was given the job of spokesman on European and EEC affairs, a mini-department hived off from Denis Healey's foreign affairs team. His deputy was the ever ardently *communautaire* George Foulkes, relations with whom had largely recovered. Cook's main brief was to rebuild Labour's public image by the time of the European poll – no mean task, so soon after the general election debacle – and to improve Labour's power base in Strasbourg; the 1979 European elections, the first to take place in Britain, had followed immediately after Thatcher's first victory and Labour, hardly bothering to campaign, had won only 17 of the 78 seats.

Having had a personal change of heart on Scottish devolution, Cook now followed up by spearheading a shift in the Labour party's stance towards Europe. Initially seeing the EEC as a threat to jobs and to other socialist concerns, the Labour hierarchy was now beginning to appreciate that Europe could become a counterweight to the Thatcher government, whose position was now stronger than in its first term. Kinnock's leadership manifesto had said: 'By 1988 Britain will have been a member of the Common Market for 15 years. That does not make withdrawal impossible. After that length of time, however, withdrawal should be regarded as a last resort that is considered only if and when the best interests of the British people cannot be feasibly safeguarded by other means.' This position formed the basis of a policy document passed by the 1983 conference. Labour anti-marketeers were stunned by the speed of the volte-face, and by Cook's willingness as an accomplice. He called for a broadening of Labour's approach towards Europe. No longer would issues be focused on EEC institutions. Labour would also tackle questions of disarmament, which were causing anxiety to people throughout Europe. 'I will be seeking contacts with our sister parties in other countries to put forward a common platform on these two issues,' he said. He suggested on one of his first visits to Brussels that all socialist parties of the EEC contest the European elections the following year on a common manifesto. 'Reflation in one country is no longer a viable strategy in the modern world,' he proclaimed. This was to become a key goal for Cook, who in later years would focus with almost missionary zeal on hopes that centre-left parties would work together in common cause, rather than for narrowly conceived national gain.

Persuading constituencies to accept the change of heart on Europe was, according to Kinnock, 'a natural job for Robin. I wanted him to turn around the policy, and fast. He always delivered. He came back never so much as a gram short.' He delivered for the party, and for Kinnock, for whom the Strasbourg elections were his first test of public opinion since becoming leader. Labour gained 32 seats in the 1984 European elections, against the Tories' 45, compared to 1979, when the Tories had 60 and Labour 17. Coming so soon after Labour's general election nadir, it was a significant achievement. 'It is suggested that if Labour's performance in the European elections shows a dramatic improvement on its abysmal 1979 results,' the *FT* had mused on his appointment the previous November, 'Mr Cook may emerge with sufficient credit to warrant a rapid promotion.'[6]

But it was not to be. Relations with Kinnock began to cool. 'Neil had always promised me that after my Europe year I would get a significant portfolio,' says Cook. 'Instead I was offered agriculture, to which I said, "No, thank you very much, I'd just rather carry on what I'm doing."' When Shore was pushed aside because of his reluctance to agree to the Europe policy switch, Cook let it be known that he saw the trade and industry job as a just reward for his efforts. But Kinnock felt too hemmed in by the veteran right-wingers – the Solidarity group members – in the shadow Cabinet, who saw it as John Smith's for the asking. Cook's supporters say that Kinnock went out of his way to show that he would not promote his former allies. 'There's a sort of Falstaff theme here. He had come from the left, from Tribune, from all the things that you know he and I shared, and like Prince Hal he felt the need to repudiate his boss in becoming king.' For his part, Kinnock was already questioning Cook's loyalty. One of the first things the new party leader tried to do was to tone down some of the institutional changes made under Foot. He suggested that the procedure for selecting candidates be opened up to one member one vote in those constituencies that wanted to take up that option; but his bid to effect this was voted down at the October 1984 conference, with Cook supporting the opponents of the motion. Cook's friends believe, too, that Kinnock resented his intellectual capability and tried to keep him down. Nevertheless, Kinnock maintained a high regard for his campaigning skills, and with constituency structures still in a moribund state, he asked Cook to take on a new job within the shadow Cabinet as campaign coordinator.

Cook agreed, though he was initially reluctant. Describing it as a backroom job, he said: 'Every politician likes to dance in front of the footlights. It would be false of me to pretend that I am a shrinking violet. But this is a vital task which Labour have neglected in the past to our peril. I am close to Neil,' he went on, but added: 'I take no credit for having won – he was going to win anyway.'[7] From his new vantage point, Cook set about trying to persuade activists to modernize their practices. Unlike the leadership of the Blair era, he had no central machinery to back him up. He wrote to all constituency parties, urging them to show greater professionalism in dealing with the local media, putting the message across, running their meetings and finances, and helping to establish a national membership list.

This was a pivotal period for the Labour left, a period of fertile thinking. The Tribune group was trying to forge a new politics, realigning policy and attitudes away from Bennite extremes while avoiding a return to the ideological listlessness of the Wilson/Callaghan years. The Labour Coordinating Committee went through several incarnations, breaking with Benn over Militant and helping mobilize support for Kinnock after 1983. Cook became a key figure in the LCC and the Tribune group from that year.

One of his first decisions on joining the shadow Cabinet in 1983 had been to appoint Nigel Stanley, who had been the LCC's full-time organizer, as his research assistant. Stanley describes Cook as consumed by paperwork, dedicated to the point of abstraction. 'He was a driven workaholic. He hasn't changed. He's a perfectionist, but was always good to his staff if they also applied themselves hard. He would use the work you did for him well.' His office, on the ground floor of Norman Shaw North, an annexe of the Palace of Westminster across the road by the Embankment, was often chaotic; he would have a boom box on the floor which would blare out classical or Scottish folk music. Stanley said that Cook was prone to unexplained moods, but did not bare his soul. 'His reaction to depressions was to bury himself in his work. He didn't mind us knocking off early to go out and do normal things, but he was always there. I would find huge quantities of new papers when I came in in the morning.' Stanley, now head of press and public relations at the TUC, remains close to Cook, but like other friends sees little of him.

Working with Cook, he says, was an intense but not a gloomy experience. The boss would crack jokes and relish a good gossip. And there was one other passion: 'We used to dread Monday mornings when Robin would turn up with bumps and bruises. He wasn't very accomplished at the beginning.' Stanley was referring to Cook's burgeoning enthusiasm for equestrianism, once described by Cook himself as 'the perfect cure for political egotism'.

It started in earnest in 1980, although even at his son's wedding Peter Cook alluded to his childhood fascination with horses. Robin and Margaret rented a self-catering holiday home at Godshill, near Fordingbridge in the New Forest. It was next to a stables, so they decided to give riding a try. It was not an auspicious start. Christopher, who was seven, fell off, and while his parents were trying to keep their own horses steady, six-year-old Peter's decided to take him solo, and horse and hapless rider had to be retrieved by the instructor. Despite this turbulent introduction, the whole family resolved to give it a go back in Scotland, and signed up with the Laswade riding school just outside Edinburgh. Margaret and the boys tried to go twice a week, once on a midweek evening and once with Robin, who joined them on his return from London for their weekend session. Margaret was thirty-five when she took up the sport. Within six months she was jumping fences. In 1986 she bought her first horse, Wendy, a Welsh cob. The boys shared a pony called Winky. Wendy went lame. Margaret fared even worse the second time: her next horse broke a leg. Robin also wanted to buy a horse he had become fond of at the stables, Diamond, but realized he would not have time to look after it. Both intrepid and less-than-youthful parents had their share of falls. Christopher remembers one particular time, just before Christmas 1985, when his father was thrown by his horse, remounted, and was thrown again. Chris was riding behind and had at the last minute to jump over his dad, cowering, hands on head, on the ground. 'When we got home Dad had to crawl up the stairs. Peter put a glass of whisky at the top of the stairs to encourage him to stagger up.' Margaret's third purchase proved considerably more successful. Together with Phyllis, a grey Thoroughbred mare, she won a national championship title. The skill gap between husband and wife was growing.

Robin and Christopher, meanwhile, devoted their energies increasingly to a more cerebral appreciation of equine grace. That first New Forest holiday had also brought them into contact for the first time with horse racing. Their visit to a point-to-point at Monmouth was to be followed by a trip to a National Hunt meeting at Newton Abbot during their next holiday in the New Forest the following year. In 1984 Robin and Christopher went to the Grand National – an event Robin never missed thereafter until 1992, when he had to be persuaded not to go as it was taking place five days before polling day. The winner that year was a horse called Party Politics. Robin and Christopher started getting the racing papers, checking form and putting on bets. For Cook, the thrill lay not in the element of chance – he had always been a bit disdainful of his friends at university who gambled on card games – but the skill in weighing up all the different factors: the going, the distance, the past form of the horse, the experience of the jockey. 'Out of politics it's my relaxation. If you are riding a reasonably good horse you can't think of anything else because otherwise you'd be on the ground. As for racing itself, the risk is exciting but anyone who thinks he can make lots of money from betting requires counselling. You should never put on more than you can afford to lose without regret,' he said.

Father and son would try to make it to a race meeting once a week – jump (National Hunt) racing for preference. Flat racing, with its greater emphasis on wealth and privilege, he regarded as second best. It was the challenge, the battle against adversity that he found so compelling: 'I think jump jockeys are still the bravest people I know. To turn up every day and know that one in every ten races you're going to take a crashing fall is an amazing form of courage and commitment. The two most exciting sights and noises I know are these: first, the colour and noise of a large field coming into a steeplechase fence, which is a tremendous spectacle; the other is the clang of the tin ballot boxes as they hit the gymnasium floor coming off the back of the trucks on election night.'[8] Cook was not shy of using racing analogies to explain the political requirements of the day. 'The reins are there to get the animal balanced and then you can get it to jump most things. I think that's a perfectly fair analogy for the reins of discipline in the party. They're not there to check enthusiasm or to stop momentum, but to make sure we go forward collectively in proper balance.'[9]

He also drew on his knowledge of the sport, and the economics of it, in the mainstream political debate. In November 1984 he proposed that local communities be allowed to run their own bookmakers' shops and off-licences, and use the profits to create jobs. Addressing a conference on community businesses, he noted that one bookmaker in Glasgow's sprawling Easterhouse estate was making £500,000 a year. 'That is an incredible drain of money out of an area where it is difficult to believe the people can afford it. One may have doubts about whether or not that is the right way for the people of Easterhouse to spend their money. But if that is what they want it seems to me that there is everything to be said for setting up a project where the profits gained can be put back into the community from which they are being taken.'[10]

In 1989, on the platform of Doncaster railway station, Cook met John McCririck, Channel Four's man in the bookies' ring, resplendent with his funny hats, big rings, polka dot bow ties and exuberant mannerisms – and an ardent Thatcherite to boot. They started talking racing straight away. They made unlikely friends, but close friends they became. In January 1990 McCririck invited Robin and Christopher on to Channel Four Racing's *Morning Line* programme, where they tipped a horse called Atlaal at Kempton Park. It was hardly a fancied runner at 10–1, but it won by a head. 'That's when the polls started to turn in Labour's favour,' says McCririck. 'He and I have joked about it since, but it's true.'

With Cook's profile in the racing world increasing, he was asked in late 1991 by Harry Reid, then deputy editor of the *Herald* in Glasgow, to write a weekly column, in which he would have to tip winners of five races every Saturday and explain the thinking behind his selections. 'It was a completely new idea having a celebrity tipster. I had read a couple of things about Robin and racing and had been impressed,' says Reid. Cook enlisted Christopher's help and set about the task with as much zeal as he applied to his politics. His early days as a newspaper tipster, however, were hardly auspicious: the first four weeks passed without a single winner. The first week Robin and Christopher selected Bradbury Star as the nap – their hottest tip of the day – only for it to fall at the first fence. The trainer, Josh Gifford, was not amused when a photograph of his hapless horse was splashed across the news pages of the *Daily Mail* the following Monday.

Riding and racegoing are not – or not necessarily – team activities, and one of the attractions of the gallop, as Cook admits himself, is the escape. This preference for solitary leisure pursuits accorded with his working habits: late nights in the Commons library, buried in books and failing to register the presence of others. Although he enjoyed a drink or two of malt whisky, it was either on his own or with one or two friends: not for him the many Commons bars, the tea room or dining room. Cook knew that his campaigning job had taken him out of Westminster for much of the time, out of the loop; but not even in his wildest nightmares did he think his absence would cost him so dearly.

The shadow Cabinet elections of 1986 saw Cook voted out. He and another Tribune group member, Bob Hughes, were replaced by David Clark and Bryan Gould, who also saw himself as a potential leader of the centre-left. Cook attributed the cut in his vote, from 106 MPs to 78, to two years 'in the back room'. Another MP, who would later join him in the Cabinet, put it more bluntly: 'We knew that Robin was brilliant, but he was hated. David Clark was useless but loved.' Martin O'Neill, to whom he was still close, says they went drinking that evening. 'He was in despair. I remember Kinnock telling me years later how his defeat in the shadow Cabinet had screwed him up.' Nigel Stanley put it down to Cook's virtual absence from the dispatch box throughout the whole parliament. 'He used to have one question on Europe during Foreign Office questions. People forgot he was around. Then he really wasn't around. When he lost he was taken completely by surprise. I suppose he was still a bit naïve, he didn't realize that the party whips had slates of candidates and each slate required working on. It took him quite some time to get over it.' The first thing Cook did the next day was to contact Gould and ask him to take Stanley on as his researcher, which he did. 'He was deeply shocked but he didn't despair,' recalls George Foulkes. 'He came to see me the next day, we analysed it, worked out why it had happened and he set his mind to getting back.'[11] That required spending time courting his colleagues, among them Derek Fatchett, who went on to become one of his closest confidants in the Commons. 'Robin realized at that point that he had been squeezed by the hard-left Campaign group and by those to the right of Kinnock. He realized after that the need to build alliances.'

Cook looks back at the period between 1983 and 1986 as the most politically frustrating of his life. He calls them the 'lost years'. For reasons he has never understood, Kinnock would not give him a job that played to his abilities – attacking the Tories on policy at the dispatch box. Kinnock admits 'there may be some justice' in what Cook says, but says that he was conscious all the time of having to balance the shadow Cabinet between wings of the party and generations. In any event, notwithstanding the election result, Kinnock kept Cook on – it became customary for one or two shadow Cabinet members to be unelected. He was given a job as trade spokesman under John Smith, shadow trade and industry secretary, and did much to rehabilitate himself in the following year as part of Smith's team. The campaigning job went to Gould.

For many on the left at the time, the mid-1980s was a period when Thatcher's control over the government and state machinery reached dangerous proportions. She did battle with the BBC, the courts and Parliament; and from the miners' strike to the poll tax dispute she was more than eager to use the police and security forces to impose her will. One of the biggest battles on this ground occurred in January 1987, and Cook, who had shown his willingness to stand up for greater openness in the 1970s, played a prominent role. Duncan Campbell – the one detained over the ABC affair in 1977 – was reporter and main researcher on a six-part series made by BBC Scotland for BBC2, entitled *Secret Society*. One of the programmes was to reveal that £500 million, disguised in the books as part of the budget for Trident, had in fact been siphoned off by the government to pay for Zircon, a spy satellite run by GCHQ. The programme not only disclosed the existence of the satellite but showed how Parliament had been deceived by government. Under pressure from ministers, the security services and BBC governors, the programme was postponed. Cook and other Labour MPs sought to have it screened in a Commons committee room. Unbeknown to ministers, the *New Statesman* was preparing to publish the full details. When the Attorney-General, Sir Michael Havers, realized what was going on he dispatched Treasury solicitors to serve an injunction on Campbell. By the time they reached the office, Campbell had taken off on his bicycle and gone to ground. No injunction could be served. Cook, who throughout the saga kept in touch with Campbell via call boxes and other discreet channels, had played a part in helping the beleaguered journalist to disappear.

Campbell reappeared the next morning in the cloisters of the Commons, close to the offices of several left-wing Labour MPs, by which time the *New Statesman* was on sale and the story had made the news. A furious Thatcher then ordered an emergency motion to be put to the Commons banning the screening of the film. Kinnock and the all-party privileges committee acquiesced. 'The Conservative government has shown an increasing tendency to use the courts against any centre of opposition – local authorities, trade unions and now journalists. It would have been refreshing to have had a clear statement from the committee of privileges that the courts could not be used against MPs going about their duties,' Cook said.[12] Days later, Campbell's home, the *New Statesman*'s offices and the offices of the BBC in Glasgow were raided. By this point the film had developed cult status and bootleg copies were being shown at community halls across the country; Cook was one of several MPs to address such meetings. It was more than a year before it was aired on television.

After the setbacks earlier in the parliament, he was back doing what he did best, and what drove him most – campaigning on issues such as personal liberty. But for some in the security services and elsewhere, Cook had gone one step too far.

6

The Face that Didn't Fit

After the lost years came the turbulent years. The third consecutive term of Conservative government saw Cook hoisted on to the national stage, his face ubiquitous on television news programmes as Thatcher's third administration stumbled into a series of crises. Yet the more prominent he became, the more he was resented by some of his colleagues. For all the vows he had made to himself after losing his shadow cabinet place in 1986 to act in a more collegiate fashion, Cook was still seen by his detractors as working by himself, for himself. Those of his rivals who had got where they were through schmoozing as much as by intellectual rigour distrusted a man who regarded raw argument as the only legitimate route to success.

Although Labour had lost again in 1987, increasing their number of MPs by only 20, the campaign itself was widely praised. Kinnock had moved policy a considerable distance from the 1983 suicide note – the party had abandoned withdrawal from the EEC, relinquished its opposition to council house sales, and beaten a retreat from manifesto commitments on job creation and public ownership. But unilateralism remained in place, and economic policy remained unequivocally Keynesian and redistributive. In other words, with Thatcher at the peak of her power, Labour did not have much of a product to sell, but sold it well. That, at least, became the perception afterwards. One man was given most of the credit, and it did not take long for the legend of Peter Mandelson to become established. Yet Cook's friends look back at this era through somewhat different spectacles. Nigel Stanley, Cook's former researcher, argues that Cook and Gould, his successor as campaign coordinator, were subsequently 'airbrushed from the memory bank' of that election.

The first tentative steps towards a more modern form of campaigning were taken immediately after the woeful 1983 election. Midway through that campaign a group of Labour-supporting advertising executives made a presentation to the election committee. This consisted of the entire shadow Cabinet and NEC, along with about twenty staffers from Walworth Road, the party headquarters. 'It was a pointless exercise,' recalls Colin Fisher of the company SRU, one of the marketing advisers. 'There was no way decisions were going to be taken like that.' The lack of organization and focus convinced Kinnock and Cook that new structures were required. A year later Fisher went to the 1984 US presidential elections and was struck by the gulf in expertise between the slick Reagan campaign and the amateur Democratic machine behind Walter Mondale and Geraldine Ferraro. On his return, he went to discuss the issue of private polling with Kinnock. But Patricia Hewitt, the leader's press secretary, was not particularly interested; nor was Larry Whitty, the newly installed party general secretary. The only enthusiast, he says, was Cook. Stanley recalls going with Cook and other party figures to a number of advertising agencies, discussing how to use focus groups and other devices that had been around a long time in the commercial world but were somewhat alien to politics. Among those they talked to were Philip Gould and Chris Powell – and thus the Shadow Communications Agency was born: a conduit through which a small team of advertising copywriters, psephologists, market researchers, graphic artists and others contributed unpaid work for the party. Initially, the agency set up a number of early focus groups. But its work was hindered by a lack of clear lines of communication and accountability within the party.

That is where Mandelson came in. A former producer on LWT's *Weekend World* programme, he had been appointed director of communications at Walworth Road by Kinnock in October 1985. Mandelson had particularly close relations with Charles Clarke, Kinnock's chief of staff, and Hewitt. The SCA, with Gould and Powell at the helm, worked directly and discreetly to Mandelson. By the time the 1987 election came around, the new structures were in place. The problem was the party, and the message. Immediately after the defeat, Mandelson asked Gould to prepare a report on how – or if – the party could ever get back into government. Gould listed a series of policy areas, from tax to public ownership, defence and industrial relations, where Labour was distrusted by voters, and said the party was entirely geared to satisfying the views of activists and pressure groups.

Kinnock had taken the defeat badly. He went into a bout of depression and was on the point of resigning several times. He saw questions about the direction of policy as a challenge to his authority. Once, when Cook, Frank Dobson and others went to see him about an impending rebellion – over an order to vote against a government motion linking an annual increase in the basic state pension to a freeze in child benefit – Kinnock launched a tirade against them. But he got over his initial gloom and concluded that the only way forward was to make a radical break with the past, a conviction confirmed by the SCA report. He ordered a review of all party policy, to be conducted by seven separate groups set up by the NEC and shadow Cabinet, which were to report within two years. He made it clear that defence policy would form an integral part of the review – this immediately after the 1987 Labour conference, at which the party had reaffirmed its commitment to unilateral nuclear disarmament. The party went, according to a colleague of Cook, into 'ideological free fall'.

The proposed policy shake-up was not matched in personnel. Only one significant opening was created, by Healey's retirement to the back benches. Gerald Kaufman took his job as shadow Foreign Secretary, Hattersley was moved from shadow Chancellor to the Home Office, and Smith was promoted from the DTI to shadow Chancellor, to be replaced by Gould. But below them a new generation was emerging. Gordon Brown made it into the shadow Cabinet for the first time, as shadow Treasury chief secretary under Smith. Cook, too, was in, appointed shadow health and social security secretary. Things seemed to be looking up at last. Within months of the 1987 election, he had had the satisfaction of seeing himself back on the official roll of the shadow Cabinet. The following year, at the party conference, he was elected on to the NEC for the first time, displacing Michael Meacher. He had doubled his vote in the constituency section. The *Scotsman*'s political editor, Ewen Macaskill, noted at the time: 'It marks what has been an extraordinary turn around in his fortunes. A few years ago his standing in the party was a long way from its present high. Few then would have betted that he would have made such a spectacular comeback.'[1]

Cook now had as his researcher Geoffrey Norris, who had been working for Giles Radice on education. Unlike Stanley, Norris was not an ideological soulmate of Cook, and their relationship was more formal, but Cook came to trust his judgement. Norris, who left Cook in 1994 to work for Tony Blair, remembers his former boss as both amusing and frustrating to work with. When an argument needed to be talked through, Cook was very collective. People that he rated he used well. But, as Cook himself concedes, hours were spent perfecting big speeches, which he saw as acts of immense political drama. His office, like previous offices, was often chaotic. 'We sat around for a long time on those orange Commons rent-a-crates. He refused to throw anything away. One weekend I stole in and threw stuff in bags,' Norris recalls.

As the policy review gathered pace, Tony Benn launched what would be his final bid for power, with a challenge to Kinnock's leadership in February 1988. The veteran left-winger Eric Heffer decided to stand against

Hattersley as deputy – as did John Prescott, who for several months had been toying with the idea of contesting the number two job. Now in charge of energy policy, he had felt shut out during the 1987 campaign despite being shadow employment secretary. Prescott had assumed he could count on Cook's support: the two shared broadly common policy positions, and would sometimes take their views directly to Kinnock as a pair. But Cook again accepted an offer by Kinnock to act as his courtier. He and Smith, who had worked for Hattersley in the 1983 leadership contest against Kinnock, would serve as joint chairmen of the Kinnock–Hattersley campaign committee, to demonstrate unity and continuity between the centre-left and centre-right in the party. Prescott took a long time to forgive Cook for assisting the leadership slate. Colin Brown, Prescott's biographer, says of that decision: 'It was a personal let-down he never forgot'.[2] Yet Cook's friends say backing Prescott then was never an option, as without Hattersley, Kinnock would almost certainly have resigned and plunged the party into chaos. In the end, Kinnock demolished Benn, securing 88.6 per cent of the electoral college, while Hattersley saw off the separate challenges of Prescott and Heffer. Prescott paid the price for his challenge later that year by being switched to transport; his job at energy was given to Tony Blair, who entered the shadow Cabinet for the first time.

That leadership contest was little more than a distraction from a more fundamental battle of ideas taking place in the shadow Cabinet. The protagonists were Smith and Gould, who thought he should have been shadow Chancellor and believed he was being sidelined. The catalyst was a document presented by Kinnock and Hattersley to the shadow Cabinet in early 1988 entitled *A Statement of Democratic Socialist Aims and Values*, which was intended to provide the policy review process with a philosophical justification of a mixed economy. Cook, Gould and others expressed concern that the paper was tantamount to abdicating Labour's historical role in redistributing wealth. Its acceptance that market forces provided a 'generally satisfactory' method for allocating goods and services seemed to undermine Labour's commitment to intervention and economic management. 'For my preference the document is a bit too fulsome in its praise of markets,' said Gould. 'The balance was wrong.' Cook then had his first taste of a new battle to come. He was seething with fury when Sunday newspapers suggested he had criticized the document because he had not fully understood it.[3] He was told that the information had been provided by forces within the party.

Cook's period as campaigns chief and his interpretation of the reasons for the 1987 defeat led him off on a different path. His view was that Labour would win back the hearts and minds of floating voters not by discarding policies lock, stock and barrel – although some changes were certainly required – but by changing its approach to the way politics is conducted. The election result in Scotland reflected an even greater disparity in geographical party allegiance than in 1983. The Tories were still dominant in England, but in Scotland support had collapsed, from 21 seats out of a total of 72 to only 10. Labour had promised Scotland after the 1983 debacle in England that it would use its strength north of the border to protect voters there from Conservative hegemony; but in reality, with power so concentrated at Westminster, there was little Labour MPs could do. In the 1987 campaign the SNP referred to Labour's Scottish contingent in the Commons as 'the feeble fifty'.

Between 1979 and 1987 devolution was strictly for the aficionados. However, a feeling of disenfranchisement brought the issue back to the fore. Thatcherism had converted a lot of Scots to devolution; Cook was not the only one to embrace it late in the day. The Tories, for their part, served notice that any change to constitutional arrangements was anathema, provoking some radicals to call for a form of UDI for Scotland – a provisional assembly of some sort. Among them was Cook, who called on Labour's fifty Scottish MPs to set up their own parliament. 'After eight years of Thatcherism, one of the reasons I find the demand for a Scottish assembly so exciting, so attractive, so appealing is because it will create an unstable situation in the rest of the British constitution,' he said. Donald Dewar, Kinnock's Scottish spokesman and as ardent a pro-devolutionist as they come, was suspicious of attempts by Cook and others on the left to challenge Westminster's constitutional supremacy; and Kinnock himself, in 1979 as staunch an opponent of devolution as Cook, was still lukewarm. He was prepared for the issue to be discussed and promoted as policy, promising for the first time in 1986 that a Scottish parliament would be legislated for in the first year of a Labour government; but he did not see it as central to his attempts to drag the party towards electability. Challenged in March 1988 on why he had failed to mention devolution in his speech to the Scottish Labour party conference, Kinnock let fly with one of his typically unguarded remarks: there were a lot of things he hadn't discussed, he replied, such as 'environmental conditions in the Himalayas'. At the same Scottish conference in 1988 a new vehicle for the left was born: Scottish Labour Action called for civil disobedience and the disruption of Parliament, and asserted 'Scotland's right to self-determination on such a basis as the people of Scotland themselves decide'.

The catalyst for this growing militancy was the poll tax, the ultimate expression of Labour impotence during the Thatcher years. Scotland was to be the guinea pig in a pilot project under the aegis of Scottish secretary Malcolm Rifkind. The first bills were sent north of the border in spring 1989. By the end of the first year, some 700,000 summary warrants had been served in Scotland for non-payment of the tax. Over three years, that figure would reach 2.5 million. The SLA coordinated the non-payment campaign, even though the Scottish party itself voted against such a policy at a special conference in September 1988. The group was a thorn in Dewar's side. Cook, although not a member, discreetly encouraged them, operating as an honorary president. Dewar, with the instincts of a lawyer, was convinced that, whatever the ethics of the poll tax, MPs had to play by the rules and not encourage non-payment. Riled at what he saw as Cook's extra-parliamentary activism, he ambushed his colleague in the shadow Cabinet and, with Kinnock's approval, gave him a dressing-down. Dewar cited media reports alleging that Cook was backing the no-pay campaign. One of these reports concerned a rally in Bathgate organized by the West Lothian Stop It campaign. Cook said he had not been asked by organizers to address the meeting; his attendance was a purely constituency matter and did not contravene any gagging order on the shadow front bench. There was nothing to prevent him speaking about the poll tax in general, he said.[4]

The legitimacy of rule from Westminster was coming under increasingly forceful questioning across a broad spectrum of Scottish opinion. The big shock to the system for Labour's leaders in Scotland was the victory of Jim Sillars and the Scottish Nationalists in the Glasgow Govan by-election in November 1988. With the SLA's non-payment and civil disobedience campaign in full swing, the Scottish Constitutional Convention – a more demure and less partisan vehicle for extra-parliamentary activity – came into being in March 1989, charged with agreeing 'a scheme for an assembly or parliament for Scotland'. At the heart of its work was not only the need to prevent a continuation of Conservative hegemony in Scotland but the creation of a new kind of legislature. Although the convention was boycotted by the Conservatives and SNP (for diametrically opposed reasons), the presence of the Liberal Democrats, along with church, women's and community groups, gave it a greater moral legitimacy than a mere in-house Labour commission could have claimed.

For the Liberal Democrats, who were being squeezed in Scotland as in the rest of the UK, some form of proportional representation was crucial. The difference now was that they were finding allies in their quest for change in the voting system where none had previously existed. During the 1970s, when Labour benefited from the traditional first-past-the-post system, only the most quirky party member challenged its fairness and efficacy. But the 1987 election had given Thatcher a majority of 57 with little over 42 per cent of the vote, and the 1983 result had embodied an even greater imbalance. The Labour Campaign for Electoral Reform began quietly in 1979, but enjoyed a period of rapid growth. Many party members saw Thatcher's summary abolition of the Greater London Council as a metaphor for untrammelled power of the central executive reinforced by an electoral system that left many disenfranchised. The issue was hotly debated by party activists. From 1983 Cook toyed with the alternative vote system, in which voters list candidates in order of preference in their constituency, but by the time he became a major player in the Campaign in 1987 he had been converted to the additional member system, in which constituency MPs are supplemented by members drawn from regional party lists to make the overall distribution of seats more proportional to the numbers of votes cast. The most powerful model for Cook at the time was Germany, where a version of this system had enabled the Green party (which shared his long-held views about the environment and the bomb) to win seats in the Bundestag. A decade later, a similar system would be used for the Scottish parliament.

Kinnock, although not persuaded by calls for change, was acutely aware that Labour had lost a voice in many parts of the country, including much of southern England. Cook would use the argument that there were more Labour voters in Kent than in Glasgow, but in Kent there were no Labour MPs. He was instrumental in persuading Kinnock to keep an open mind on the issue. With many in the party wondering aloud whether it could ever rule again on its own, Kinnock agreed to set up an independent commission on electoral systems to answer growing calls for change among party activists. Originally its remit was confined to looking at devolution, giving power to the regions, changes to the House of Lords and other constitutional proposals. However, with the NEC divided, the 1990 conference voted to extend its remit to cover the Commons. Cook, who was at the forefront of the campaign for this extension, launched a blistering attack on Hattersley, who argued that the issue was an irrelevance. 'There is to be a ring fence around the Commons. This is a no-go area in which the electoral system is not to be examined. This is the politics of the ostrich,' Cook told a fringe meeting.[5] Led by Raymond (later Lord) Plant, professor of politics at Southampton University, the commission held its first meeting in December 1990.

For all the hackles raised in discussions of electoral reform, from its inception in 1987 it was clear that the most contentious area of the Labour party's policy review would be defence. Kinnock was still an ardent unilateralist when he succeeded Foot. Not long after becoming Labour leader he made a public appearance to address CND's largest London rally, in which 400,000 people had gathered in Hyde Park, on 24 October 1983 – days before the arrival of the first cruise missiles. Yet defence had proved the party's Achilles' heel at the 1987 election. Kinnock himself had cause to rue one particular interview when, asked to outline Labour's response to a

Soviet invasion of Britain, he said it would be to 'make any occupation totally untenable'. This spawned Tory posters that read 'Labour's defence policy' above a picture of a soldier with his hands up as if in surrender.

The retention of unilateralism at the subsequent party conference convinced Kinnock, and more particularly his backroom team, that he would have to be more proactive in changing policy. Backed strongly by Kaufman, Hattersley, Smith and younger shadow Cabinet members, he started using interviews to put out feelers for a change. Kinnock hinted that Labour could no longer propose going into international disarmament talks as a nuclear power without using its deterrent as leverage. The suggestion that Labour was moving away from what Kinnock called the 'something for nothing' policy led Denzil Davies, a convinced unilateralist, to resign as shadow defence secretary. Kinnock says he toyed with giving Cook the job, but that it would have been too controversial an appointment. He opted instead for Martin O'Neill, who had been Davies's deputy and would be a safer choice than Cook – who had said only months earlier that it was 'nonsense on stilts' for Britain to posture as a nuclear power. One of the more trenchant attacks on his line appeared in the *Mirror*, written by its then political editor Alastair Campbell. When Campbell took over as Blair's press secretary in 1994 he saw the article pinned to a peg board in the office of Anna Healy, the press officer for the parliamentary Labour party. He asked her diplomatically to take it down.

Unilateralism was finally dumped, at the third attempt, at the 1989 conference. A few months earlier Kinnock had secured one of his most important successes by persuading the NEC to agree that Britain's weapons should be put into international negotiations. The rearguard action was led by David Blunkett, a new arrival on the Labour front bench although, by virtue of his former position as leader of Sheffield City Council, an NEC member since 1983. Blunkett sought a formula that would allow for the unilateral option to be preserved, in the event of international talks failing. Cook, with Kinnock's agreement, introduced a weaker amendment, stipulating only that, if the START II talks failed to achieve the scrapping of Trident in a multilateral deal, Labour would be able to enter into a bilateral deal with the Soviet Union to rid the UK of nuclear weapons. Once more, Cook had found a rationale for dropping a view he had once held strongly. 'It was very useful for me that Robin, after presenting several amendments and after a degree of divergence, had come along with the mainstream. It was very important that we got him on side. I would not say I abused this, but I certainly exploited it,' says Kinnock. To Cook's detractors, this was a further example of going with the flow. Any remaining ambiguity in defence policy was dispelled by Kinnock in 1991 when he said that the British deterrent would be retained 'until the extermination of nuclear weapons'.

As the policy review was in full swing, Cook was enjoying his most productive period as a pursuer of hapless Conservatives. Although he had told Kinnock in 1987 that he would have preferred an economic portfolio, he was very happy to be given health and social security, a brief that put him in the front line of Labour attacks on government policy.

Thatcher had gone into the 1987 election promising a revolution in the way the NHS and the benefits system were run. Easy applause could be won at Tory conferences by haranguing so-called 'scroungers'. 'Choice' was the buzzword; increasing disposable income was the key aim. The Social Security Act of 1986, the latest in a series, had been designed to stem the seemingly inexorable rise in the welfare bill, largely by simplifying claims. The legislation had been taken through the Commons by Norman Fowler, who had been Secretary of State for Social Services for six years and was moved on after the election. The new incumbent was John Moore, a man catapulted to fame after only a year as transport secretary, who helped to encourage the creation of his own myth – only to see it blown away just as quickly. Thatcher was letting it be known that, with her tenth anniversary as Prime Minister just a couple of years away, she could see someone like Moore stepping into her shoes. Television profiles echoed that sentiment. He was suave, good looking and had – so his mentor hoped – a certain 'presence' that comes with clarity of political purpose.

When Cook heard that Kinnock wanted a new broom to shadow Moore, replacing Dobson and Meacher, he rang Hewitt from an Indian restaurant to express his interest. Kinnock gave him what he wanted – a move that was to usher in a dramatic rise in his fortunes. One of the most pivotal tasks of opposition is to identify the government's weak point and harry it, producing a barrage of negative publicity for ministers. Health, social security and, initially, Moore himself became that weak point. From 1987 until the 1992 election there were weeks when Labour was 'running' almost entirely on health. Moore started badly, failing to impress the 1987 Tory conference. He then got a viral infection which affected his throat and kept him away from work in the crucial months at the start of 1988. Cumulative cuts in health spending in recent years came to a head that winter, with doctors and nurses marching on Downing Street, health authorities going broke and up to four thousand beds closed. A former Treasury man, Moore felt it his duty to work within the budget allocation and did not fight the department's corner in Cabinet.

The social security changes embodied in the act of 1986 were due to come into force in April 1988. The timing could not have been worse. A month earlier Nigel Lawson introduced his great giveaway budget to the better-off, with the top rate of tax slashed from 60 per cent to 40 per cent. Cook played on the fears of many at the opposite end of the spectrum. He condemned the budget as a 'budget for the greedy, paid for by the needy'. At the Labour conference in September 1987 he had warned Moore that the Tory minister was 'not going to launch his campaign for the party leadership on the bodies of claimants'. He predicted that 700,000 welfare claimants would be excluded by the new social security bill. He asked Tony Newton, the minister of state responsible for health, how putting up dental charges encouraged people to look after their teeth. His attacks struck a chord with many.

Moore was only just recovering from protracted illness when he was forced to defend the social security changes in a Commons debate. The mauling he received from Cook that afternoon earned a prominent place in the annals of one-sided parliamentary debate. Cook found the perfect mix of emotion, generality and specific example, meshed together in a menacing deadpan delivery. His main argument, corroborated by evidence from several outside organizations, was that the changes would do three times the damage the government had admitted. He noted that the government had tried to ignore the findings of the Social Security Advisory Committee, set up by the government as a source of independent advice, when in its annual report it put the number of losers not at 12 per cent, as ministers claimed, but 43 per cent of claimants. He cited harrowing examples of infirm claimants who would suffer more under the new system. 'Those who lose most are the old and the sick. That is not surprising, because a key feature of the new scheme is that it sweeps away all the extra additions for the special needs of the disabled and frail, such as diet, heating and laundry: all the additions to which a former minister of state with responsibility for social security – now the minister for health – once referred in a television interview as the twiddly bits of the system. It is, of course, those "twiddly bits" that made life bearable for the disabled.' His conclusion was withering, contrasting the budget with the benefits assault. 'There need not have been any losers from the social security changes. We know that the government had the money to prevent there being any losers. We know that because the Chancellor found £2.08 billion to give to 750,000 top-rate taxpayers only last month. There was no talk of targeting there in the budget speech; no talk of concentrating help where it was most needed last month. The Chancellor actually gave away more money to 750,000 of the rich than the entire increase in the social security budget for twelve million claimants. That tells us all we need to know about the government's priorities.'[6]

Moore floundered. The cumbersome department was rudderless. Proposals to reform the NHS had made little progress. Cook spread the message that the government intended to 'privatize' health, playing on public perceptions of a government that promoted greed over compassion. His anger was genuine – the NHS that his hero Nye Bevan had founded was being threatened. Of all the issues gauged in opinion polls, health consistently and comfortably gave Labour its biggest lead. Thatcher responded to Cook's onslaught by splitting the DHSS as part of a reshuffle in July 1988. By reforming the very structures of Whitehall, she was paying tacit tribute to Cook's success. Kenneth Clarke was appointed to health; Moore was left to preside over social security, and was even knocked off the Cabinet committee conducting the health service review. He lasted in his new job only a year, and eventually quit Parliament in 1992 for a life in the City of London. It was an ignominious fall, and it was attributable in no small measure to Cook.

Thatcher hoped that Clarke's more charismatic and pugnacious approach would neutralize the opposition attacks. Cook urged Kinnock not to follow her in splitting the portfolios: he could manage both, he said. Given Cook's success, it was hard for Kinnock to ignore his request. With Scottish schools having their summer holidays earlier than English ones, Cook almost always made good use of August to raise his profile. In party terms, this happened to be traditionally when constituency activists sent in their ballot forms for NEC elections, and Cook was to profit from that. This year, Clarke had barely read himself into his new job when Cook struck again. It was August 1988, and the nurses were in dispute over a low pay settlement. Civil servants in the new stand-alone Department of Health had failed to coordinate diaries, resulting in Clarke, his new number two David Mellor, and other ministers all being out of the country at the same time. Much to his amusement, Cook found himself on the *Today* programme debating with Timothy Yeo, a member of the social security select committee, who was the highest-profile figure the government could muster, in his car in a motorway layby on his mobile phone. 'I suddenly had this wonderful vision that there was nobody else around, and so we had two wonderfully happy weeks running rings round them on health. That's when I wrote to Mrs Thatcher saying that I was distressed there were no ministers able to run the department. I was home in the country and available if she would like to send for me.' By the start of the following year Clarke had finally got to grips with the grand plan for the NHS. However, Cook triumphantly announced that part of the white paper had come into his possession. Clarke squirmed in an interview when told that Labour had details of the purchaser/provider split, the transformation of directly managed NHS hospitals into self-standing trusts, and the plan to give general practitioners the right to purchase hospital care on behalf of patients. Mandelson told Cook afterwards that it was the first time he had ever 'heard somebody sweat' on the radio.

By summer 1989 Cook believed that his success at the dispatch box merited promotion to one of the main economic portfolios. He had done his extra year combining the health and social security jobs, but the two functions of the department were becoming increasingly separate and it was becoming difficult to keep them both on in opposition. Charles Clarke, Kinnock's chief of staff, phoned Cook and asked him to stay on. 'It says a lot about their relations that Kinnock didn't even bother to call him,' says a friend of Cook. 'Robin asked if anyone else was on the move. He no longer had that kind of relationship with Neil to tell him straight that he'd been eyeing trade and industry.' Cook told Clarke he was prepared to stay on for a year, but on the assumption that he would be moved 'somewhere significant' next time. Kinnock assured him that would be the case. But Cook was not told that the reshuffle of 1989 was going to be a radical one, aimed at forming the core of the team Kinnock wanted to take into the next general election, and that there were not going to be major changes in 1990. When he found out the results of the reshuffle he was livid. Cook was doubly aggrieved to see that the job he coveted, the DTI, was going, unbeknown to him, to Brown. A close friend of Kinnock says that if Cook took the changes as a snub 'that's more of a comment on him than us. There was no way he was getting one of the top three jobs. As for the economic jobs one rung below, they were up to Smith. If Robin had a grudge he should have directed it at John, not Neil.'

For all the attempts to undermine him, often from within the top levels of the party, Cook's public and media profile was by no means all bad. The *Mail on Sunday* suggested on 9 June 1991 that when William Waldegrave, the latest incumbent in the health job, 'closes his eyes at night, one face dominates his dreams. It is the impish, slightly diabolic visage of his "shadow", Robin Cook. More than any other Labour politician – more than John Smith, Gordon Brown, Neil Kinnock – Cook is the main reason why the government is languishing eight points behind Labour in the opinion polls.' Yet such praise told only part of the story. Cook's strength was in attacking Tory policy. When the spotlight was turned on a policy of his own, he would be evasive. Gordon Best was director of the King's Fund, a medical charity – a key player in the health world and a Labour supporter. In 1991 Norris arranged for him to meet Cook. Best was about to start a sabbatical. 'I arrived and said "I'm offering my services for free to do what I can to help get Labour elected." But instead of welcoming me with open arms he asked me what I was looking for. I told him, "to make your policies more specific", to which Cook replied, "Whatever for?" Robin said he was happy for me to develop some ideas but that until the election I should keep them to myself. "I don't want policies that are too specific," he said. At that point he rummaged inside his top drawer, threw a folder on his desk containing a printout. "This is the latest focus group, giving us an 87 per cent rating on health. When it starts going down I'll start thinking about a new policy," he replied.'

Cook was now using the NEC as his own vehicle. Kinnock had central-ized power to a degree, but this was a period of intense debate about the future direction of policy in the formal meetings of the party upper echelons, and the NEC and shadow Cabinet were anything but a pushover. As now, deals were hatched, moves were plotted, in smaller coteries, but those whose views were not aligned with the leader's office still carried considerable weight. Cook worked closely with Clare Short, who like him had been elected on to the executive in 1988 and who was now a junior frontbench spokeswoman. Dobson and Meacher were allies, as was Blunkett.

It was in the late 1980s, as Cook hogged the headlines with his health campaign, that his friends believe the briefings began. The finger is pointed at Mandelson, although after 1992 Gordon Brown's camp came into its own.

Mandelson believed the future lay with Brown and Blair. Kinnock also took pride in nurturing the pair of young modernizers. Blair had entered the Commons in 1983 as MP for Sedgefield, and was instantly spotted by Kinnock and Smith as someone to watch. Smith asked Brown and Blair to work on the employment select committee at a time when a further bout of Tory trade union legislation was being considered. At this point Blair was very much the junior partner, but he was moving quickly. He was given a low-ranking shadow Treasury job in 1984 and was planted by Smith into Gould's DTI team in 1987. Still, according to Cook's colleagues, Blair 'barely appeared on his radar screen at that point'.

It was Brown who was making waves. After his precocious brilliance in university days, he had taken longer than he had liked to gain a seat in parlia-ment. He was desperately upset not to win the nomination for the Hamilton by-election in 1978, when he had chosen to stand even though it was assumed that George Robertson would get the seat. Brown pleaded with a third candidate, Alf Young, to stand down and ask his supporters to back him instead. Young, a former senior party officer in Scotland who is now deputy editor of the *Herald* in Glasgow, stood his ground. Brown withdrew from the race, hugely disappointed. The following year he secured a nomination, but the seat of Edinburgh South at a time when everyone seemed to be deserting Labour was well-nigh unwinnable. Cook had joined Brown in canvassing for Robertson and, while the relationship was very much one between a senior and a junior partner, they were reasonably good acquaintances. With boundary changes impending, they would discuss their future career paths, where the next opportunities lay. For Cook it was Livingston, for Brown it was Dunfermline. By the time Brown made it to Parliament in 1983 there was no reason why they could not have worked together. They might not have been natural bedfellows – Brown was much the more gregarious of the two – yet they shared the same political views and inheritance.

Cook was well aware that Brown was held in high regard by the leadership even before he came to the Commons. Kinnock had invited Brown for dinner during campaigning for the Glasgow Hillhead by-election in March 1982, and had listened intently to the prospective MP's economic theories. Brown took to oppositional politics easily, making a name as a junior DTI spokesman exposing the growth of poverty under the Tories and attacking their welfare cuts. This was roughly the same ground as Cook, and inevitably they were rivals in the arts of identifying news stories and leaking documents to journalists. But, whatever professional jealousy might have set in, they still cooperated. There is little evidence to suggest any bad feeling after the 1979 devolution campaign, in which they were on opposite sides. After all, many a friendship had survived those divisions.

So when did the rot set in, and why? Cook says he was not aware of any problem until 1987. One theory, put forward by Brown's biographer Paul Routledge, is that Cook first antagonized Brown by letting him down in 1982. Brown came down to London to drum up support among Scottish MPs for his bid to become chairman of the Scottish party. He was meeting Murray Elder, an old friend who was then general secretary of Labour in Scotland. They invited Cook for a Chinese meal in Soho, but when Brown asked for backing, Cook replied: 'I am sure you will do very well, Gordon.' Brown took that as a refusal to help.[7] Not only do Cook's friends not recall the evening at all, they doubt the veracity of this story, arguing that it would have seemed strange to lobby for a job that is rotated anyway, that Cook would not have been able to influence it even if he had wanted to and that Brown, a prominent figure north of the border, was well capable of getting it without much effort.

Furthermore, if Brown felt betrayed, why would he ask Cook to contribute to another of his political books? Just before the 1983 election, Brown enlisted the help of an old friend, Bill Campbell, to publish an updated analysis of the social and economic problems affecting Scotland, taking forward the issues set out so strikingly in the *Red Paper on Scotland* a decade earlier. Campbell had established Mainstream Publications out of the student publications board of Edinburgh University and turned it into Scotland's largest independent publisher. Brown invited Cook to co-edit the new book, to be published by Mainstream, and to supply an essay on housing and deprivation. Brown wrote the introduction, arguing that the government was resetting the poverty line 'at only a few pence above destitution level and a few calories above starvation level'. He wrote that the common theme of every contributor was 'the need for redistribution of income and wealth', and that 'taxation should rise progressively with income. What is needed is a programme of reform that ends the current situation where the top 10 per cent own 80 per cent of our wealth and 30 per cent of income, even after tax.' The book did not have the same impact as its predecessor, but it still received reasonable publicity in Scotland.

Bill Campbell gives another possible catalyst for the Cook–Brown falling-out. The launch of the book, on 30 October 1983, took place in the publisher's Edinburgh office at 25 South West Thistle Street Lane. Campbell recalls that Cook arrived before Brown, greeted the assembled journalists and started the launch without his partner. 'He breezed in and started, saying, "We might as well just start." When Gordon got there it felt as if they were all wrapping up, that Robin had hijacked his show. It had been Gordon who had pulled the whole thing together.' However trivial this event might seem fifteen years on, it says a lot about the grudges that were subsequently borne. Brown concluded from it that Cook could not be trusted; Cook only later came to the same view about Brown, but he was already feeling uncomfortable about the claim of the young pretender to the conscience of the Scottish left.

That would be the last of their joint ventures. By the time of the 1987 election, Brown had marked himself out in the Commons, and resentment was building up. It had taken Brown only two years to get on to the front bench, while Cook was only now re-emerging after his setback in the shadow Cabinet election of 1986. Immediately after the general election, Brown joined him in the top ranks, as shadow Treasury chief secretary, the person responsible for costing policy commitments. Labour had been dogged in the 1987 election by Tory assaults on its spending plans, claiming they amounted to £35 billion. Kinnock decided that the only way to stop this happening again was to make the shadow chief secretary a member of the shadow Cabinet, with the power to excise from policy statements and speeches anything that might be construed as an uncosted pledge. Cook's friends say Brown suddenly switched from poacher to gamekeeper, always arguing in shadow Cabinet meetings about the spending implications of policy projects on health and social security but still presenting himself as a true socialist to the rank and file. This they saw as duplicitous. 'Here was someone, Gordon, who had made his reputation out of links between economic growth and poverty, and who was still making weekend speeches to the rank and file about it, but who was objecting to increased spending on social security,' says one Cook ally.

With Kinnock as mentor to the 'modernizers' and Mandelson in charge of the message, Cook felt isolated. He performed strongly in shadow Cabinet and NEC elections, but was shut out of the heart of decision-making. Worst of all, stories started to appear: that he was plotting to challenge Kinnock for the leadership; that he was at odds with policy because he had not understood it; and that his looks and manner precluded further promotion.

'A lot of it had to do with Mandelson rather than Brown,' says a long-standing Cook supporter. 'Mandelson had adopted Brown and Blair and had plainly decided that one of them – in those days it was thought to be Brown – would be a future leader of the party. It was a breathtakingly ambitious perspective ten years out, but he tailored everything to promote them. Robin could have lived with it, yawned and turned the other cheek if Mandelson hadn't seen as part of that project cutting down anybody who was seen as a potential rival. Things started to go rocky when Robin discovered stories, negative stories, planted by those he knew. This started just as Robin was becoming successful.'

Not only was Cook portrayed as 'a loose cannon', 'unreliable', 'slippery' and 'untrustworthy', but jokes about his appearance started doing the rounds. 'He wants to be leader, but plastic surgery hasn't got that far' . . . 'He's Lenin but without the human touch.' The one that really stuck was the 'garden gnome'. Denis Healey acknowledges authorship of the term. 'It just happened. Robin's always looked like that. You can't do anything about it. I tried to shave off my eyebrows once and my trousers fell down. You become the butt of all cartoonists, but you learn to grin and bear it.' Healey says that to Cook's credit he never resented him for using the phrase. But Healey is convinced that Cook could never have led the party because of his looks. He thinks the same of Gordon Brown, with 'his slack jaw and odd eyes'. That, he says, is the price to pay for the television age.

The caricatures came thick and fast. A profile in the *Sunday Times* said he could 'easily be mistaken for an elderly jockey'. It fell back on the usual compliment, that he was probably the best parliamentary debater of his generation, but added, with a sting in its tail: 'On television, he comes over less well. On a bad day, unblinking and unsmiling, shooting off a rat-a-tat-tat of statistics, he looks like a loss-adjuster from an insurance company.'[8] The journalists writing these profiles invariably draw anonymously on the comments of other MPs. There would be no shortage of colleagues who would enjoy putting him down. Cook was well aware of the limitations of his image. He once told a shadow Cabinet colleague that he was 'too ugly' for the modern soundbite age. It was, he said on another occasion, 'part of the small change of politics. It doesn't bother me in the slightest. Never since I started out at primary school have I ever thought I looked like Clint Eastwood or that my strength was my looks.'[9]

Cook had met Barbara Follett and her thriller-writer husband Ken when he was head of campaigns in the mid-1980s. Their work for the anti-apartheid movement was a natural link, but they also saw eye to eye on politics generally and on constitutional reform. Follett would remark to friends that she regarded Cook as one of the cleverest people she had ever met. The three of them would go out for dinner frequently, Margaret Cook joining them on the rare occasions she was down in London – such as her habitual Christmas shopping trek. Sometimes they would be joined by others. Follett remembers going to see a performance of the Buddy Holly tribute show with her husband and Cook, accompanied by Harriet Harman. They had a great evening. The Folletts would always give Cook the same birthday present – a bottle of malt whisky.

Follett is credited, or lampooned, for her role in sharpening the appearance of Labour MPs. For her, the sight of Michael Foot at the Cenotaph in what was described in the media as a donkey jacket was the point of no return. In the minds of the British public, woolly hats were equated with woolly heads. Most of the main players, Cook included, subjected themselves to the Follett makeover. Apart from making them look less rumpled, Follett encouraged them to feel more comfortable about their own appearance. Cook, with his complexion and height, was urged to ditch black suits and white shirts and to opt more for autumnal colours. What she wanted to do was to neutralize appearance, so that what an MP was wearing was not noticed by a television viewer. 'Once he began choosing "browns and oysters" he was surprised at the number of people who came up saying how well he looked.'[10] Still, there remained a lack of confidence that often perplexed Cook's friends. His looks – or at least his perception of them – were seen as either cause or excuse for his unremitting quest for perfection in his speech-writing and other work. 'He would think that what he was doing was not quite good enough,' said one.

The Folletization improved matters, but the personal criticism continued. 'The question being asked about Robin Cook is whether he could become Labour leader. Conventional wisdom has it that he is just too odd-looking – small, with lots of springy red hair and a pointy beard, and features which somehow all manage to be prominent – eyes, ears and nose,' said the *Independent on Sunday* by way of introduction. Cook told the interviewer: 'I have never been under any illusion that I got elected because of my classical good looks.' Then, in a caveat whose significance would only later be understood, he added: 'although curiously, men always seem readier to comment than women.' As to the attitude of other MPs, the paper suggested: 'Cook has no close friends in politics – colleagues are respectful rather than warm,' to which Cook replied: 'I wouldn't want to embarrass any of my colleagues by suggesting I was close to them. When I came to Westminster, adapting to the heartiness of political life took an awful lot of effort.'[11]

Cook was not the only one in the shadow Cabinet in feeling beleaguered and outmanoeuvred. Bryan Gould also found himself edged out of economic decision-making by Smith and Brown. After a series of demotions, he quit British politics angrily to return to his native New Zealand. The job of vice-chancellor of Waikato University was about as far as he could get from the ferment of Westminster. In his autobiography, Gould said of Mandelson:

> He became rather contemptuous of most members of the shadow cabinet as he began to see his own fortunes linked to those of the leading figures of his generation – like Gordon Brown and Tony Blair. Some members of the shadow cabinet had begun to feel that their positions were being undermined by briefings of the press by Peter Mandelson. John Prescott, Robin Cook, Michael Meacher all felt that from time to time their stock would mysteriously plunge as unfavourable stories appeared in the press . . . It was widely believed that he acted with Neil's authority in planting stories, even those unfavourable to shadow cabinet colleagues.[12]

A former aide to Cook tells a similar story: 'Every time Gould or Cook went on TV it was portrayed back to friendly journalists as a gaffe.' John Prescott, too, recalled the period, referring to Blair, Brown and their sponsors as 'the beautiful people'.[13]

Alliances and animosities consolidated in the late 1980s would last the best part of a decade. Many of the leading players were consumed with grievance and obsessed with plotting. What troubled Cook's friends was his refusal – or inability – to build alliances. Prescott's resentment, kindled in the leadership contests of 1988, lingered. Others on the left were similarly cool. Until her promotion to the shadow Cabinet in 1989, Margaret Beckett was a member of the health and social security team under Meacher and then Cook. Her friends say that whenever she developed an idea, or an area for which she was directly responsible suddenly became a hot issue, Cook would pull rank and brush her aside. She was particularly aggrieved at her treatment during the Commons deliberations on the 1988 social security bill. The same applied to Gould, who shared Cook's views on Europe and economic management, and yet could not always count on his support when the chips were down. Cook resented the ruthlessness of the modernizers, yet not once did he take them on directly. He made it clear that he did not share their world view, or the way they were going about achieving it, which meant that they never trusted him fully; yet at the same time, those who were trying to resist them never quite knew where they stood with him. Cook thought tactically rather than strategically. He believed he could, through force of argument and ordering of fact, win any battle he chose to fight.

Kinnock insists that 'there was no strategy for the discriminatory promotion of those two [Blair and Brown]'. He acknowledges that those who complained of negative stories in the press had a 'circumstantial case', but that nothing took place on his instructions. 'I knew that these stories were being written, but I didn't have time to deal with them. This was all gallery bar gossip. What has happened in the years since is a lot of post-hoc rationalisation.'

Mandelson's friends say that anything that may have been done was done in the single-minded pursuit of making Labour electable. They deny that any particular individual was targeted; the task was simply to get 'the message' right. They say he appreciated Cook's campaigning skills, and his willingness to help out, even at the last minute. One particularly important occasion was the Monmouth by-election in March 1991. Mandelson, who was running the campaign, had turned the focus on to allegations that the government was about to privatize the local hospital. He asked Cook to go down there – a round trip that took the best part of a day – just to do a three-minute local television discussion on the state of the local health service. Cook went. A true blue seat fell to Labour. On specific tasks like that, Mandelson felt he could trust him.

On broader policy issues, what struck some on the left of the party as Cook's untrustworthiness was seen by some modernizers as a sign of his flexibility and openness. 'He has never been a factional politician,' says Derek Draper, Mandelson's long-time adviser. He remembers as a student volunteering to help Cook in the Kinnock–Hattersley leadership campaign in 1988. He phoned Norris, who arranged that Cook would call. Cook asked him where he stood in the party. Draper replied that, by way of example, he thought the idea of a joint slate for the soft-left Tribune group and the hard-left Campaign group was 'ridiculous'. It was only in mid-sentence that he remembered it was Cook's original idea. 'As you no doubt know, I have slightly different views on that subject,' came the reply. 'But that needn't affect matters.' One of Cook's adversaries admits: 'Robin is not sectarian. He will listen to all types of opinion and will not be so paranoid about personal loyalty.'

Brown's big break came in 1988. He was forced at the last minute to deputize for Smith in the debate on the Chancellor's autumn statement: John Smith had just had his first heart attack. Brown gave one of the great parliamentary performances of the period, demolishing Nigel Lawson at the height of his reputation. It was from then that he started to be talked of as the Labour leader of the next generation. Brown started to amass followers and topped the shadow Cabinet poll that year. He nurtured his friends, both giving them and demanding of them intense personal loyalty. Cook both resented and envied Brown's tactics. His assiduity was well recognized.

Once, walking through Speaker's Yard at the Palace of Westminster, he came across Frank Field, the singularly independent-minded MP for Birkenhead. 'How're you doin'?' Brown greeted him. 'Fine, Gordon,' came the reply, 'but you don't need to ask. I've already voted for you.'

Cook did not cultivate MPs in the same way. He enjoyed discussing policy, but – for all the lessons of his setback in 1986 – still failed to 'work the tea room'. Not playing the game, he came over as aloof, even when that was not the intention. First impressions would often grate. Sometimes he would unintentionally antagonize uncommitted Labour MPs by putting them down or not giving them the time of day if he felt they had not mastered the issue they were discussing. This is a matter of some regret for those who did stick by him. By the late 1980s, say Cook's friends, Brown had begun to build bunkers, assembling a group of friends in his trench. 'The biggest single problem was that he and Robin drifted out of contact, and neither of them made an effort to wrest it back,' says one member of the current government. Out of contact they may have been; out of mind, certainly not. A party worker remembers his first meeting with Brown, in a car on their way to a party meeting he had helped to organize in the early 1990s. Brown asked him immediately what he thought of party policy, and added virtually in the same breath: 'So what d'you make of Cook?' As for relations with the existing leadership, Cook did not fall out with Kinnock any more than many others in the shadow Cabinet. By the time of the general election of 1992, Kinnock and Prescott were barely on speaking terms. But the perceived lack of appreciation rankled with Cook more, as he had twice organized Kinnock's campaign. That, according to the Kinnock camp, was irrelevant: 'Neil never owed him a favour for his leadership election victory. He was never going to lose it. Robin was just the front man. Anyone could have done that job.'

Of all the battles over policy direction, the most pivotal concerned the economy. John Smith's main aim, having taken over the party leadership, was to rid himself of Gould. During the 1987–92 parliament Brown was moved from shadowing the chief secretary to take his job at trade; Gould was put out to pasture at environment; Beckett, who had just been elected on to the shadow Cabinet, was promoted from being one of Cook's deputies to chief secretary; and Blair, having done energy for a year, displaced Meacher at employment. Smith now had in place an economic foursome that would steer policy for the next few years. The special status of this quartet was first institutionalized in April 1991 in a party political broadcast involving Kinnock and all four of the others. Kinnock gave almost carte blanche to Smith and Brown. Some on the left say he felt intimidated by them, and would defer to them, and to his economics adviser, John Eatwell, who in turn was close to Brown, on all issues of importance. Smith had been taken aback at Brown's rapid rise and was somewhat wary of him; yet he saw him as closer to himself on many aspects of economic policy than anyone else. The collective view of this group was that Labour had to show that toughness on spending was not just an electoral tactic, but was proof that Labour had turned its back on devaluation as a means to monetary stability. In other words, the party had to embrace the economic orthodoxy of the day, explicitly distancing itself from anything that smacked of Keynesian reflation. Support for sterling's entry into the exchange rate mechanism of the European monetary system was a prerequisite. By May 1990 Labour's latest economic policy document, *Looking to the Future*, had erased all traces of Gould's paper, *Meet the Challenge, Make the Change*, that had been approved as part of the policy review a year earlier. Keynesianism was discarded. ERM membership was demanded 'at the earliest opportunity'. The rate at which sterling would be set would be aimed at 'maintaining an anti-inflationary stance'.

Margaret Thatcher's removal by the Conservative Party in November 1990, and her replacement by the more conciliatory and down-to-earth John Major, proved double-edged for Labour strategists. On the one hand, they were dealing with an opponent more likely to command public affection, or at least quiescence. But on the other, attention would be diverted away from Labour's internal travails, giving the party more leeway to enact change. During this period a vast swathe of policy was ditched: unilateral nuclear disarmament; Keynesian economic expansionism; renationalization of the privatized utilities; support for the trade union closed shop. Labour's spending commitments became, due in large part to Brown, more modest.

Privately, Cook was having increasing doubts about the direction of party policy. He spoke of his fears for the bottom 20 per cent of society, saying he feared the rise of a fascist movement, with neither main party seeking to represent the urban poor as jobs were shed. 'He spoke with an almost religious concern,' recalls Harry Reid. Cook would often use the party conference to distance himself from the leadership. In 1990 he and two other shadow Cabinet members supported a motion to use the 'peace dividend', quantified as a one-third cut in the £21.2 billion defence budget, to increase spending on health, pensions, housing and education and to eliminate low pay. Such gestures only goaded his detractors to brief journalists against him. In spite of the negative stories that would periodically appear about him, Cook maintains that in this respect he has always been more sinned against than sinning. On several occasions, he says, members of his staff or political allies have gone to him and offered to plant a negative story against Brown and others; but he has refused to allow this. He maintains that he has never briefed against Brown.

Sometimes the stories against Cook and other left-wingers were manufactured out of thin air. Sometimes a reasonable enough remark was deliberately taken out of context and distorted. On other occasions there was no conspiracy. One such example, which particularly exasperated Kinnock, came during an interview for BBC Scotland's *Left, Right and Centre* television programme in February 1992. Cook said that when a Scottish parliament was set up, according to Labour's manifesto, he did not believe it would be possible for him, as a Scottish MP, to continue as health secretary for England and Wales. This was his answer to the West Lothian question, originally posed by Tam Dalyell, as to whether Scottish MPs should have a say in English affairs at Westminster once a Scottish parliament had been set up. Dewar was cross; Kinnock was furious, issuing a terse statement that it was for the Prime Minister of the day to determine who should be health secretary. Cook backtracked, saying in a statement: 'Our programme is for a full parliament and I intend to see it implemented in full throughout that parliament. In a future Westminster parliament, elected after the creation of a Scottish parliament, it will be for Neil Kinnock to decide whom it would be appropriate to appoint as secretary of state for health.' The Tories made hay over the issue, with John Major using the constitutional issue, and the unresolved anomalies behind Labour's plans, as ammunition in the election he called for 9 April 1992.

Labour went into the campaign in comparatively good spirits. Cook, though, was going through another patch of self-doubt and frustration. He joked to a friend that if Kinnock won the next election he would make him 'ambassador to Paris'. Yet despite the undeniable friction, Kinnock ensured that Cook was part of his 'leader's committee' preparing strategy for the election. Jack Cunningham, shadow leader of the House and campaigns coordinator, was officially in charge. Mandelson was not at the heart of the battle as he had been in 1987; this time, for the first time, he was contesting a seat of his own, Hartlepool. With Kinnock often on the road, Blair and Brown felt shut out during that brief period by the older hands, especially Cunningham and Hattersley.

The campaign got off to a bad start, with Smith's 'shadow budget' turning into a public relations disaster, and culminated with the notoriously triumphalist Sheffield rally. In between was the débâcle of Jennifer's Ear. Cook, as a senior member of the team and responsible for health, had ensured that the issue was one of the strongest on which Labour could challenge the Tory record. On 24 March 1992, the fourteenth day of the campaign, Cook and Cunningham invited journalists to a party election broadcast to expose the effects of government health policy. The highly emotive film, contrasting the fates of one girl waiting nine months for an ear operation on the NHS, and another who had jumped the queue thanks to private health insurance and a £200 cheque, turned out to be a catalogue of errors. Cook introduced the video, set to B. B. King's 'Someone Really Loves You', but he and Cunningham steadfastly refused to identify the suffering girl. Unbeknown to them, Kinnock's press officer, Julie Hall, started giving clues to journalists, which led to the torrid tale of Jennifer Bennett, her father who was happy that the issue was highlighted, and her Conservative-supporting mother who said that Labour had misrepresented her daughter's case entirely.[14] Amid the recriminations after the election, the senior politicians blamed the backroom team for not checking the facts against the case histories presented to the media. Cook says he never saw the film before it was put out. 'The whole broadcast was prepared without the participation or knowledge of the spokespeople involved,' he said.[15] A second broadcast highlighting the Tory record on health was junked.

Lessons had been learned. 'We have to remain in control of the message,' said Cook. Better organization was one thing. But what kind of message would he be asked to sell?

7

Friends Again?

Neil Kinnock announced his resignation on Sunday, 12 April 1992, three days after polling day. John Major had defied his critics and the odds to secure an historic fourth successive victory for the Conservatives. A majority of 21 would be adequate to see him through the first few years at least. For Kinnock, defeat was devastating. He had spent nine years as leader of the opposition trying to reposition Labour as an unthreatening centre-left alternative. Hattersley and he had no alternative but to go. Within hours, Cook received a call from Smith: once again, he was being asked to play kingmaker. Smith believed that Cook would deliver the left for him. Cook was close to Smith and sympathetic to his less presentationally driven brand of politics. They had had their differences in the past – on policy, they had disagreed vehemently on devolution, Europe and some aspects of economic management – but Cook did not think twice about accepting, and started working the phones to prepare a new campaign team. Smith knew better than most how to handle Cook; but he would confide to friends that he never quite knew where Cook was coming from, or where he wanted to go.

Nobody had been preparing for defeat. Brown, Blair, Mandelson and other modernizers had worked from the assumption that, several years down the line in government, Kinnock, the Labour Prime Minister, would hand the baton to the younger generation. But in 1992 Smith was the obvious choice, a stabilizing figure. Kinnock's dash to shed policies had left many of the party faithful disorientated. They had been prepared to go along with it, so long as it paid dividends: but it did not, and nor did the brash excesses of the campaign itself. The main jockeying for position was over who should run for deputy. Both Brown and Blair thought long and hard about it: Brown was dissuaded because the presence of two Scots at the helm was seen as untenable; Blair vacillated, his doubts fuelled partly by fear of antagonizing Brown. Kinnock wanted Gould to take the job, despite their disagreements during the policy review; Cook backed this idea and tried to persuade Smith to endorse him. But Smith had got on particularly well with Beckett in his economic foursome, and felt comfortable with her position both on policy and on dealing with the party. She was also less of a threat.

Gould responded by challenging Smith himself, but without a power base and with precious few supporters he was never going to stand a chance. Prescott threw his hat into the ring again, but the Smith–Beckett ticket had the support of the main trade unions, many constituency organizations and most MPs. Yet the campaign began badly. Cook had had only twenty-four hours to organize the inaugural press conference. Smith parried questions uncertainly and received a strikingly bad write-up for someone long seen as a safe pair of hands. Cook rang Mandelson at home to seek his help. He told him that there was a problem with Smith's image in the media and urged Mandelson to 'do the kind of job for him that you have done for others'. Mandelson declined, saying he wanted to make his own way as a new MP, although he suggested enlisting the support of Brown and Blair. (They helped Cook write Smith's manifesto.) Within days stories emerged about the modernizers riding to the rescue of Smith's faltering campaign. Cook was disappointed but only slightly surprised. He was accustomed to reading Sunday papers running him into the ground, but he had hoped that the election defeat would have brought at least a temporary halt to this kind of briefing. But there was more of this to come: much more.

Kinnock still had one last function to perform as leader. A meeting of the NEC was due to endorse changes to internal structures that many in the party had finally come to realize were vital to recovery. The election defeat appeared to have swung the balance towards change. The principle of 'one member one vote' – quickly dubbed Omov – to end the block vote in the choice of leader and on conference resolutions, was supported not just by modernizers but by some in the union movement. Kinnock had tried it once before, in 1984, and had been outgunned. He had grown to live with backroom deals – indeed, union barons helped deliver victory for him in several policy clashes in the late 1980s. Yet between the first NEC meeting in May and the follow-up in June, the mood among several union leaders turned against the proposed reform. One of these was John Edmonds, whose GMB union supported Smith. He became increasingly nervous of loose talk suggesting that Omov was the precursor to a more fundamental break in the party's links with the unions. With Smith's approval, Cook proposed that the whole issue be referred back for consultation with the unions and that no decision be taken until the following year. Smith was convinced that he would not have been able to push Omov through the 1992 party conference; a year on, after the slimmest of victories, he would look back on the NEC decision as the correct one. But to Brown and Blair, his hesitancy – at a time when his stock could not have been higher – was not a good omen.

The message from the Smith camp during the leadership election was one of consolidation and gradual change. So badly was Gould's campaign going that his manager, Blunkett, tried to persuade him to give up a few weeks before the vote. Smith romped to victory on 18 July with 91 per cent of the electoral college. Beckett secured 57 per cent for the deputy leadership, with Prescott on 28 per cent and Gould trailing on 15 per cent.

Whereas Kinnock in 1983 had felt hamstrung by the number of grandees at the top of the shadow Cabinet, 1992 saw a clear-out. Hattersley and Kaufman were the two most prominent to stand down, making room for significant changes of personnel. Smith was fully aware of the rivalries among his colleagues, but he took a more relaxed attitude than Kinnock towards dealing with them. He saw no reason to keep the protagonists apart, or to allow one clique to dominate policy-making in any particular area. Rather the reverse. He had Brown as shadow Chancellor, Cook at the DTI and Prescott at employment – all interdependent economic portfolios. They were joined by Beckett, the deputy leader, in the economics committee of the shadow Cabinet. Smith would happily drink whisky with Cook in his room, and talk; he would do the same with Brown and others. Cook says he did not openly lobby for the position of shadow Chancellor, indeed he assumed that Brown – having just done the DTI and the shadow chief secretary's job – would be the natural choice. The DTI was a good second best for him, as long as he was pivotal to economic decision-making.

Smith was far less fixated than Kinnock on party organization. He also had a certain disdain for outside advisers. He believed the Shadow Communications Agency had acquired too much influence, and had it disbanded. He also made a point of keeping Mandelson out of the picture, on the pretext that he was now a backbench MP and had to do his time like the rest of them. Smith tolerated, even encouraged, open discussion. Dissent – something Kinnock or later Blair would call disloyalty – was not punished.

Notwithstanding the new leader's more relaxed approach, intrigues continued unabated. Each of the combatants would ask others in the party what his rival was up to. Shadow Cabinet meetings were often tetchy. The body language between many of the members was bad, between Cook and Brown particularly so. They did not need to say anything to make their mutual disdain apparent. Cook used to get particularly annoyed by Brown's squeaky thick felt-tip pen.

For Brown this was a tricky period. Five months on from his spectacular election victory, Major was presiding over a government close to collapse. Black Wednesday, 16 September, saw a tidal wave of speculation against sterling, forcing two heavy increases in the interest rate and culminating in the government's humiliating exit from the European exchange rate mechanism, two years after Britain had joined. Some £2 billion had been lost in a vain attempt to defend the pound. Labour exploited the disaster, but was also hamstrung by the policy it had set for itself.

All summer there had been turbulence in the currency markets as traders sensed that several currencies inside the ERM basket were ripe for devaluation. The pound, at DM2.95, was the most obvious. Cook, as usual assuming the role of chief spokesman during August, had said everyone in the party was agreed on the need for a general revaluation. Brown refused to fall in behind this line. Cook urged Smith to rein Brown in. In a shadow Cabinet meeting on 10 September, Gould, Meacher, Blunkett and Cook pressed Brown to acknowledge that the pound was overvalued. Again Brown did not budge. 'Our policy is not one of devaluation, nor is it one of revaluation or realignment,' he replied. At the party conference two weeks after Black Wednesday there was little overt criticism of Smith, who had backed Britain's decision to join the ERM. But there were rumblings against Brown. Gould, by now a dwindling force as shadow heritage secretary, walked out of the shadow Cabinet and into political oblivion on the eve of the conference, complaining: 'We do not yet recognize the futility and damaging consequences of putting the defence of the exchange rate at the heart of economic policy.'

It was around this time that several newspapers speculated that Cook was in line to step in as shadow Chancellor. Cook and his entourage deny having anything to do with the stories, saying they were flights of fancy by journalists. Brown's position was never seriously threatened, but he was subjected to two years of pressure from the soft left, both within the shadow Cabinet, where it emanated from an informal group composed of Cook, Prescott, Meacher, Blunkett and Dobson, and outside it. A genuine battle of ideas, and pamphlets, was waged during the short period of Smith's leadership. The Tribune group, with Peter Hain and Roger Berry at the helm, was at the forefront of a campaign to push Smith and the party back towards Keynesian first principles. Hain, who first rose to prominence as an anti-apartheid campaigner in the early 1970s, played a major role in various left-wing caucuses for the next decade and more, making repeated attempts to bring together the party's hard and soft left factions, with no success. In 1995 Blair would bring him into the fold as a whip, followed by an appointment as junior employment spokesman.

Shortly after the 1993 spring budget, the Tribune group issued a document, *Labour and the Economy*, calling for a return to demand management economics. They also argued that the convergence criteria under the terms of the Maastricht Treaty for joining European economic and monetary union – emphasizing low inflation, low borrowing and low debt – would further damage workers' rights and increase unemployment. Brown was furious and tried to order them to withdraw it. With tacit encouragement from Cook they went ahead regardless. Brown's position was weaker than for some time, but he and his friends were still determined to act. Hain was ousted as secretary of the Tribune group at a meeting later in the year ambushed by Blair, Brown, Mandelson and an army of supporters. They had previously seldom attended. By neutralizing the group, they deprived the soft left – and Cook – of a platform in the PLP.

Brown's approach to the media was to seek saturation coverage. Cook would do the same, and – at that particular time – was doing it rather more successfully. Towards the end of 1993 Brown was also taking more of a beating than usual in the Commons at the hands of the ever-pugnacious Kenneth Clarke. Mandelson, perturbed at the turn of events, sought out one of the trade union movement's better media managers. He asked Charlie Whelan during the Labour conference that year if he was prepared to give up his job at the Amalgamated Electrical and Engineering Union and work for Brown. Around the same time Brown enlisted Ed Balls, a 27-year-old leader writer at the *Financial Times*, as his economic adviser. From that moment his fortunes began to recover, and Cook's difficulties increased.

Blair, while close to Brown, was disturbed by the continuing coolness between him and Cook. Attempts had been made by shadow Cabinet members, MPs and others in the party to engineer a reconciliation. Frank Dobson had tried once, even though John Smith had warned him he was wasting his breath, quoting Wordsworth at him:

> For old, unhappy, far-off things,
> And battles long ago ...

One attempt did come close to success. Colin Fisher, the management consultant who had served as midwife to the Shadow Communications Agency, had long since stopped taking an active part in Labour campaigning, but he had kept in touch with the leading players. A burly, bearded, no-nonsense figure, Fisher got on reasonably with all the key figures and had been especially close to Cook, who would come around on his own from time to time. Fisher also helped Mandelson, who on winning the nomination for Hartlepool had been forced to stand down as director of communications in January 1990, by giving him a job at his company, SRU, to tide him over. Strangely, Fisher's name appears virtually nowhere in histories of the modern Labour party. But he served an important function – his house at 74 Clapham Common South became a venue for Labour get-togethers over dinner. Some were purely social, others had a specific agenda. His wine cellar and the quality of his cooking, especially roasts, were in themselves incentives to attend. A year after the 1992 defeat, he and Blair discussed the Cook–Brown saga and Blair agreed to invite the protagonists – Brown, Cook and Mandelson. At the last moment, Brown sent his apologies. They tried again in October 1993, and this time Brown came. Seated around an oval table were Brown and Cook next to each other, Mandelson on his own opposite them, and Blair and Fisher at either end. Fisher began by inviting the guests to look for common ground in their approaches, to keep the discussion general. They went headlong into intense argument about policy. Mandelson said virtually nothing, sipping his wine excruciatingly slowly as the others drank more copiously. The dinner was civil – 'very sensible and sociable' was the Cook verdict – and they agreed to try a bit harder. But the promises came to nothing.

For all the jockeying for position, for all the acrimony, Cook enjoyed the trade job at least as much as he had health. The job description was largely the same – to harry the Tories – and two opportunities fell into his lap. On 13 October 1992 Michael Heseltine, trade and industry secretary at the time, announced that thirty-one of the mining industry's remaining fifty pits would close, with the loss of up to 30,000 jobs, many of them compulsory redundancies. Some of the closures would begin within days. Cook tapped into the public outcry. Heseltine was forced to go to the Commons on 19 October and announce a U-turn. The closures would be submitted to review and the pits would be kept open in the interim. Cook taunted Heseltine: 'Does the Secretary of State understand that his statement will be judged by whether it is a genuine attempt to save miners' jobs or a manoeuvre to save ministers' jobs? In order that they may judge which it is, will the Secretary of State tell us whether his statement means that a single pit on last week's list has a secure future or whether a single miner has a secure job?'[1] The jobs were saved, but only for a year or so.

In two weeks Cook fitted in several high-profile visits to coal mines between a succession of press conferences and television appearances. Martin O'Neill, who was in his trade and industry team, said that Cook identified the coal issue early on, and ran with it 'incredibly well – he outshone me, although I was supposed to be responsible for the issue'. (By this point Brown had developed a tactic of persuading Smith to include one of his placemen in each shadow department. Brown had both O'Neill and Nigel Griffiths at the DTI. However, at the height of the pit crisis Cook gave much of the work to Fatchett, the team member to whom he was closest.) By the time the review was completed, the following March, the issue had subsided. The public and the workforce had largely become reconciled to the virtual elimination of the industry. But Heseltine, such a sure-footed performer, had been badly damaged. Some of the credit for that went to Cook.

Then came sleaze. By the time Major was hounded from office in 1997 his government had been riddled with accusations that his ministers and MPs had either acquiesced in or directly engaged in a series of shady enterprises. The most serious case was the arms-to-Iraq affair. The scandal came to light in November 1992 when Alan Clark, a former trade minister, was asked to testify in a prosecution brought by Customs and Excise against executives of Matrix Churchill, a west midlands machine-tool company accused of breaking the arms embargo against Iraq in the late 1980s. Clark admitted that the government had secretly relaxed the rules and should have known all along that the equipment was not for peaceful purposes, but was instead destined for Iraqi arms factories – just as the defence lawyers had argued. The judge then overruled public interest immunity certificates – gagging orders – signed by government ministers that would have prevented disclosure of state documents vital to the defence. Major responded to the uproar by setting up a public inquiry led by Sir Richard Scott, a court of appeal judge.

Cook seized the moment. He pared the issue down to a simple charge: 'Britain armed Saddam Hussein. Ministers engineered a cover-up, then they were prepared to let three men go to gaol simply for doing no more than what ministers had agreed they should do.' He became omnipresent on television screens, his moral indignation reinforced by a flawless command of the minutiae. Coming so soon after his successful campaign against pit closures, this earned him the description in one profile as a 'one-man opposition'.[2] This was Cook at his forensic best. Smith told him once that he would have made a good barrister – his own previous profession.

Scott's public hearings began early in 1993. They made for gripping theatre, with Tory ministers or former ministers bridling in indignation at the tone of the inquisitor-in-chief, Presiley Baxendale QC, and she in turn using every device in the book to encourage them to implicate themselves. Cook would join the queue most mornings bright and early for the small number of seats reserved for the public and press. His most enjoyable day was when Thatcher was asked to testify, on 8 December 1993, the first former or serving Prime Minister to give evidence before a public inquiry. In heated exchanges with Baxendale, Thatcher claimed she had never been informed officially of the relaxation in dealings with Baghdad. She also denied approving the export of machine-making tools by Matrix Churchill, and said she was aware of intelligence reports warning they were to be used in the making of weapons and shells. Cook knew the timing of news bulletins by heart and was always on hand to supply his views, often in memorably pithy form. Thatcher said during her testimony: 'If I had seen every copy of every minute that was signed in government I would have been in a snowstorm. Delegation matters in government.' Cook later responded: 'I have to say that I don't remember this style of government.'[3] A month later he was back, first in line at seven in the morning on the day of Major's testimony, 17 January 1994.

Tory scandals apart, Cook ran into more of the same tension on mainstream economic decision-making. Early in 1994 he produced a policy document on promoting trade and investment which alarmed Blair and Brown. To them, it appeared to signal higher taxes for middle-income groups and a return to more state involvement in strategy planning by industry. Brown was achieving considerable success in trying to turn the issue of tax to Labour's advantage. The previous year he had tried to persuade his own party to swallow the pill of an end to 'tax and spend' policies. In a speech to the Labour Finance and Industry Group on 17 August 1993 he announced that 'the next Labour government will not tax for its own sake. Labour is not against wealth, nor will we seek to penalize it. If we cut taxes – and I hope that we will be able to do so – we will ensure that everyone benefits and not just an elite few as has happened under the Tories.' Brown, and his shadow chief secretary Harriet Harman, secured a coup by forcing the government to admit that the overall burden of income tax and national insurance on an average family had risen since 1979. The last thing Brown wanted was for anyone in the shadow Cabinet to advocate raising taxes as a desirable option in itself. Yet, in spite of the continuing internal warfare, Cook looks back on those two years of Smith's leadership as 'blissfully happy'. They ended abruptly.

At eight-thirty on the morning of Thursday, 12 May 1994, Cook was joined by friends in his cramped office in 1 Parliament Street. Among them were Derek Fatchett, Frank Dobson, Michael Meacher, Jim Cousins, Geoff Norris. Cook told them he had heard from the policeman outside the gates of New Palace Yard that Smith had had a heart attack. The group sat and waited, hoping for the best but presuming the worst. Official confirmation of the Labour leader's death came two hours later. For a while the group sat stunned, unable to grasp the magnitude of what had happened. Smith should have been with Cook that morning to announce a new industrial policy initiative. The meeting would later be portrayed by critics of Cook as an unseemly plot to push for the vacant leadership. 'Of course the subject of Robin standing cropped up,' said one person present. 'I said I would support him, but that was all that was said. All our thoughts were with John's family.'

Cook, like each of the other main players in the shadow Cabinet, spent the next few days writing tributes and touring television studios to give his own personal appreciation of Smith. Less publicly, within hours the Blair bandwagon was quietly up and running, much to the chagrin of Brown and his supporters. Cook asked Peter Hain to make a few discreet enquiries about his own chances, but by the first weekend Blair was already being regarded as a runaway favourite. Cook and Hain agreed a strategy that Hain would telephone Sunday journalists on Saturday, telling them that Cook was being encouraged by his supporters to stand. But the Press Association overplayed it and suggested that Cook had made up his mind and would enter the race. The following morning Mandelson, who had been hovering between Brown and Blair, appeared on television expressing disappointment that any member of the shadow Cabinet was even thinking of standing at this dark hour, several days before Smith's funeral. But the real disappointment for Cook that day was an interview by Chris Smith, shadow environment spokesman, during which he said he wanted a candidate who could appeal 'safely to all parts of the British electorate'. This was interpreted by all as a tacit endorsement of Blair. Chris Smith, who had always had good working relations with Cook and was similarly positioned on the 'soft left' of the party – indeed, as a member of the Tribune board, he could not have been politically closer – was the kind of person whose support Cook needed if he was to stand the remotest chance. Cook has always privately felt personal disappointment at Smith's line, but in retrospect does not quibble at the logic he used. Smith himself later said of Cook: 'He jumped too late. He genuinely dithered about whether to stand or not for quite some time, and with hindsight I think if Robin had stood for deputy he might have done extremely well.'[4]

Cook certainly did dither. His first intention was to stand. Then he thought better of it. Not only was he, like the rest of them, still in shock at Smith's sudden death, but he also had to cope with the death of his father-in-law, Arthur. He and Margaret had asked Anna Healy if they could borrow her car to drive down to the west country that first weekend to pay their last respects to him. Cook's own father, Peter, had died only the previous January.

The following week Cook was back in his constituency taking stock. Jim Devine, his agent, remembers the two of them sitting in the Harthill service station on the M8 between Edinburgh and Glasgow going through the arithmetic. 'I told him he didn't have enough of a machine. He wasn't going to get the numbers. It was traumatic.' Norris also warned his boss that he would not do himself any favours by standing. 'He was very open in talking to me about it. He took my assessment in good heart. He could have shunned me; instead he said he would understand if I went off to work for

Blair,' says Norris. Mo Mowlam, one of the 1987 intake with views not dissimilar from Cook's on many issues, especially constitutional reform, phoned him to tell him, in her usual direct and charming fashion, that he should not bother and that he should join her and others in helping Blair's campaign. He concluded to Hain, with wry resignation, that apparently he was 'not pretty enough'.

What made this especially hard for Cook to take was that less than a year earlier, in the 1993 shadow Cabinet elections, he had once again taken top spot. Dobson and Prescott were tied in second place, with Brown only fourth and Blair sixth. That contest, however, was all about MPs listing a selection of candidates as part of a team, a choice based as much on respect and personal ties as on electability. It had little to do with the choice of a single individual with broad voter appeal. Even so, on that count, Cook reckons he would have received the support of at least four, probably five, other shadow Cabinet members – Dobson, Meacher, Ron Davies and Joan Lestor. Early on he was also contacted by David Blunkett, who privately urged him to stand. Blunkett, now seen as one of Blair's most loyal lieutenants, was chair of the party that year. His support would have been extremely important. In fact, Cook's supporters were fairly confident that they could have mustered declarations from seventy MPs, more than a quarter of the parliamentary party. A poll of MPs by Tribune put Cook in second place. That assertion was to remain untested.

Two weeks after Smith's death, the focus of attention was firmly directed towards Blair and Brown. A *Scotsman* poll of Scottish Labour MPs on 25 May put Brown ahead, but gave Blair a surprisingly large share of the vote in his rival's heartland. What should have sealed it for Cook was the survey's finding that only three out of the forty-two Scottish MPs who had expressed a preference said they would back him. He was even trailing Prescott in fourth place. But still, according to Fatchett, Cook was toying with standing, leaving a message with Fatchett's wife Anita that he was thinking of going ahead. Even the day after Brown had bitten the bullet, 1 June, Cook appeared with Cunningham at a press conference for the European elections and would not say whether he would stand. He was prepared to give his favourite for the Derby, he said, but not for the leadership.

Cook only finally ruled himself out after Brown's decision not to stand was confirmed. This period, according to a close friend of Cook, proved a bad miscalculation. 'We scrabbled around looking for nominations, but when it was clear that Tony would walk it I got brutal with Robin. I told him: "Your mission is to jump ship and support Tony before Gordon does." But he let Gordon jump first. Being first into Tony's camp would have done him immeasurable long-term good, but he couldn't bear the thought of Gordon running and not him.' That friend believes that had Cook 'jumped ship' early, not only would he have emerged a stronger player in the Blair set-up, but that as a consequence the soft left would have been harder to ignore.

The real problem for Cook was his failure to strike a deal with Prescott. Not that either of them would have thought of trying. Prescott, still resenting Cook's failure to support his 1988 bid to oust Hattersley, still believed that he could not trust him, while his own stock among the rank and file had been boosted enormously by his passionate speech on Omov that saved the day for Smith at the 1993 party conference. As for Cook, 'It was a measure of his cold and clear judgement that we totted up the votes and realized they weren't there. Robin didn't want to stand unless he was sure he could run Blair close,' says Hain. Cook finally told his supporters in a circular that 'reluctantly and with a heavy heart' he had decided not to stand. 'It has not been an easy decision, and I have kept an open mind about whether to run for as long as possible. It is clear from the many approaches I have received that I have a considerable basis of support among the active members of the Labour party. However, it is equally clear from the soundings my colleagues and others have taken that there is not sufficient support among the wider membership of the party and the trade unions for my candidacy.' The subtext appeared to be: those who had been around for a long time and active in the party appreciated the merits of Cook; the more fickle *arrivistes* would opt for the Blair gloss.

Hain phoned Rodney Bickerstaffe, general secretary of Unison, and Dick Caborn, MP for Sheffield Central, to tell them that Cook was not standing either for leader or for deputy, and that the coast was clear for Prescott to fight the left's corner. Brown backed Margaret Beckett for deputy; Cook supported Prescott, but there was no love lost between them. 'John was running for leader because he desperately wanted to fulfil his ambition of being deputy leader, and had worked out that his best prospect of becoming deputy leader was to run a high-profile campaign for leader,' said a friend of Cook. 'John would have been aghast if he had ended up winning.'

Members of Blair's team had already put out feelers to Cook about whether he was prepared to be his number two on a joint ticket. These were only tentative offers, but they were quickly rebuffed. Cook went round his friends asking: 'Should I back Tony, or should I not back Tony?' That was code for: 'Should I stand, or should I not stand?' Several colleagues of Cook asked him then, and subsequently, why he did not go for the deputy leadership. His credentials – his ardent support for constitutional reform and green issues, and his broadly Keynesian approach to economics – would have delivered the left for Blair. Some believe he bottled out, and would have had far greater clout with Blair, and thereby far greater power to press the left's cause, as his right-hand man. On the contrary, argues Cook: such a stance, rather than consolidating his position, would have constrained him. It would be loyalty without power. 'As deputy leader he would have been silenced,' says Ken Purchase, one of Cook's staunchest allies who is now his parliamentary private secretary.

Blair then asked Cook if he would consider running his campaign, as he had done for Kinnock in 1983, Hattersley (for deputy) in 1988, and Smith in 1992. Cook said that whatever else he did, he would not be typecast. He told Blair: 'Look, I'll support you, but we are in serious danger of making a caricature out of me.' Blair then turned to Jack Straw, who did the job with Mo Mowlam. For the next six weeks Cook kept his head down, helped to fight the European elections, but let Blair know he was tacitly supporting him. If Cook had wanted to endear himself to Blair he would have accepted the offer to run the show; but he had learnt the hard way that running a campaign produced few rewards. Now the inner sanctum was forming without him.

8

The Right Revolution

'This is a modern party living in an age of change. It requires a modern constitution that says what we are in terms that the public cannot misunderstand and the Tories cannot misrepresent. It is time we had a clear, up-to-date statement of the objects and objectives of our party. John Prescott and I will propose such a statement to the NEC. Let it then be open to debate in the coming months.'

The bombshell had been revealed in advance to only a few. Three months after sweeping to victory in the leadership contest, Tony Blair set about a transformation in party structures and policy that dwarfed anything Kinnock had tried. The modernizing camp had grown increasingly frustrated at the slow pace of change in the two years between the 1992 election and Smith's death. Blair had spent the summer mulling over his first big move – to abandon Clause Four, the party's symbolic commitment to nationalization that had stood virtually unchallenged since penned by Sidney and Beatrice Webb in 1918. Blair and his new press secretary, Alastair Campbell, plotted their course with precision. Three weeks before his first keynote address to conference as leader, on 4 October 1994, Blair brought Prescott into the picture. Prescott was shocked but was persuaded to back his leader. Then, almost by stealth, Blair made the necessary oblique references to the clause towards the end of his speech; Campbell filled in the gaps to journalists.

With Prescott's cooperation assured, Blair had felt no need to involve Cook and several others in the shadow Cabinet and NEC until the morning of the speech. Cook was appalled when he heard what Blair was going to say. He told Blair, with acerbic understatement, that he was 'not enthusiastic' about the plans. He privately urged Prescott to help rally opposition, but

Prescott had already signed up to Blair. Two days after the speech, once the significance of Blair's announcement had sunk in to delegates, the conference agreed to discuss it in an emergency debate. Cook was, by chance, in the chair, and – so Blair's supporters suspect – deliberately chose a series of speakers in favour of retaining Clause Four. The Blairites saw this as a last hurrah of the old left. But in the coming months they had to work extremely hard to swing enough party members and unions behind the reform. Blair took to the road to spread the message, talking to 30,000 activists as he criss-crossed the country. The support of the soft left was crucial.

It took Cook a week formally to line up behind the leadership. He told Blair in private conversations shortly after conference that he wanted to play a part in reforming the party's constitution.[1] In his heart it took him a while longer to be convinced of the merits of change; but by the turn of the year it had become clear to him that in resisting it he was in a minority. The constituency parties were steadily moving to back the reform. Cook collected his closest confidants from the centre-left to help him sell his conversion. One was Meacher; another was Fatchett. 'It was classic Cook,' says Fatchett. 'He came down on the side of the leadership, yet put down a radical marker.' The other version is less complimentary. 'He opposed it, saw which way the wind was blowing and left others in the lurch,' says a shadow Cabinet colleague of that time.

On 25 January 1995 Cook made what he considers a seminal speech, harnessing the aspirations of those who still considered themselves on the left of the party with the Blairite project of yanking Labour towards the centre ground. A new version of Clause Four could be 'a fuller, richer statement of our ideology', 'more radical and more relevant' than the old blanket commitment to nationalization. It should, he said, set six objectives: a just society, an opportunity economy, common ownership 'where appropriate', a stable environment, an open society and equal rights. He had been convinced, he said, that his initial opposition to change was wrong. 'Common ownership is not the sum of Labour's ideology and has never represented the totality of our programme.' The old document, he pointed out, said nothing about tackling inequality, unemployment, the centralization of power or the blighted environment, and did nothing to promote women's rights.

The speech was an attempt to forge a new path for those on the left of the party from within the emerging Blairite agenda. Having reluctantly been forced to shelve aspirations towards a more overtly redistributive fiscal system in the latter Kinnock years, Cook now sought a new solution through a different kind of politics. He saw constitutional change as pivotal, not peripheral. His ideal settlement would see parties forming alliances on the basis of individual policies, and groups of politicians thrashing out ideas on the basis of logic and argument, rather than traipsing through division lobbies at ten o'clock each evening to demonstrate some form of tribal loyalty.

Cook's intervention was timely – it was on the eve of Blair taking to the road in an attempt to win over the party rank and file to change. Cook took an active part in the various discussions to form a new Clause Four. Still, for even engaging in the Clause Four debate, Cook was accused of betrayal by some on the left. They dubbed him and others 'the emperor's new clothes parade of frontbenchers'. Blair, for his part, expressed his gratitude for Cook's change of heart and praised his working draft of the clause as one of the best submitted. On one area Cook was adamant. Blair and some of his supporters were pressing for a reference to social behaviour, possibly a mention of the nuclear family as the best model. Cook, who from his first years in parliament had been a staunch libertarian opposed to any form of moral prescription, helped to fend off those attempts, reminding their proponents of how spectacularly Major's 'back to basics' campaign had backfired on the Conservatives. One of the turning points was the conference of the Scottish Labour party that March: even there the verdict was narrowly in favour of change.

By the time the NEC's special conference took place in London on 29 April, the result was a formality. Even before the Clause Four announcement, however, Cook had found himself left out of Blair's inner circle. He had been moved from trade and industry to become shadow foreign secretary. In most people's eyes that would have been a promotion; Cook felt, however, that he had been shunted upstairs, to a job that was set apart from the central concerns of economic and social policy. The belief that he had been ostracized, albeit to a glamorous world that came with the position in government, was not unjustified. Brown had been determined to keep him away from any form of economic responsibility. Blair had seen little merit in Smith's idea of putting his heaviest hitters in rival jobs. Prescott's deputy leadership was geared towards party campaigning. This gave Brown, for the first time, hegemony over the shadow Cabinet's economic policy committee in which Cook no longer had a role. Cook's friends have not the slightest doubt that he was moved at Brown's behest, as some compensation from Blair for standing down in the leadership contest.

The reshuffle had its genesis at another sensitive dinner hosted by Colin Fisher at his Clapham house. This time Cook was not there: it was for Blair, Brown and Mandelson only. The gathering took place in June 1994, a few weeks after Brown had stood down in the leadership contest, leaving the coast clear for Blair, and it was an especially difficult evening. They sat around the table for six hours. Brown was barely on speaking terms with Mandelson, who he blamed for betrayal. He sought an explicit guarantee from Blair that he would not contemplate giving Cook the shadow chancellorship, as had been rumoured. Furthermore, he was insistent on gaining a promise from Blair that as a consolation he would have an agreed agenda giving him complete control over economic policy, to the exclusion of Cook. Blair said little, but the point was registered. Cook was outmanoeuvred.

When news of the reshuffle came, Cook made no secret of his unhappiness. He had wanted to stay where he was, but he accepted that such an argument might strike some as odd. 'Part of the weakness in resisting the offer was that one can hardly say he offered me the whole world and it wasn't big enough for me.' Cook admits that it took him time to work up an interest in foreign affairs. But he got on with it, ploughing through piles of papers about issues of which he had only perfunctory knowledge; and his past antinuclear activism gave him at least a grounding in some defence-related areas, even though he would now have to come at them from an entirely different angle. He would later say that for all his initial disquiet about the move away from the DTI, no one could accuse him of not applying himself to the new task. On taking up the new post he remarked: 'I had only been doing the job for two years and, yes, I was very keen on what I was doing and there was work I wanted to complete. Tony took the view that the European debate was going to be so important in the development of British politics in the subsequent two to three years that he wanted to have someone senior handling it. I can't say I am unhappy doing the job I am doing.'[2]

Andrew Hood became Cook's first researcher on foreign affairs, chosen from six hundred applicants. He had not worked for the party before, but had been a ghost writer for Tony Benn. He remembers being terrified during his interview, having to fend off a series of questions on foreign and domestic policy, including his suggestions for an updated version of Clause Four. He got the job on a Tuesday, which gave him nine days to prepare Cook's response in the foreign affairs section of the debate on the Queen's Speech. Cook did not give explicit instructions. Part of the skill of working for him was to anticipate what he wanted.

One of Hood's first tasks was to liaise with the Foreign Office on planning a series of trips for the new shadow Foreign Secretary to build up his contacts. Trips were organized across the European Union, central Europe (where he sought out former dissidents, both those now in positions of power, such as Vaclav Havel in the Czech Republic, and those outside it, such as Adam Michnik in Poland) and the Middle East, to Hong Kong and elsewhere in Asia. Sir John Kerr recalls a visit he made to Washington, where Kerr was then British ambassador. Cook, as was the custom with senior politicians on official business, was staying at the residence. 'We arranged a series of meetings for him. In the evenings after dinner we would chat. This was usual for a visitor, to get up to speed for the following day's discussions. But Robin did this for all five nights. The first night was US politics and diplomacy, the next two were Europe, then came Greece, Turkey and Cyprus, then came

China, Japan and human rights.' Kerr was astonished, not just by Cook's grasp of detail and thirst for information, but that two months later he phoned to go over with him some of the minutiae of their five nights burning the midnight oil. 'I can only assume he had gone up to his room at the end of each evening and written everything down.' When Rifkind, then Foreign Secretary, decided to appoint Kerr as permanent secretary from 1998, Cook was consulted to confirm the bipartisan nature of the appointment.

But Cook was wary of staying out of the country for too long, and made sure most visits were tightly scheduled to enable him to get back as soon as possible. He went out of his way to try to continue influencing the domestic debate. Blair had discarded much of Smith's collegiate style, as a result of which Cook often had to find out what was going on himself. Mandelson, after two years in enforced purdah, was back in his role as unofficial minder/spin doctor. Blair's use of outsiders to coordinate strategy was beginning to worry Cook and others who found themselves outside the charmed circle. The hackles were first raised when newspapers disclosed an informal meeting held at the Hampshire home of Chris Powell, the former chairman of the SCA and now chief executive of BMP, Labour's advertising agency. Those present included Mandelson and Brown. Prescott was furious about not being invited. From then on he and Cook insisted on being kept better informed on strategic decisions. Then came disclosure of a memorandum written by Philip Gould for Blair earlier in the year that called for a 'unitary command structure leading directly to the party leader' who would be 'the sole ultimate source of authority'. The fallout from this revelation during the 1995 TUC conference led Blair to institute regular 'big four' meetings with Brown, Cook and Prescott.

Blair realized the need to pay at least lip service to the official structures and hierarchies. In the week before the 1995 party conference Brown was officially named election strategy chief. With Major's government reeling from one crisis to the next, with its majority dwindling and Euro-rebels jumping ship, that election could have taken place at any moment, and Blair wanted to be ready. Prescott was put in charge of the so-called Key Seats Strategy, focusing on the hundred marginal seats Labour would need to take to secure an overall majority. Cook was formally in charge of campaign policy – although in practice Blair would make sure that his imprint was on just about every word. The major carrot given to Cook was the chairmanship of the National Policy Forum. The forum was created on the back of a decision by the 1990 conference to draw all the various party groups into a more flexible 'rolling programme' for policy-making, as was the case in many other European centre-left parties. It was a device to minimize the influence of the NEC and the union block vote, and to give added moral weight to resolutions the annual conference might find hard to stomach. The forum started meeting in 1993 but assumed a forceful role only when Cook became its chairman two years later. Despite this key position, Cook told friends that he felt lonely in the party, that he was one of a small minority carrying forward genuinely left-wing ideals to alleviate the plight of the poor.

By early 1995 Brown was back in his stride. He had waged a powerful campaign denouncing the 'fat cat' bosses of the privatized utilities, raking in excess profits on the basis of undervalued sales of former state assets. He and Blair cemented a new economic orthodoxy that had been gestating for several years. Blair set out the building blocks, including tight monetary control, when he gave the annual Mais lecture on 22 May 1995: 'The control of inflation through a tough macroeconomic framework is even more important than the Tories have said. Low inflation is not simply a goal in itself, it is the essential prerequisite both of ensuring that business can invest and that supply-side measures can work to raise the capacity of the economy to grow.' A document setting out the rationale, entitled *A New Economic Future for Britain*, was approved by the 1995 conference. More difficult for traditional party members and MPs to take were sudden changes to the component parts of Labour economic thinking. In June 1995 Harriet Harman, then employment spokeswoman, declared that instead of the government announcing the level of Labour's promised minimum wage, it would be set by a Low Pay Commission. But the two biggest controversies were still to come.

Charlie Whelan had added a new steel to the Brown operation. He was working to several agendas, and the same speech would be 'spun' several ways according to the audience. For Conservative-supporting newspapers Brown was invariably portrayed as the next 'iron chancellor', a man prepared to take on Labour vested interests; to the rank and file, speeches were peppered with references to heroes of the Labour movement and for good measure, Brown would throw in the odd reference to 'comrades'. What particularly exasperated Cook was that he almost always got away with it. If anybody saw the double game, they rarely mentioned it.

In November, fresh from the party conference, Brown gave an interview to the *Daily Telegraph* in which he suggested that unemployed people who unreasonably refused any of several work or training options created by a Labour government would have their benefits cut. He referred favourably to US workfare schemes. His announcement caught almost everyone in the shadow Cabinet by surprise. Prescott, Blunkett and Chris Smith complained privately to Blair. Prescott was already railing against Brown's ambitions to broaden the scope of the Treasury, expanding it into 'both a ministry of finance and a ministry for long-term economic and social renewal'. Cook joined the chorus of disapproval at the next shadow Cabinet. He complained that Brown had failed to consult his colleagues and that, in any case, this was not party policy as determined by the National Policy Forum. Cook was backed by the three who had complained earlier, as well as Frank Dobson, Jack Straw, Mo Mowlam and Doug Hoyle, the chairman of the PLP. Cook asked in exasperation why they had all joined the Labour party in the first place if they could countenance such a scheme. Blair listened to them all calmly but made clear that Brown had his backing '101 per cent'. He demanded an end to sniping and warned that the contents of the meeting should not be revealed to the press. He referred specifically to the *Guardian* and *Observer*, the two in-house papers for Labour activists. The following Sunday a full account of the row appeared on the front page of the *Observer*. 'Shadow Chancellor Gordon Brown has been accused by senior Labour colleagues of endeavouring to establish himself as leader-in-waiting,' wrote Andy McSmith. 'Extensive soundings taken by the *Observer* suggest up to half the shadow cabinet – and many lower ranking front-bench spokesmen – are angry at Mr Brown for flouting party discipline by speaking out of turn on policies outside his responsibility. Some front-benchers speak bluntly of Mr Brown being "out of control".'[3]

More was to come the following April. Brown was giving the John Smith Memorial Lecture at Edinburgh University. Its theme was equality of opportunity; but the story that appeared, courtesy of Whelan, had an altogether different gloss. Brown floated the idea of scrapping child benefit for 16- to 18-year-olds, and reinvesting the £700 million saved in training opportunities for teenagers from families with low incomes. This flew in the face of just about everything anyone in the party had stood for. For years Labour had defended child benefit against Thatcher's unfulfilled ambitions to abolish it. The first Chris Smith heard of the proposal was when he read the papers the following morning, on a plane on his return from a confer-ence. He and Blunkett were furious – they had just prepared a policy document reiterating the case for maintaining the universal benefit against those arguing for means testing. Cook, who was in Beijing at the time, was so outraged that, without consulting anyone in the leader's office, he proclaimed witheringly in a radio interview that the proposals were 'not carved in stone'. On his return he put a conciliatory gloss on the argument: 'What Gordon Brown announced two weeks ago was a review. It was not a policy, and I think that Labour has to be able to continue with its review of that idea floated by Gordon Brown without it being dressed up as a row.'[4] Privately, Cook commented to a friend on the prospect of Brown running the economy: 'God help us.'

They kept the amount of time they had to spend in each other's presence down to a minimum. Cook's supporters say he went to Brown shortly after Blair became leader and tried to sue for peace, arguing that a war of brief-ings was damaging to both of them. They say Brown agreed and accepted a suggestion that he nominate Cook as chairman of the National Policy Forum. But, they say, Brown did not show up at the next meeting.

Blair had come to loathe shadow Cabinet elections. Rather than demonstrating Labour's democratic credentials, they exacerbated in-fighting and factionalism. Senior figures would spend the summer months wooing uncommitted Labour MPs in an unseemly scramble for supporters. More fundamentally, they constrained Blair in his attempts to tailor his top team to the platform on which he wanted to fight the next election. Under the rules, he would have to take his outgoing shadow Cabinet to form his first Cabinet in government, after which he would be free to make his own choices. But he was impatient to act before this. As soon as he heard the rumours that Blair would confront the party by unilaterally scrapping the elections, Cook made one of his classic interventions – bringing the subject to light, while coating his remarks in expressions of loyalty. 'I was with Tony Blair for two and a half hours yesterday afternoon and this was never discussed. I have no reason to believe there is any such proposal. As one of those who is concerned, as one of those elected, I would expect to know.'[5] Instead of scrapping the elections, Blair brought them forward from November to June to avoid another summer of jockeying and sniping.

The shadow Cabinet elections also fuelled the hostility between Brown and Cook, which by now was getting out of control. Each was desperately keen to outshine the other. The 1996 results were double-edged for Cook. He retained the top spot, but the contest gave Brown, his power base growing steadily, the chance to persuade Blair to put his friends in all the key economic positions. Chris Smith was moved from social security to health, opening the way for Harriet Harman, a close ally of Brown. Harman had just scraped back in, at the bottom of the poll. Clare Short was shunted from transport to overseas development, Meacher from employment to environmental protection. Blair and Brown had agreed the changes over breakfast at Simpsons in the Strand.

Although Cook had lost much of his influence in economic policy, Blair allowed him to keep one specific area of his old DTI portfolio. After many months of delay, Sir Richard Scott was due to publish his report on the 'arms to Iraq' affair in February 1996. The inquiry had been acrimonious; Tory ministers past and present took every opportunity to rubbish its proceedings and to cast aspersions on Scott's credibility. Now the government, fearing that his conclusions would be damaging, possibly fatal, undertook a damage limitation exercise without precedent. Everything about the presentation of the findings was gerrymandered. Some twenty copies of the report were handed into the Cabinet Office eight days ahead of the 15 February publication date to give Major, his aides and the ministers implicated in the scandal – William Waldegrave, the Treasury chief secretary, and Sir Nicholas Lyell, the Attorney-General – a head start in constructing their response. The Speaker had to intervene to ensure that Cook got more than the thirty minutes the government was planning to give him to do the same. The report was two thousand pages long, in five confusing volumes. Even for someone who had followed the saga day by day, and who had such an ability to assimilate facts and figures quickly, it was an awesome task.

The night before he was due to speak on the report, Cook rehearsed what he might say with Hain, who as Labour whip on European issues had become one of his closest friends. Hain recalls that they were both going to a dinner with the Norwegian ambassador. 'Robin had already done his speech almost word for word, leaving gaps to insert paragraphs of detail from the report. It was staggering to watch, he showed an incredible mastery of detail.'

The restrictions put on Cook that day were a cross between Whitehall farce and the dying days of a one-party dictatorship. He had two hours with the report inside a small room at the DTI, with only a pen and paper to help him. He was not allowed to take any documents in or to make any phone calls out, and would be accompanied if he tried to go anywhere. After conducting media interviews outside to stress the absurdity and inequity of the arrange-ment, he buried himself in the papers, on his own. He then returned to the Commons, where he had only a few minutes to brief Blair and other shadow Cabinet members before having to reply to the statement delivered by trade and industry secretary Ian Lang, prepared over the previous week with the full weight of the ministerial and Civil Service machine behind him.

It was a make or break moment. Cook delivered a tour de force, heaping scorn on attempts by ministers to extricate themselves from the squalid affair. With controlled anger, with a mixture of mockery and menace, he delivered one of the best parliamentary performances for many years in a Chamber hardly replete with great orators. His contempt and verbal dexterity rained down on the government like hot lead. Ian Lang was no match for him. Was Lang, Cook asked, 'really going to ask the House to accept a report which, over five volumes, demonstrates how this govern-ment misjudged Saddam Hussein, misled Members of Parliament and misdirected the prosecution, then tell us that no one in the government will accept responsibility for getting it wrong?' He went on: 'The report goes beyond the career of individual ministers or the reputation of some officials. It reveals the price that Britain pays for a culture of secrecy in government. The report documents how ministers changed the guidelines, but were more worried that Members of Parliament and the public might find out than they were about what Saddam Hussein might do with the weapons.'[6]

Even as Cook sat down, to the roar of Labour backbenchers and the relief of Conservatives, the body language here and there on the Labour front bench suggested he had done a bit too well for his own good. Brown, when invited by a colleague to acknowledge Cook's performance, snapped: 'Yes, it was very good,' and hurried off.

The next day, at a joint press conference with Menzies Campbell of the Liberal Democrats – a new departure in cross-party cooperation – Cook accused ministers of turning the supposedly non-partisan Civil Service into a 'Tory lie machine'. In a letter to Sir Robin Butler, the Cabinet Secretary and head of the home Civil Service, he said: 'It is not good enough to claim that civil servants must always put out the government line. When the government line is a lie, they must be free to refuse to take part.' He followed up his initial parliamentary assault in a full debate on the scandal on 26 February. By then it was clear that, politically, the government had got away with it. Lyell and Waldegrave were safe. But morally the Tories' credibility had been badly damaged. They won the vote by the narrowest of margins, 320 to 319, but only after another Cook speech full of sarcastic barbs that had reduced the Tory benches to silence. 'The government are fond of lecturing the rest of the nation on its need to accept responsibility. Parents are held responsible for their actions; teachers are held responsible for the performance of their pupils; local councillors are held legally and financially responsible; yet, when it comes to themselves, suddenly not a single minister can be found to accept responsibility for what went wrong. It is a government that knows no shame,' he proclaimed.[7]

Cook believes Scott himself was found wanting. 'The big problem we had with Scott was not actually the length of the report, nor with this extraordinary affection the man had for double negatives which obscured the power of his conclusion. The big problem was that he took so confoundedly long to write it. If he had produced it a year earlier I've not the slightest doubt that we'd have been in government,' he said. Using his favourite racing analogy, he likened his own task over Scott to the Grand National, the biggest test of courage and endurance in the sport. 'In horse racing terms it was Becher's. So, you do get psyched up and put a lot of emotional and mental energy into it. When I sat down I knew my colleagues were pleased, but my staff always say I'm unbearable for 24 hours after such occasions.'[8]

Cook's friends believed that the Scott debate had made him indispensable to Blair; but they still needed to be convinced that the Blair camp shared that assessment. Within days Cook received a letter from Blair – a letter to which he attached great significance and of which he was very proud. 'Dear Robin, I really thought your performance was one of the highlights of my time in parliament. You were not merely brilliant, you lifted the whole morale of our troops,' Blair told him. For the next year he had it pinned to the noticeboard of his cramped office in 1 Parliament Street. When he got into government he had to take it down. That letter was last seen in one of the orange packing crates piled high in his new Commons office.

9

What About the Poor?

There was one occasion when Cook was not surprised to see a controversial headline about himself. 'Cook flies banner for the left – keynote STUC speech to emphasise Labour's commitment to traditional socialist values', proclaimed the *Scotsman*. He was due to give a speech to Scottish trade unionists on 17 April 1996, and, unusually for him, had decided to brief about it on the evening before. (His refusal to trail speeches and announcements in advance – an increasingly common practice, designed to put the desired spin on a story or float reaction to a particular announcement ahead of time – was not driven by any principled objection; he finds it very hard to complete a final draft of a speech the day before delivering it.) Cook had becoming increasingly concerned that the thrust of the Brown–Blair economic agenda was tailored exclusively to what came to be known as the Middle England voter. To reach out to that voter, Conservative-supporting tabloid newspapers were used as the medium. Policy was based on the need to make Labour seem non-threatening. Cook and others acknowledged the demographic and electoral exigencies; but they felt the presentation had gone too far, that Labour's traditional constituency was being ignored. After all, where else did it have to go? In his STUC speech, Cook called on the party to speak for the poor: 'We must do it because our values of equality and community make us the party of social solidarity. Because each of us understands that if we accept a society that does not help those who are vulnerable and weak, then it will not help us when we are vulnerable and weak.' He then turned to speculation about Labour loosening its ties with the trade union movement. 'The relationship between the Labour Party and the unions is not a marriage of convenience. It is a recognition of our shared values.' The standing ovation showed no signs of abating. After more than a minute Cook urged delegates to sit down to get on with the rest of the business.

A week earlier, Blair had been in Wall Street convincing American financiers that Labour was a party of the centre. Blair was, his office said, 'perfectly happy' with what Cook had said; his concern for the poor was shared by all at the party's helm. In fact, Blair was annoyed. Everyone was on election alert, and still Labour had momentary lapses of discipline. The party had barely got over the furore among Labour MPs over Harriet Harman's decision to send her son to a grammar school when Clare Short speculated on television about the need to raise the top rate of income tax.

The centre-left, the stalwarts of the old Tribune group, were in a quandary. They did not want to rock the boat and stand accused of letting the Tories back in for the fifth time; and so they were gripped by a sense of powerlessness. Cook, and to a degree Prescott and Dobson, were fighting their corner in the shadow Cabinet. But they had to pick their battles extremely carefully. Hain tried to revive the caucus by hiving off the rump of the original Tribune group into a more informal bunch. What's Left – the double entendre intended – arose out of a pamphlet Hain wrote in September 1994. It has no membership or constitution, just a network of around fifty Labour MPs. Cook addressed it several times. In 1996, as the guest speaker, he thanked the assembled MPs 'for keeping the flag of John Maynard Keynes alive'. He would joke about his role as the agitator inside the camp, announcing himself in calls to journalists: 'Robin Cook at revolutionary headquarters here.'

Cook revealed some of his frustration at the time in an interview with the *Herald*: 'Politics must be about something other than how you win favour in places that matter. One of the problems today, I sometimes think, is that American-style politics is becoming more dominant in the sense of our calculating the pay-back from every statement rather than the social gain, or social pain, of any specific policy proposal.' As for Brown, he would say only: 'Gordon is a valued member of the shadow cabinet, and a colleague. I have to tolerate an awful lot of things being said about me, and I have no intention of saying them about anybody else.'[1]

Blair had just sprung another surprise on the NEC: a proposal that an early draft of Labour's election manifesto be put to a vote of all individual party members at the October conference. By getting ordinary members involved – a large proportion of whom had joined only since Blair had taken over – he would increase internal democracy, while further sidelining the old power bases of conference and the NEC. *New Labour, New Life for Britain* was launched in July 1996. Brown and Blair dominated the press conference at Labour's new high-tech Millbank headquarters, presenting Labour's five pledges for government on a card the size of a credit card. 'We have rejected the worst of our past and redis-covered the best. Keir Hardie would sign up to this. Clement Attlee would sign up to this. Harold Wilson would sign up to this,' proclaimed Blair. Cook, sitting at their side, scowled and tried to intervene twice during the question and answer session. Each time he spoke the other two chatted between themselves. Blair and Cook had had several sessions together to go over the main points in the document; but in the end, Blair's finger-prints were all over it, and Brown had written the economic sections himself. Cook felt marginalized.

On foreign policy, Blair was extremely agitated about some areas, but less concerned about others. When it came to preparing the party's main foreign and security policy paper, his office was exercised by only one section – the wording of Labour's commitment to keep Britain's Trident nuclear missiles. After all the years of controversy about unilateralism, there were to be no hostages to fortune. Jonathan Powell, Blair's chief of staff, who had come to the Labour leader's attention as a senior diplomat in Washington, dictated the wording on the nuclear deterrent. Powell was to become increasingly influential in guiding foreign policy. He and Cook would not always see eye to eye. When *Fresh Start for Britain* was launched on 25 June, Blair – himself a member of CND until the mid-1980s – was asked whether he would press the button. 'These are enormously difficult decisions. You have to envisage the circumstances in which your deterrent can be used, but I don't think it is ever sensible for a prime minister to spell out those circumstances. I believe in retaining our nuclear capability – that is important whilst we have a nuclear threat in the rest of the world, and that will be done under a Labour government,' he said.[2]

The closer the election came, the more superfluous Cook felt. His friends saw Mandelson as manipulating the message for short-term gains, Brown as unprincipled and shallow. But instead of confronting his detractors, he turned more in on himself. He had few confidants. One was Anna Healy, a long-time party official who had helped his press operation, and that of other shadow Cabinet members, before being moved to Blair's office for the final haul.

The atmosphere in the second half of 1996 was febrile. David Blunkett, one-time favourite of unionists and other activists, vowed at the start of the TUC conference that a Labour government would not tolerate 'armchair revolutionaries whose only interest is disruption'. Stephen Byers, whose meteoric rise since entering the Commons in 1992 had led him to the employment brief under Blunkett, had provoked uproar by suggesting, over dinner with journalists during the conference, that Labour would work to sever its financial and organizational links with the unions. Blair was happy with that message. He was preparing for the party conference a few weeks later, at which trouble was expected from Barbara Castle over Brown's refusal to link the state pension with increases in wages rather than prices. Blair was looking to his senior figures to help minimize that trouble.

But no sooner had Cook arrived in Blackpool than he was embroiled in further controversy. He had given an interview to the *Sunday Times*, which he had believed at the time to be thoroughly uncontroversial. When the paper came out, the headline read: 'Cook rounds on Blair for his neglect of poor'. The message was an extension of the concerns he had expressed a few months earlier to Scottish trade unionists.

> It's very important that as we reach out to these new voters we also remember that the coalition on which we're building a Labour victory includes the dispossessed and those who have had the toughest time under Thatcher. There is a very real danger that we're ignoring the needs of a minority in society who find themselves in a very difficult position, usually through no fault of their own, so much so that when someone like me comes along and tries to redress the balance we're accused of having an odd political agenda. I would very much resist the idea that the function of the Labour party is to speak only for a minority of the poor, but I do think it is part of our job to do so. I would like to see that complemented by more work with focus groups from the bottom 30 per cent of society, those who have suffered most in the past 20 years.[3]

Blair was furious. Cook released a transcript of the interview, complaining that his remarks had been taken out of context and condemning the news story as 'mischievous, wrong and wholly unprofessional'.

Still, it was not a bad conference for him. He saw his NEC vote go up by 30 per cent, and Blunkett overtaking Brown into second place. But MPs were being warned this was no time for individual rivalries. The leadership's mantra at that final conference before the election was 'discipline'. Tom Sawyer, the party general secretary, urged delegates to 'avoid mistakes' in the ensuing months. Prescott reminded them of the consequences of playing to the enemy. He recalled the shock of defeat in 1992: 'I will never forget that day, burned in my memory.'

Cook was desperate to find a new niche for the left within New Labour, and the main vehicle had to be constitutional reform – not just a worthy end in itself, but a means towards creating a new kind of politics. For all his successes at the dispatch box, which encouraged the Rottweiler tendency in protagonists of the two main parties, Cook was eager to see a change in the way politics worked in Britain. Too much power was in the hands of a single and secretive executive in London. A more open politics would lead to greater diversification and would bring more people into the fold. He told a conference fringe meeting organized by Nexus, an offshoot of the LCC:

> Part of the mindset which produced the conservatism of the left in the eighties was an unhealthy nostalgia for the vanished society. It is important that we resist the attractions of a retreat to a sepia-tinted Hovis socialism. Believe me, nobody who lived through the real experience of a working class community of 50 years ago feels remotely tempted to return to it now. Life today, with all its problems, is richer, more diverse and more free for my constituents now than it was then.[4]

Shortly afterwards the *Guardian* columnist Martin Kettle wrote: 'Robin Cook is probably the most generally admired politician in Britain today. Only Tony Blair runs him close. Cook has come to be seen by Labour members as the custodian of the party's conscience.' At the same time, Kettle wondered whether Cook's brand of politics – open intellectual engagement with interest groups on specific policies – had any place in Blair's centralized and highly disciplined unit. He wondered whether Cook would have any power in government. 'If you were Cook, how would you prefer to spend the next decade? Ten years of trying hard but probably failing to bust the alliance of Blair and Brown in a Labour cabinet?' This was a barely veiled hint that Cook was considering upping sticks if he could secure the job of head of a devolved Scottish parliament.

Cook was now unchallenged as the leading light in the party working for constitutional reform. He had been instrumental in persuading Kinnock not to close the door on the idea. Smith was thoroughly uninterested. Blair was more amenable but, like others in the leadership, saw it as a bit of a distraction, an issue for the chattering classes. His eyes would glaze when asked for the umpteenth time his position on proportional representation. He saw the issue as indicative of the kind of 'rainbow coalition' approach to politics, in which interest groups held undue sway over politicians, but would concede that, if packaged properly as part of the modernization of politics, it had long-term merits. In the pre-election period he gave Cook his head in this area. Cook had started discussing cooperation with the Liberal Democrats soon after Blair became leader, before a formal bipartisan working group was set up. Although its conclusions were fuzzy, the Plant Commission had crossed a watershed. The principle had been established that the various elections – for the European Parliament, for the proposed Scottish parliament and for possible future English regional assemblies, as well as for the Commons – could require different voting systems. Cook saw pluralism as enhancing the power of the centre-left in the UK. Blair, although unpersuaded by the merits of PR, saw considerable advantage in structures that would harness the support of the Liberal Democrats. Relations between him and Paddy Ashdown were particularly close.

A joint committee on constitutional reform headed by Cook and Robert Maclennan, the Liberal Democrats' president and a former Labour minister under Callaghan, reported on 5 March 1997. The Liberal Democrats had been forced to discard some of their more radical proposals; but the final shopping list marked a sea-change for Labour. By any historical standards it was extraordinary, including not only a confirmation of the commitment to devolution, but also the removal of the right of hereditary peers to speak and vote in the Lords, a code on human rights, freedom of information legislation, independence of the national statistical service, greater scrutiny of quangos, a modernization programme for the Commons, a commitment to regional assemblies in England where required, a referendum for a mayor and assembly for London, a pledge to change the voting system for the European elections at the first opportunity – and, crucially, an independent electoral commission charged with providing a 'proportional' alternative to the first-past-the-post system that would be put to voters in a referendum. (The alternative vote system favoured by some in the party, including Mandelson, is not considered proportional, and, its detractors believe, would centralize power even more. But AV with a proportional 'top-up' would suffice.) Hugo Young suggested that Blair was more on board than he was letting on. 'It's not a case of the shadow cabinet's ablest radical, disappointed by its economic conservatism, going off on a constitutional frolic of his own. Once this reform programme gets under way, based on the radical critique both parties now agree on, it's not easy to see how a progressive prime minister would put his name to stopping the momentum.'[5]

This was politics at its most progressive – Cook, in harmony with the Liberal Democrats and some in his own party, trying to break out of the stale atmosphere of Westminster. At the time the report was published, some shadow Cabinet members scoffed at Cook's efforts. They saw it as a hobby – something to keep him occupied, but away from the 'main event', discussions around the economy and public services that were central to election strategy. But within a few months of the report being issued most of its proposals would be accepted components of a constitutional package that would provide a radical underpinning to Blair's early period in government. Before 1997 PR had been a minority interest among Labour MPs. By that summer an electoral commission under Lord Jenkins had been established and many more were engaging with the possibilities. To advocates of change, there would be no going back. Rather than seeing constitutional reform as a diversion, Cook saw it as a means of saving the left and enhancing a political pluralism that was being snuffed out at the centre.

Shortly after the 1996 conference, Cook had to face further trouble. On 14 November *Tribune* published an anonymous 700-word article under the pen name Cassandra. Claiming to express the views of a senior Labour MP, it warned that Blair could become the shortest-serving Prime Minister, ousted by a palace coup the following summer. He would be replaced by Cook. 'Behind the façade of unity and discipline the reality is that Tony Blair's position as leader of the Labour party is weaker than that of any leader in memory,' it said.

With Robin Cook having built the strongest parliamentary reputation since John Smith, there will be no shortage during next year's summer of discontent of MPs prepared to accept that the damage caused by an internal palace coup will be less of a problem in the long run than the greater risk of being led by a leader whose policies and personal beliefs are shared by only a small minority of the PLP.

Cook was furious and embarrassed, and quickly sought to assure Blair that neither he nor anyone authorized to speak on his behalf had anything to do with it. Mark Seddon, *Tribune*'s editor, refuses to reveal the culprit, but says it was not anyone close to Cook. Hain was chairman of the *Tribune* board at the time. He was confronted by Blair before a meeting of the National Policy Forum and told that the exercise had been 'extremely unhelpful'. Blair, not a man prone to lose his temper, was seething.

Cook had used his speech to the 1996 conference to set out his particular agenda for foreign affairs. On Europe, his message was based on arguments similar to those he had set out in 1983 when helping to shift policy away from opposition to the EEC. Cook suggested that political links between like-minded centre-left parties, which ran a majority of states in the EU, were strong enough to overcome national differences. They would help to develop 'a people's Europe', in which institutions would be more responsive to the ordinary concerns of voters. This was an updated version, with all the required modernizers' buzzwords, of his long-held credo of socialist internationalism. By way of demonstration, Cook introduced video messages from three EU heads of government – Wim Kok from the Netherlands, Austria's Franz Vranitsky and Portugal's Antonio Guterres – each of whom signed off by chanting the mantra, 'New Labour, New Life for Britain, New Hope for Europe'.

Cook was concerned to broaden his foreign affairs remit, Brown to rein it in, especially when it came to the planned European single currency. The formula had been agreed back in 1991. Labour declared it was in favour of EMU in principle but would join only if the conditions were right for Britain. It was refined several times later, on one occasion by Brown, on another by Cook. The former would push the merits of EMU, the latter would speak of the hurdles in the way. In December 1994 Cook tried to harden Labour's conditions for joining EMU, requiring a politically accountable bank as well as convergence on employment and economic growth to go along with the Maastricht criteria of low inflation, low deficits and low debt. As for rejoining the ERM, Cook said a month later: 'No, we've said quite clearly that the ERM poses very clear problems for Britain.'

The differences burst into the open during the 1996 conference. Whelan, dining with journalists from the *Sun*, reacted furiously when bleeped with news that *The Times* was running a story the following morning that said: 'The Labour leadership is edging towards a decision to stay out of the first wave of a European single currency if it goes ahead in 1999. The party's most influential figures are privately voicing serious doubts over whether a Labour government coming to power next year would want to make such a momentous move so soon after entering office.' Whelan, characteristically, called it 'bollocks'. It transpired that the story had come from a lunch with Cook, but the leader's office was prepared to endorse it. Cook's caution about EMU was largely shared by Blair, although Blair's reasons were geared more to what could be sold to a sceptical press and public than to any concern over the tight financial criteria.

A few weeks later, Cook infuriated Brown when he expanded his views. Jobs, he insisted, would be the bottom line to determine whether to join a single currency. There was a very serious problem for Britain joining in the first wave, in 1999, but – by contrast – Britain would find it extremely difficult to stay out of a successful EMU 'in the medium term', a reference to the full introduction of notes and coins in 2002. What particularly riled Brown was Cook's assertion that it 'could be very risky for Britain to give up the option in future of devaluing, if that was necessary'.[6]

Within minutes, Brown's team was briefing the press. 'On the margin, Mr Cook may have damaged his chances of becoming chancellor. The reason is that he used the "D" word, devaluation, which is frowned on in New Labour circles,' the *Financial Times* wrote. It quoted an MP close to Brown as saying: 'The whole thrust of Gordon's approach has been to convince the markets that Labour is no longer the party of devaluation. Can you imagine the interest rate penalty the UK would have to pay if we stayed outside the single currency in the first round and Robin was chancellor?'[7]

Shortly after this episode, Brown was forced by Blair to accept a policy shift to match the Tories' requirement of a referendum before any Cabinet decision to take Britain into EMU. But Brown was always pushing the cause. At a speech in the City of London in November 1996, while accepting the need to keep Britain's options open, he said that 'genuine and active consideration' of the merits of the single currency would be Labour's policy in government. Undaunted, or rather goaded, Cook repeated his view in several interviews in subsequent months that Labour had all but decided that it would not take Britain in in the first wave, but that 2002 was an altogether different matter. Relations had reached rock bottom.

Whelan was a past master at planting stories with friendly journalists. Brown was having trouble accounting for a revenue shortfall from an estimated £1.5 billion in privatization proceeds earmarked by the Conservatives for projects that Labour would not continue in government. Brown and Blair were keen to dispel suggestions of any renationalizations. But what about a privatization of their own? The fate of the Tote, a state-run betting organization that helps subsidize the sport of horse racing and was at that time headed by one of Thatcher's staunchest supporters, the former Labour MP Lord Wyatt of Weeford, was hardly something that would set the nation's pulses beating or raise the hackles of committed socialists. Yet the Tories, not ones to shun a quick privatization deal, had looked at it several times, but baulked. A review conducted in 1996 by Michael Howard, the Home Secretary, concluded that 'complex issues' made the idea impractical. Brown's team were not to be deterred; after all, the sale would raise up to £400 million. The story duly appeared in the *Sunday Telegraph* on 16 February. It had a certain ring of authority to it, and the Sunday news bulletins began to refer to it as settled Labour policy. Jack Straw's office, which was in charge of the area, was unsure how to react when confronted with this apparent sudden change in policy and hedged its bets. Few had reckoned on an intervention from Cook. After all, what did a shadow Foreign Secretary have to do with the issue? Immediately he weighed in – his passion for the racing industry combining in a heady cocktail with resentment of the scheming of Brown's aides. Cook told *The Times* for the following morning, in one of the most devastating rubbishing operations of an announcement by a colleague: 'I can authoritatively bring down the curtain on this story. There have been no discussions in the shadow cabinet about the sale of the Tote. There will be no proposal by Labour to sell the Tote.' Prescott backed him, accusing Labour's 'press guys' of 'running around with their little stories for the Sunday papers'. Whelan's reaction was to laugh off the furore: 'We are going to be exposed to difficult questions about how to fill that black hole,' he said. 'That's why it was a huge mistake of Cook to rubbish the idea of privatising the Tote. Anyway, Cook was talking bollocks. Is he saying we can't do anything? Tony Blair wouldn't be where he is now if he'd had to make sure everything he said was party policy, nor would Labour be where it is in the opinion polls.'[8] Downing Street eventually swung behind Cook's rearguard action, and the idea was reluctantly dropped by Brown. Subsequently, however, in government, Brown would have the last laugh.

A few weeks later the *Independent*'s political editor, Anthony Bevins, who is close to Alastair Campbell, reflected a widespread view in the party leader's office that Brown was going over the top in doing down his colleagues. Citing negative stories that appeared about Cook, Chris Smith and, ironically, Mandelson, the report said:

> High-level complaints have been made to Tony Blair about the 'uncom-radely conduct' of Gordon Brown's friends, with some frontbenchers comparing the shadow chancellor's office to a killing machine. A run of newspaper reports, denigrating and vilifying shadow cabinet members, have appeared over the last week, and senior Labour sources have noted that Mr Brown is fingered as the beneficiary of the assassinations. Comparisons with *Terminator* and *Reservoir Dogs* were being made at Westminster, though sources close to Mr Brown denied involvement in the reports.[9]

The report referred to two apparent 'gaffes' by Cook. The first had occurred on 5 March. Cook, Brown and a host of shadow Cabinet members and Labour veterans had attended a party at Brown's restaurant in Covent Garden to celebrate the sixtieth anniversary of the *Tribune* newspaper. Food and drink were plentiful, and everyone was in high spirits. The election that they had waited for and prepared for so long was around the corner. John Major had ignored the two previous deadlines, and although he had not announced it, 1 May was the only possible date that remained. Shadow ministers were joined on the platform by Michael Foot and Barbara Castle, and Brown, as was customary for him at such occasions, turned in one of his barnstorming paeans to socialism. Cook's offering was more muted, but he prefaced his remarks by saying: 'What better year could we have to celebrate the sixtieth anniversary in which we are going to see the second Labour landslide of this century.' He then got on with the evening like the rest of them. The next morning he was staggered to hear the BBC quoting him as predicting an election landslide and suggesting this flew in the face of Blair's strict edict against triumphalism. Cook protested that his remarks had been taken out of context. But Blair's office did little to dampen down the story, and a few hours later Blair himself delivered a slap-down, telling daytime television: 'What Robin was saying was there was a great sense of hope and excitement. I tell you, if you take people for granted they very quickly remind you who's boss. We take nothing for granted.'[10] He then issued a circular to all candidates reminding them of the electoral arith-metic – that Labour would have to achieve the biggest swing of the century to wrest power from the Conservatives. Was the original story a conspiracy? Nick Robinson, the BBC journalist concerned, says he was not briefed by anyone but had simply registered that Cook's remarks could be seen as controversial.

More was to come the following Saturday. Cook was in Inverness addressing the annual Scottish Labour party conference. The day before, delegates had heard a stony warning from Blair that they had to accept change, that unless Labour won Middle England, the people of Scotland would continue to be denied a voice. Cook decided to play to the gallery with more traditional Tory-bashing oratory. He said that recent speeches by Michael Portillo, then defence secretary, and John Redwood, the right wing's defeated candidate against Major in 1994, had shown that 'chauvinism and xenophobia are the parents of bigotry and racism'. The Conservatives called on Blair to take action against Cook over his 'scurrilous and irresponsible charges of racism'. It was left to Chris Smith to back Cook 'to the hilt'. Was this a conspiracy? One of Cook's closest friends says he saw a member of Brown's camp outside the hall immediately after the speech talking to a journalist on his mobile phone. 'It was amazing how that story got legs so quickly and ran and ran for so long.'

Real or imagined, the sense of grievance grew ever deeper roots. One of Cook's friends says that incident taught him a lesson. 'If there was a problem there, it was precisely that he didn't have a Charlie Whelan-type spin doctor to go round all the press or even talk it through beforehand, saying "you know this is the story", because, perhaps naïvely, he tended to leave it to the press to decide what was the story in the speech. On that occasion the story they found was not necessarily the one he'd have pointed them to, but at the same time, he wouldn't resile from what he said.'

What frustrated Cook was the propensity of the media, encouraged by spin doctors, to gauge each speech purely on its 'gaffe quota' and its loyalty-to-the-leadership level. Paucity of debate is a common private complaint of his. He expanded on his frustration in an interview with the *Sunday Telegraph* at the end of March, saying he was not at ease with

hairstyles and opinion polls. I see nothing wrong with somebody who's going to appear on television for an extended 45-minute interview making sure they don't look offensive to the viewer. But it is not just a question of 'is the blow dry right?' It is also a question of 'what is the substance?' Politics should be about the quality of ideas and the relevance of policy to problems, plus the competence of ministers to carry through those policies. If instead we turn politics into an evaluation of personality, then you are going to end up with some very anomalous outcomes. Nobody runs a business on the basis of whether someone has a pleasing personality. I do think if you want to have a parliament, and therefore a government, that is representative of the people as a whole, you have to recognise that you cannot have a parliament of 630 perfect people. The manifesto focuses quite rightly on the importance of having an environment for children in which they are brought up properly and given a fair start, and that's a perfectly legitimate concern. But how people choose to spend their private life is for them.[11]

Only a few at the time knew the true significance of his plea.

On 17 March, Major went to the country. His attempts to repeat the Tory miracle of 1992 got off to a bad start, with Blair securing the support of the *Sun*. The Labour machine at Millbank headquarters was finely honed. Blair was almost constantly on the road. So was Prescott, barnstorming the one hundred marginals. Brown was in charge of day-to-day operations, with Mandelson working uneasily alongside him. Cook made the odd appearance at press conferences, but was confined mainly to helping Prescott's campaign. Neither Brown nor Mandelson wanted to know. He and Brown had met earlier that month and agreed on the need to arrange to be seen together campaigning for unity. On one Saturday, Cook was to do a photocall at Huntingdon racecourse in Major's constituency; he asked Brown if he wanted to appear with him. Brown could not find the time. He tried again with Musselburgh, a course near both their Scottish constituencies. Somehow they never managed to timetable it. As for better links with Mandelson, to whom Brown had barely spoken since the 1994 leadership contest, an aide of Cook said: 'Peter was determined to keep Robin out during the campaign. There was no use suing for peace after.' One of Cook's friends said a modus operandi could have been possible, but nothing more: 'They are not natural allies, not because of anything personal between them but because they come from different historical traditions and have different political perspectives. Nobody would expect them to be natural allies or close friends.' Mandelson believed Cook and Cunningham had panicked over the notorious 'Jennifer's ear' broadcast of the previous campaign and that the experience of 1992 reinforced the need for central control.

The Cook team had a desk at the far end of the Millbank operations floor, in what was called the 'horseshoe', close to Prescott's and far from the heart of the action. His staffers mounted tongue-in-cheek acts of defiance. A stuffed stoat that adorned his parliamentary office was brought in, as was a bottle of whisky that was put on the desk in spite of Mandelson's edict of teetotalism to all during the campaign. 'That sort of thing brings out the natural rebel in Robin,' says a friend. Cook had very little say in how the election was being run. He would sometimes become frustrated that everything was being geared towards the natural but doubting Conservative voter, such as when he had to toe the line in baulking at an EU directive on part-time workers' rights. Cook saw no electoral difficulty in accepting it. He also suspected that some in the campaign command were trying to dilute a long-cherished commitment to restore the right of union recognition to workers at GCHQ, the government's intelligence-gathering centre in Cheltenham. His team would write press releases on the European social chapter, talking it up in regional visits in a way that was not happening with the national campaign. Asked what they were doing, some of Cook's underemployed aides would say, tongue half in cheek: 'We're preparing for government.' Cook himself would joke about the tight control. Once, when his bleeper went off during a speech in Dundee, he told the audience: 'I've been told to phone John Prescott. I must have committed Labour to a policy'.[12]

He was not even consulted on issues that bordered his patch, such as EMU. On the eve of the launch of the party's manifesto Blair was in Derby, the first stop of his election bus tour. Journalists were briefed by Campbell that the manifesto would harden Labour's stance towards a single currency, referring to 'formidable obstacles' in the way of UK membership. 'What is essential is genuine convergence among economies that take part, without any fudging of the rules,' Blair told a party audience. 'There is no question of it being imposed on a country, slunk through under cover or by a side wind.' Cook was not uncomfortable with the statement, but given his calls in the past for tighter controls on media monopolies, he had reservations about the prime motive – to keep Rupert Murdoch's News Corporation and other Eurosceptic media moguls sweet. Still, he was in no position to complain. When Mandelson posed with a bulldog to reinforce these new pseudo-nationalist credentials for the tabloids, Cook merely smiled.

Blair made his only foray into broader foreign policy issues in a curious speech in Manchester on 21 April. The audience consisted of London-based foreign diplomats, but the message appeared to have been designed almost exclusively for the domestic audience. Speaking of a new international role for Britain, Blair said: 'The British people want to count for something in the world.' Many a former great power had seen its influence reduced, but this should not be Britain's fate. 'New Labour is the internationalist party – outward looking, confident in our ideals, and our capacity to take them abroad for the good of Britain and the wider world. A narrow, crabbed nationalism, the old force of the right, is reborn in the Conservative party. It is a natural reaction to insecurity and fear in a changed world. New Labour is the genuinely patriotic party in Britain today.' There was no mention of some of the issues to which Cook attached high priority, such as tighter control of arms sales and a stronger focus on human rights. In fact, the original draft of that speech, written by Jonathan Powell, even had Blair proclaiming his fondness for the British empire. Such thoughts were excised at the last moment.

Out on the road, Cook bit his lip. He found himself challenged time and again by traditional Labour activists accusing Blair of selling out the cause – as, for example, in Birmingham, when he agreed to be a guest on the *Ed Doolan Show* on Radio WM. Cook winced as his old friend, sitting opposite him in a Pebble Mill studio, derided the New Labour makeover. The electorate, Doolan said, was being asked to choose between two ugly sisters, 'and they're not exactly wild about either'. Doolan is a figure of folklore in the west midlands, a good old-fashioned radical who portrays himself as the friend of the common man. Cook got to know him in the late 1980s when, as shadow health secretary, he shared his fury at cuts in the NHS. Now the shoe was on the other foot: Cook was having to defend Labour's new-found fiscal prudence. 'Where's the beef, Mr Cook?' Doolan demanded. 'Where's the socialism?' Cook's reply was pained. He went through the motions of defending the economic policy, but added: 'Anything that smacks of originality or innovative thinking is written up as "off message". It shows a certain lack of maturity in our political process.'[13] Cook has long been troubled by what he sees as the trivial obsessions of the media, and the tendency to dress any new idea up as an embarrassment or challenge to the leadership – which, in turn, breeds an obsession with control by party managers.

As if to prove his point, the only coverage for his one appearance on the *Election Call* television and radio phone-in revolved around his penchant for horses. Cook was annoyed. 'I've never hunted. I've never shot. I've never fished. I ride, yes, but lots of people ride who never ride to hounds. I'll freely admit that I have ridden horses that have followed hounds. I hope that doesn't make me guilty.'[14]

He found humour a useful outlet for his frustration during the campaign. During a rare visit to his constituency – among Labour's safest – he watched teenagers from a gym class dance around a community hall. 'New Labour discipline,' he said, one eyebrow raised, the equivalent of a grin. 'Peter Mandelson would be proud of them.'[15] A few days later, Cook tried to explain to another audience why he was sitting tight. 'I know there are many people in the grass roots of the party who identify me with their values. I understand that I represent these values within the collective leadership. Having me there in the collective leadership greatly strengthens Tony's position,' he said.

On another visit to Scotland, he went into a bookie's to put a hundred pounds on William Hague becoming the next Tory leader following the election defeat that everyone in the party believed, but dared not say, was inevitable. The odds, at 4–1, were 'not particularly generous'; but, he joked, the bet helped the Labour cause. It meant that 'every Ladbrokes in my constituency has a board up saying "£100 on William Hague to win the leadership contest which will follow their defeat".'

The penultimate Friday of the campaign saw Cook back in Livingston. To rally the troops, he agreed to call the bingo numbers in the Loganlea miners' welfare and charity club in the village of Addiewell in his constituency. He then introduced his unlikely comrade-in-arms, the racing celebrity John McCririck. McCririck had lost faith in John Major's dithering Conservatives and, reassured by Cook's scepticism on EMU, he was about to break the habit of a lifetime and vote Labour. McCririck was at his avuncular best that night on stage. How, he asked in mock grief, could an amateur like Cook keep on stealing a march on one of Britain's best-known pundits? 'I don't know how you do it, Robin. It sickens me to my gut. I'm jealous. Just how do you do it?' he proclaimed, puffing on his torpedo-size cigar. That part was fine, but the evening became decidedly more tense when the wayward guest turned to politics. He launched into the Scottish Nationalists. 'What party with the word "national" in it has ever done anything for anyone? Look at them: the British National Party, the National Front, the National Socialists.' What about the ANC? shouted someone from the audience angrily. 'The jury's still out on them,' McCririck replied.[16] Theirs is a close and curious friendship, one that speaks volumes for Cook's own independence of thought.

As the campaign moved towards its final week, Jonathan Powell was working flat out on preparing for government. This was all top secret – the press was not to be given the impression that Labour saw the result as a fait accompli. Powell's main task was to finalize a Cabinet list and fill the most important second-ranking jobs. With the Amsterdam EU summit looming weeks after the election, the job of minister for Europe was vital. Cook had asked to retain the same team he had in opposition, with Joyce Quin, a soft-spoken former MEP, taking the Europe brief. Powell made clear Quin was not going to get the job: she had gone too native in her ten years in Strasbourg and might not negotiate hard enough for Britain. Cook reluctantly accepted that, but tried to ensure an equivalent job for Quin in another department. (She became a minister of state in the Home Office.) Shortly before polling day Cook found himself in Leeds at the same time as Fatchett, his old friend who is one of the city's MPs. The two sat for half an hour in Cook's car in the car park of Leeds United's Elland Road ground discussing how the campaign had gone. The fact that he could not even choose his own number two confirmed Cook's worst fears.

Election night itself was a surreal experience. Cook emerged from Bathgate Academy school, the polling station for the Livingston and Linlithgow constituencies, with Tam Dalyell, the neighbouring MP, in the early hours of the morning. Both had secured easy victories. The streets were empty. In spite of Labour's impending landslide, Cook was depressed that night. He had told his wife Margaret and other friends over dinner that he ought to have felt joyful on taking office but wondered what was in store. Now, with his entourage – Jim Devine, his agent; Peter Hastie, an ultra-Blairite former chair of Scottish Young Labour who he had taken on to look after his profile in Scotland; David Mathieson, a long-standing researcher who had been seconded back to his campaign; and Gaynor Regan, his diary secretary – Cook drove to Edinburgh airport to catch a flight down to London. As they arrived at the small separate section reserved for private planes they were surprised to see Gordon Brown, together with his team of Whelan, Balls and Sue Nye, who was running his office. Cook's team had phoned Brown's office five days before the election suggesting they share planes. They rang again, but Brown's aides said they had not yet decided on their exact plans. Cook's team booked a larger Lear jet, Brown had a twin-prop Cessna. Meeting at the airport, they saw on the television monitor that Jim Murphy, the Labour candidate, had just taken the Tory stronghold of Eastwood. This presaged a Conservative wipeout in Scotland. 'This is quite extraordinary,' said Cook. Brown agreed. Then they went their separate ways.

Cook arrived in London first and headed straight for the Royal Festival Hall, where Labour's victory party was due to get under way at dawn. As the team approached in the car, they realized they were too early. They drove around the area for several minutes to make sure their arrival coincided with the start of the live television feed.

10

Flying Start

Shortly after lunch on 2 May 1997, Cook got the call. After toiling away in opposition for eighteen years, he was driven into Downing Street to meet the newly installed Prime Minister, Tony Blair. The landslide that he had been ordered not to predict had happened. A majority of 179 defied all expectations. Blair had that morning signalled a new dawn, arriving at No. 10 past a carefully choreographed crowd of Labour well-wishers. The two spent half an hour together, reflecting briefly on the astonishing turn of events, but quickly getting down to business. The following Monday the Labour government would represent Britain at an important meeting of EU ministers preparing for the Amsterdam summit. Blair asked Cook to offer some names as minister for Europe. He suggested first Clive Soley, then Peter Hain. Both came from the same Tribune centre-left stable, but Soley, after winning the Hammersmith seat in 1983, had not progressed beyond junior frontbench level. He was an unlikely choice. Hain had been praised by Blair for his handling of the Maastricht Bill while opposition whip for Europe; but after being appointed a junior employment spokesman, he had had several run-ins with the Blair camp over policy. Blair told Cook he would consider his preferences, and suggested they talk on the phone over the next forty-eight hours and meet again at Blair's Islington house (which he was preparing to vacate) on Sunday evening.

On leaving No. 10, the plan was for Cook to meet Sir John Coles, the long-serving Foreign Office permanent secretary, at the Ambassador Steps, the grand entrance hall that leads up to the Foreign Secretary's office. Coles had expected him to go through the usual entrance in King Charles Street. But Cook had other ideas. He wanted to go through the grander iron gates that lead directly from Downing Street – and had not been used for years.

His request sent Downing Street and Foreign Office officials into a frenzy as they searched for the key. 'I walked out of the door of Downing Street and straight across the street and through the big gates of the Foreign Office and into the main building,' Cook recalled. 'It's the only time I've ever gone that route, the rest of the time one goes in the back door. But it was quite good to have those big gates opened again, and we must do it some time again in the future. It would have been a bit of an anti-climax if I'd come in the back door for my first appearance.'[1]

He was shown to his office. There, he and his most senior officials – Coles, William Ehrman, his principal private secretary, and Nigel Sheinwald, head of the news department – worked until late in the evening on their first set of papers. The next three days, over the May Bank Holiday, saw three dozen meetings. The civil servants had, as is customary, spent the long six weeks of the campaign bringing themselves up to speed on the manifesto proposals of both main parties. But in reality they were preparing themselves for Cook – the politics and the person. They were anticipating a new approach. They got it straight away. On the following day, Saturday, Cook asked that one hour be set aside in the early afternoon to allow him to watch the Two Thousand Guineas from Newmarket, the first Classic of the flat racing season.

The first full day of Cook's new job began inauspiciously. The *Financial Times* reported that Blair had offered Sir David Simon, chairman of British Petroleum and an ardent advocate of EMU, the job of minister for Europe and a peerage. This was the first Cook had heard of it. Alastair Campbell, who as anticipated took over as Blair's press secretary in government, rebutted only part of the story. 'In the past there have been discussions about whether he might be able to help in some capacity, but not as minister for Europe,' said the new Downing Street press team, still unpacking its boxes. Cook had been concerned about the Europe job for some time. More than a year before the election the *Daily Mail* speculated that Mandelson – an ardent pro-European – was seeking not just that position, but a separate department hived off from the Foreign Office. Mandelson, keen to move away from his coordinating and spin doctoring past, had spoken of his desire for the job. Jonathan Powell had looked at the possibility of a different department, but concluded that it was unworkable. Blair, for his part, was desperate to harness business leaders to the government as a signal of Labour's rapprochement with the private sector. He had met Simon during his many business conferences and the two had got on well. The word around the Millbank HQ during the campaign was that Simon was on the cards for a Europe-related position.

Simon is adamant that the story did not come from him and that the first time he was sounded out by Powell for a job was on election night itself.

That first call, he says, was a general one. Over the weekend the offer was firmed up, but he was reluctant to leave BP. He insists that, with legislation on Amsterdam and other EU issues requiring participation in long and complex Commons debates, it would have been difficult to have a Europe minister based in the Lords. In the end, he was offered the post of minister for European competitiveness, based at the DTI under Margaret Beckett.

On Saturday 3 May, Cook took a call from Blair: the Prime Minister had made up his mind. The new minister for Europe was to be Doug Henderson, MP for Newcastle North. On the face of it, he could hardly have picked a less likely candidate. A long-time official at the GMB union, Henderson – as he admitted himself – knew next to nothing about European negotiations. That, Blair believed, was the beauty of it. He was also industrious and reliable. Cook accepted the decision in good grace, although another member of his team remarked several months later: 'I've still not totally worked out that appointment.' Initially, Cook saw it as a genuine threat. Henderson was closely allied to Gordon Brown. Was his job to report back to his mentor? Indeed, when the full government list was published, it became clear that the new Chancellor had emerged as second among equals. He had his placemen in just about everyone's departments, while the Treasury was entirely his own bailiwick.

As compensation for losing out on his choice for the Europe ministry, Cook was allowed to retain two colleagues from opposition in the other minister of state jobs. The most important to him was Fatchett. A former university lecturer and member of the hard-left Campaign group in his early days as an MP in the mid-1980s, Fatchett quickly saw Cook's more incremental approach to change within the Labour party as the most effective. The two became very close friends. Fatchett shared most of Cook's views, but on one area they were poles apart: Fatchett headed a group of Labour MPs who believed firmly in retaining the first-past-the-post electoral system. The other job went to Tony Lloyd, MP for Stretford, considered both an ally and a safe pair of hands. The junior appointment in the department was another surprise. It was given to Liz Symons, a close friend and political soulmate of Blair. Cook had struck up a good working relationship with Symons during the Scott Inquiry, when she was head of the top civil servants' union, the First Division Association; she was also a member of the Cook–Maclennan committee on the constitution. She was to play an important part in modernizing the Foreign Office and opening up its selection procedures.

One of Cook's first resolutions on going into the Foreign Office was to try to make the place less stuffy. There was no grander office in Whitehall than the Foreign Secretary's – large enough, as the last Labour incumbent David Owen had pointed out in the late 1970s, to accommodate three double-decker buses. 'This', acknowledged Cook, 'was built to impress foreigners. Sometimes, I must confess, particularly in the earlier days, it quite intimidated me.' To lighten the tone, Cook brought in his stuffed stoat – which he had bought from a taxidermist at the Badminton horse trials – and ordered a copy of the *Sporting Life* to keep him abreast of horse-racing news each morning. He also asked that the huge picture standing over the fireplace, a portrait of the Maharajah of Nepal, be replaced by something more up-to-date. That, he was told, would not be so easy. Pointing to the hapless potentate, he said: 'That fellow over there, I felt, is not the modern image I would like. My problem is finding something to replace it, because you need something that big and the trouble is all the paintings that are that big are all backward looking and ideologically unsound. But we are working at it.'[2] He eventually got it out: his old friend Brian Lang, now chief executive of the British Library, wrote to him asking for it back. 'I suppose he was thankful to get rid of it,' says Lang.

A man so used to running his own life, Cook now had to come to terms with a team of officials, protection officers and drivers wanting to know what he was up to all the time. He caused consternation initially by leaving his room, not by the door through his private office (where his four main officials sit), but directly into the corridor, into the lift and up to the staff canteen. No Tory had ever been seen there, queuing up, tray in hand. Nobody had told him it existed. He had found it out by accident from one of his bodyguards. 'At first they weren't very happy about it next door. Indeed, they talked about locking the door so they would know that he couldn't get out of the door unannounced and disappear on his own,' said an aide. Cook's first phone call to his US opposite number, Madeleine Albright, caused instant mirth. After speaking to her he suggested to his officials that, with hindsight, it might have been better if one of them had been listening in. 'Don't worry, minister, two of us were,' said Dominic Chilcot, one of his private secretaries.

According to the established convention, Cook was allowed to bring in two special advisers from his opposition staff. Andrew Hood and David Clark had been working in tandem since late 1994, Clark doing Europe, Hood more or less everything else. Prior to that, Clark had spent six years working for various Labour MPs – Doug Hoyle, John Reid and John Home Robertson. Cook insisted on a third adviser. David Mathieson had first come to his attention in 1987, at which point he had been working part-time for Frank Dobson, shadowing health, while finishing a PhD on 'the declining and rising fortunes of the Labour party 1947–64' and running NHS Unlimited, a doctors' group lobbying to combat the spread of private medicine. He spent the next five years working part-time for Cook alongside the more demure Geoff Norris, thinking up stunts to draw journalists' attention to the failures of Tory policy. At the same time he enrolled on a law course and qualified just before the 1992 election. He spent two years as an articled clerk, but after just three days in practice decided it was not for him and went off to live in Mexico with his girlfriend, who teaches for the British Council. Cook met Mathieson again early in 1995 and, six weeks before the election – stung by all the so-called gaffes spun to the press – asked him to work temporarily as his spin doctor. In the first few days in government, Mathieson rarely left his boss's side. Coles, Ehrman and Sheinwald had no idea what he was doing there. Cook asked the party to pay his salary on a one-year rolling contract.

It took Cook three weeks to move into his official London residence, 1 Carlton Gardens. A grand but lifeless building, its two lower floors reserved for official functions and the two upper ones containing the Foreign Secretary's private flat, 1CG is perhaps best known now for serving as the headquarters of de Gaulle's wartime resistance movement in London. Cook scattered horse-racing paraphernalia and framed cartoons of his finer moments at the dispatch box around the flat. He found a bust of Ernest Bevin, Labour's postwar Foreign Secretary, collecting dust behind an aspidistra in the conservatory and had it taken to his office. All these efforts notwithstanding, he took some time to get used to the place. 'I don't particularly like the flat. A great big bloody mausoleum,' he confided.

There's a wing of guest bedrooms which, incredibly, has MFI furniture. Douglas Hurd must have spent a couple of weekends assembling the kits. It's very gloomy. When I go out of my bedroom in the morning there's a picture of three rather sad peasants in a cart on the river, looking at the sky and mouthing, 'it's going to rain'. I feel like rushing back in for my raincoat. The most cheerful painting in the place is the one that greets you when you come in the front door – the murder scene from Hamlet. Plus the lights are very dim. This is not a normal existence. There's no point pretending that it is. I wouldn't deny that there isn't a serious problem in not being able to find any private space to recharge your psychological batteries. I didn't take this job for the trappings. The main difference in lifestyle is that your time is measured and parcelled out in fifteen-minute intervals from 7 a.m. till midnight.[3]

He set off as he would continue – at a brisk pace. In his first fortnight in the job, Cook started to reshape relations with Europe, announced an international initiative to combat the sale of landmines, spoke out against the arms trade, promoted human rights and the environment, and ended the ban on trade unionists at GCHQ. The first announcement came as he left his Islington meeting with Blair on 4 May, on the eve of Henderson's debut on the European circuit: 'We will tell our European partners that we want the rights and benefits of the social chapter to extend to the people of Britain. It marks a fresh start in Europe for Britain, working with other members as a partner, not as an opponent.'

Four days later, the new Foreign Secretary made his first foray overseas. 'Welcome to Cook's tours,' he told his team as his ministerial BAe 146 took off from RAF Northolt for Paris. For a man who had not been in a plane before becoming an MP, this was an altogether new experience. 'The trouble with the Conservative position,' he told a small group of accompanying journalists, 'is that they said "no" so often that people lost track with which were the essential "noes" and which were simply "noes". I'm not in the business of creating goodwill. I'm in the business of negotiating a deal, but constructive negotiation produces an environment which will get that deal. By not fighting needless battles we will be able to focus energies on the battles we must win.' Nigel Sheinwald, straining to hear what Cook was saying, was learning his new lines. The man who had sought to explain Rifkind's policy of non-cooperation with Europe would now espouse the merits of close ties. That was his job. 'We've been told to be more informal and open, so give us points at least for trying,' he said. Cook would not take long to get used to the breakfasts of bacon, omelette, hot rolls and Fortnum and Mason marmalade, meticulously served on china. But he and his team wanted to enjoy this one. 'This beats flying Britannia to Tenerife,' said Henderson as he disembarked at Villacoublay military airport.

First stop was the headquarters of the French Socialist Party, in the midst of their own elections. After a tête-à-tête with Lionel Jospin, Cook was asked if he had passed on any thoughts about campaigning: 'It would be very presumptuous of us to suggest that we have got anything to teach. But if they wish in any way to study our experience we should be very happy to share it with them.' The French were keen to reciprocate the words of goodwill. In the pouring rain, the Quai d'Orsay produced the Republican Guard, a welcome which went far beyond the requirements of protocol. This, after all, was supposed to be only a working visit. Cook tried hard to conceal a smile as he walked past the fourteen soldiers lining the sodden red carpet, resplendent in their gold braid and Beau Geste képis, sabres drawn. Lobster, lamb, red fruits and ice cream comprised the first of what would seem a lifetime of lunches. Cook and his host, Hervé de Charette, announced a trilateral deal, with the Germans, to scrap production of anti-personnel landmines.

It was then on to Bonn, appetite more than satisfied by an RAF cream tea, and a less effusive welcome from Klaus Kinkel. In case anyone was in any doubt, the British would have gone to Germany first, Kinkel said, but he himself happened to be in Egypt that morning. He acknowledged the work of Rifkind, although he described relations with Britain as 'unspectacular and sober'. Cook pledged to draw a line under the 'sterile, negative and fruitless conflict' between the UK and its neighbours, vowing that Britain would join Germany and France in a 'triangular' leading role in the EU. 'We want there to be three main players in Europe, not two,' he declared. Kinkel was quick to allay any misunderstanding. 'All these countries must play a leading role, but we shouldn't speak of triangles.'[4] They then went off for some seasonal asparagus, and the best Auslese that the Rhineland could offer, before Cook finished his long day with a visit to Oskar Lafontaine at the headquarters of the SPD. Lafontaine, an old friend from the Socialist International, espoused policies that Cook had long been persuaded to relinquish. The two gave each other a bear hug, for old times' sake.

On his return Cook was confronted with his first minor diplomatic fracas. The Italians were seething at his talk of a tripartite axis. 'Perhaps minister Cook doesn't yet fully understand the rules of the European Union where, fortunately, there are no leading countries and no countries are led,' said an Italian official.[5]

Cook's early trips convinced him that the flummery was one of the least attractive parts of the job. 'I could, frankly, do without some of the meals. I'd rather just get on with the business over sandwiches,' he commented. 'The problem is, particularly in the European context, diplomacy is inseparable from gastronomy and there's a broad view among many European foreign ministries that if you're not eating at the same time you're not sincere.'[6]

The senior Foreign Office officials may have wondered what Cook's third special adviser was there for, but Mathieson himself was in no doubt. His 'big idea' was a mission statement, of the kind that had become so fashionable in the corporate world. This would send the right modernizing signals, while giving Cook a platform to set out his own distinctive agenda. The Foreign Secretary enthusiastically agreed. They had ten days to prepare it.

The great and the good from embassies and think tanks assembled in the ornate Locarno Room on 12 May for a spectacle the likes of which the Foreign Office had not seen. Cook and his team took their places at the rostrum to the accompaniment of a video extolling Britain's role in the world – at the forefront of peacekeeping, technological breakthroughs and environmental improvement, setting the pace in fashion and the arts. A bank of television monitors 30 feet high cut from images of British soldiers helping Bosnian refugees, to Eurostar racing into the Channel Tunnel, to models strutting on the catwalk, to brokers making money in the City. Coles, the permanent secretary, shuffled awkwardly. But Cook was enjoying the hype. Britain, he proclaimed, would 'once again be a force for good in the world'. The mission statement supplied 'an ethical content to foreign policy and recognizes that the national interest cannot be defined only by narrow realpolitik. Our foreign policy must have an ethical dimension and must support the demands of other people for the democratic rights on which we insist for ourselves'. The new message was to be spread to all British embassies and consulates in a video put together by Lord Puttnam, the Labour-supporting film director. However, *Cook – The Film* never happened. It was overtaken by events.

In the subsequent months there would be considerable argument over just what Cook had promised that day. What did he mean by an 'ethical dimension'? And how important was it to broader strategy? Foreign Office officials would later stress that neither Cook nor anyone in his team used the term 'ethical foreign policy'. Close textual analysis of the statement appears to bear out the theory that ethics and human rights were intended only as one cog, and not a particularly prominent one, in the wheel:

The mission of the Foreign and Commonwealth Office is to promote the national interests of the United Kingdom and to contribute to a strong world community. We shall pursue that mission to secure for Britain four benefits through our foreign policy:

1   Security. We shall ensure the security of the UK and the dependent territories and peace for our people by promoting international stability, fostering our defence alliances and promoting arms control actively.
2   Prosperity. We shall make maximum use of our overseas posts to promote trade abroad and boost jobs at home.
3   Quality of life. We shall work with others to protect the world's environment and to counter the menace of drugs, terrorism and crime.
4   Mutual respect. We shall work through international forums and bilateral relationships to spread the values of human rights, civil liberties and democracy which we demand for ourselves.

To secure these benefits for the UK we shall conduct a global foreign policy with the following strategic aims:

1   To make the UK a leading player in a Europe of independent nation states.
2   To strengthen the Commonwealth and to improve the prosperity of its members and co-operation between its members.
3   To use the status of the UK at the UN to secure these strategic aims over the next five years of this parliament.

In the next 12 months we shall focus on the following immediate priorities:

1 The success of the British presidency of the European Union, by opening the doors to enlargement and completing the single market.
2 An enlarged NATO and strengthened security partnerships abroad.
3 A successful transition in Hong Kong which promotes its security and preserves its freedoms.
4 An agreement on specific measures to protect the world's environment at the forthcoming UN conferences.
5 A productive Commonwealth summit which promotes trade, investment and good government for all its members.
6 A deeper dialogue with the countries of Asia through a successful Asia–Europe summit.
7 A vigorous effort to develop our relations with key and emerging partners.

The government will use the professionalism, the expertise and the dedication of the staff at the FCO in Whitehall and abroad to achieve our mission. I invite them to join with us in working together to deliver these benefits for the British people.

The document was less of a break with the past than was 'spun' at the time. But, even if it was not Cook's intention to overplay the ethical dimension, that certainly was the result. The atmosphere of the moment was not conducive to caution, to measured responses. The honeymoon was in full bloom. The government was making waves, and receiving plaudits for virtually everything it did. Brown's announcement that he was giving the Bank of England independence to set interest rates had set the mood. Two days later, Cook delighted many inside and outside the party by formally announcing the end of the ban on trade unions at GCHQ, imposed in 1984 by Thatcher. 'The government have signalled their commitment to open and fair relations in the workplace. As part of that commitment, I am righting a long-standing wrong,' he said. Former employees who lost their jobs for continuing union membership would be free to apply for re-employment under the new conditions of service. Cook had had to fight hard for this, and without him it might not have happened. During and after the campaign several key figures were advocating either scuppering or delaying the plan. The last impression they wanted to give was of a new Labour government giving concessions to the unions.

During the 1980s Labour could be crudely divided between, on the one hand, so-called Atlanticists, and, on the other, advocates of unilateral disarmament who would tend to regard Washington with suspicion. In his early years in Parliament, Cook had belonged to the latter camp, and omission of any explicit reference to the United States in the mission statement reinforced suspicions that he would seek to elevate relations with Europe at the expense of the much-vaunted but ill-defined 'special relationship' with America. His first meeting with Madeleine Albright, who had been appointed Secretary of State early in 1997, had been difficult. The pair were atypical for their offices, both feisty, outspoken and lacking some of the gloss of traditional diplomacy. Their working breakfast at the start of a visit to Washington in May was altogether different. Cook astonished the US team by talking for an hour and three-quarters without briefing papers; Albright referred to a big book she had with her, but impressed her opposite number with her imaginative thinking on difficult issues. Their mutual respect would later turn to good friendship, the closest between British and US foreign ministers for some time. That, in itself, was no mean achievement.

Cook also saw William Cohen, the defence secretary, and Sandy Berger, President Clinton's National Security Adviser. However, one meeting overshadowed the rest – an encounter with the legendary Jesse Helms, the North Carolina Republican who chairs the Senate foreign relations committee. Visiting delegations to Helms's office are asked to sit against the wall. Before the talking begins they are asked to pose, in a line, for photographs. He and another old gentleman, his sidekick Admiral Nance, would sit on rocking chairs declaiming on the woes of the world. 'It was bizarre theatre, like a Southern colonial balcony in *Gone with the Wind*,' said one participant. Cook was genuinely taken aback by their ignorance of world affairs, beyond generalities. They began with an argument over US late payments to the United Nations. Helms waxed lyrical about the high number of staff the UN had; Cook responded by saying that the ratio of staff to senior people was smaller than in Congress. Helms responded that the Europeans owed the Americans money for the UN, because the Americans had bailed them out after the Second World War. He then, on a completely different tack, said: 'Since you guys are in favour of NATO expansion, we're not going to pay for it.' Cook, for his part, criticized the Helms–Burton Act, devised in part by his host, which penalizes foreign companies that deal with Cuba. The meeting, scheduled for half an hour, ended after twenty minutes. Helms abruptly stood up and ushered Cook to the door. The pair were described as having 'disagreed disagreeably'. Albright, similarly averse to many of Helms's views, had learned to flatter him.

Cook saw a considerable amount of Blair during this period. The two men made several trips abroad together, using their time on board government aircraft to go through business. An informal summit in the Dutch coastal resort of Noordwijk gave EU leaders their first opportunity to test Blair's proclaimed *communautaire* credentials, while Cook kept more on the sidelines. On the detail of negotiations they worked well together. After all the talk from Michael Howard and other Conservatives that the nation-state would be imperilled by Labour, Blair and Cook played hardball on several issues at the Amsterdam summit; they came away having gained concessions on border controls and blocked Franco-German proposals for an eventual merger of the EU and its defence arm, the Western European Union. 'We have made very substantial progress in getting Britain's national interests. It is quite clear to me from the conversations I have had with my opposite numbers that to a large extent we have made that progress because there is a new negotiating climate,' said Cook. During one of the breaks in fraught late-night negotiations, Chancellor Kohl said to Blair of Cook: 'He's extremely impressive.'

On a more conceptual level, Cook was less comfortable with some of Blair's utterances. But he kept his counsel. One such occasion was a speech Blair gave to fellow party leaders at a congress of European socialist parties in Malmö, Sweden. Blair, to the chagrin of the newly elected French premier Jospin, dismissed much of the economic thinking that had long been the norm for European social democracy. Urging fellow leaders to accept radical welfare reform and Anglo-Saxon labour market flexibility, Blair proclaimed, in a quintessential Campbellism: 'We must modernize or die.' Over the past decade, he said, the left had 'looked like defenders of a fading industrial past'. Instead, governments should 'give the people the education, skills, technical know-how they need to let their own enterprise and talent flourish'. The one word that did not flow from Blair's lip was the dreaded S-word, socialism. Yet it was those same proponents of what Blair believed was a dying creed, people like Oskar Lafontaine, with whom Cook spent the late evening drinking in the hotel bar.

In other contexts Cook could allow his public pronouncements to mirror his personal convictions. The previous Tory government's reluctance to set the pace on efforts to secure an international deal on landmines had struck even many in their own party as odd. For Blair this was one of those policy shifts without a downside. On 21 May, Cook announced a complete ban on the use, production, transfer and stockpiling of anti-personnel landmines, which kill or maim an estimated twenty thousand people a year. British stockpiles would be destroyed by 2005. A treaty was eventually signed on 3 December in Ottawa requiring signatories to destroy their stocks even earlier, within four years. The United States, Russia, China and some other states did not sign, but it was a start. This was early and uncontroversial proof of a greater emphasis on the ethical dimension.

Much of the pressure for such a ban over the spring and summer had been brought to bear by Diana, Princess of Wales. In June, she asked to come and see Cook to discuss the new government's approach in detail. It was a meeting that left its mark on Cook, in more ways than one. As she arrived, Mandelson was leaving Cook's office – the two of them were trying to develop a better working relationship in government. To the embarrassment of officials, Diana marched towards Mandelson, greeted him with a 'hello, Peter', and gave him a kiss on the cheek. She then went in for a discussion with Cook, his special adviser Andrew Hood, and Clare Short, Secretary of State for International Development. Cook began with a quick tour d'horizon, mentioning that there were a hundred thousand mines in existence; Diana immediately corrected him with the more precise figure. After the meeting, Cook introduced her to his private office, and to the secretaries in the next-door 'engine room'.

A week later, at the Earth Summit follow-up meeting in New York called by the UN to set new targets for greenhouse gas emissions, Cook was at his most outspoken. His passion for tougher environmental regulation is one of the least appreciated parts of his political makeup. He was the UK government's first delegate to speak, and went in head first: 'At the moment the biggest single problem is that the American public has not yet grasped that if it continues with its present lifestyle then it is going to make it impossible for its children or grandchildren to enjoy the kind of environment and lifestyle that the American public have today'.

Underlying Cook's attempts to refashion the way Britain approached foreign affairs was recognition of the growing interdependence of nation-states, and their need to work collectively to make progress in any number of fields. He would argue that citizens across the world, whatever the democratic credentials of their government, were united by a common set of concerns and ethical bottom lines. He developed this theory in a speech delivered on 17 July under the title 'Human Rights into a New Century'. His twelve-point plan, based on the Universal Declaration of Human Rights, said Britain would:

1   support measures to isolate regimes 'who grotesquely violate human rights';
2   support sanctions, notably against Iraq for seeking to develop weapons of mass destruction;
3   refuse to supply weapons 'with which regimes deny the demands of their people for human rights';
4   condemn child labour and all forms of exploitation of children;
5   support non-governmental organizations and others working for human rights;

6   seek dialogue on the observance of human rights in all bilateral
     contacts;
7   support proposals for a permanent International Criminal Court;
8   provide more resources to existing criminal tribunals;
9   re-target a British training programme for foreign security forces
     more towards human rights;
10   give stronger support to media under threat from authoritarian
     regimes;
11   publish an annual report on its activities in promoting human rights;
12   incorporate the European Convention of Human Rights into British
     law and sign other agreements still outstanding.

A self-standing human rights policy department had been established
under Douglas Hurd in 1992. Cook wanted to give it a higher profile within
the Foreign Office and to use it to help improve consultations between
NGOs and British diplomats. Amnesty International and other groups
welcomed the commitment as evidence of a change of attitude.

As MPs and ministers prepared for their long summer recess after the
slog of the election campaign and the first three months in office, there was
widespread praise in the parliamentary party and Whitehall for the way
Cook had applied himself to the job – a portfolio he had three years earlier
been reluctant to accept. The hectic schedule, however, had kept him
almost completely out of the picture on the domestic social and economic
agenda. He seemed unwilling to make waves on domestic policy in the way
that he had in opposition. An early sign was the postponement of a speech
he was due to give to the First Division Association. The senior Civil
Service union had held an annual lecture on behalf of the GCHQ workers
since 1984. Cook had accepted the invitation to address the gathering in late
May 1997, and had volunteered the contentious subject of trade unions in a
modern society. The speech had to be cancelled because of foreign commitments, but Cook did not get back to them to offer an alternative date.

Cook found himself peripheral to many areas of domestic policy. He was
not included in many of the key Cabinet committees, and headed only one –
the Europe subcommittee, where he was regarded as an able chairman. For
the first few months at least, the 'big four' meetings continued to take place,
just before the full session of Cabinet on Thursdays. The constitutional
reform committee was run by Lord Irvine, the Lord Chancellor; Cook
became less and less involved in its detailed workings, even though he had
been responsible for many of the proposals it was examining. Although he
was named as a member of the Labour delegation in the newly established
joint Cabinet committee with the Liberal Democrats, that show was
dominated by Blair and Ashdown. Cook was not even in the loop when the

decision was taken in mid-July to hold the 1999 European elections under proportional representation – although he was thrilled at the victory this represented.

On one decision he would not compromise. He and other members of the shadow Cabinet who were on the NEC had been asked by Blair to stand down from the National Executive. The Prime Minister was determined to ensure that a committee that had dogged the Wilson and Callaghan governments, and made life difficult for Labour opposition leaders, notably Kinnock, would not become a rival centre of power. The NEC was Cook's most powerful base of support, much more so than the shadow Cabinet: it was his direct channel to the rank and file, among whom he remained immensely popular. So, in contrast to Brown, who had decided at the start of the year not to stand, Cook ignored Blair's request, even though he knew that impending changes to party structures would make it impossible for Cabinet members to sit on the NEC from the 1998 conference on.

Cook's meetings with Blair were businesslike, structured and devoted almost entirely to foreign affairs. Brown, by contrast, was omnipresent – running Cabinet committees on a broad range of policy, as well as popping into Blair's office once or twice a day, or meeting in the evening for a drink on the terrace overlooking the Downing Street garden. The living arrangements – with the Blair family having the larger No. 11 flat, and Brown the smaller apartment above No. 10 – further cemented that relationship. Brown, meanwhile, was assiduously courting the army of new Labour MPs at Westminster. Each one received a letter of congratulation on his or her arrival, and groups were invited to Downing Street for drinks. Even Jim Devine, Cook's long-standing agent and friend, received a mail shot in Glasgow from Brown's office about how well the first few months had gone for the Chancellor. Cook believed he had done equally well, but preferred not to advertise it.

11

The Ethics Business

The article was entitled 'The Tragic Cost of Britain's Arms Trade'. It detailed how a Labour government had restocked Middle Eastern governments whose inventories had dwindled after a series of wars. It called into question the morality and economic wisdom of a desperate chase for arms contracts when the UK was owed £90 million by countries that had not paid up. As for the sale of Hawk aircraft to Indonesia, this was 'particularly disturbing as the purchasing regime is not only repressive but actually at war on two fronts: in East Timor where perhaps a sixth of the population has been slaughtered in Indonesia's continuing efforts to consolidate its invasion of 1975; and in West Papua where it confronts an indigenous liberation movement'. As for the Labour defence secretary, he had 'sought to defend the sale on the ingenious ground that the Hawk is only a trainer aircraft'. The author bemoaned that President Jimmy Carter had been obliged to discard his good intentions to reform US foreign policy and its approach to arms sales because of a rearguard action by the defence industry and a lack of international support for his efforts. 'Labour got Britain into this sordid trade in a really big way by ordering the Defence Sales Office in 1966 "to ensure that this country does not fail to secure its rightful share of this valuable commercial market". It would help make amends if Labour were to start us on the first few steps towards getting out of it.'

The article appeared in the *New Statesman* on 30 June 1978. The author was its defence correspondent, Robin Cook. The wheel would turn full circle.

This is what Cook told the Labour conference in September 1995: 'A Labour government will not license the export of arms to any regime that will use them for internal oppression or external aggression.' He did not bother with qualifications.

In February 1997, to mark the first anniversary of the publication of the Scott Report, Cook set out a plan to ensure that a British firm would never again break the rules to sell arms to pariah nations. 'Britain is a leading arms exporter. We have a right to maintain our competitive edge in this market, but we must also accept our responsibility to ensure that the arms trade is properly regulated.'[1] His programme included:

1   a ban on all anti-personnel landmines and a moratorium on their use;
2   stricter monitoring of end-user certificates;
3   measures to prevent UK companies from manufacturing, selling or procuring equipment such as electric shock batons and other instruments of torture;
4   an annual register of arms sales setting out the state of controls and their application. This would list the total value of defence exports to each country, giving details of licences granted and refused. Commons committees on defence, foreign affairs, and trade and industry would examine the report. Efforts would be made to establish a similar register for the EU.

Three days earlier, Blair was extolling the virtues of UK arms companies. He, and the leaders of the other two main parties, had been put a series of questions in writing by the chief executive of British Aerospace, their answers destined for the company's internal newsletter. The Labour party issued a press release, drawing attention to Blair's response: 'A new Labour government will be committed to creating the conditions in which the [defence] industries can thrive and prosper. Winning export orders is vital to the long-term success of Britain's defence industry. A Labour government will work with the industry to win export orders.'

In opposition, Cook had vowed radically to alter Britain's approach to arms sales. It was never going to be easy. In 1997 Britain accounted for almost a quarter of the global arms export market, second only to the United States, with sales abroad valued at over £5 billion a year. France had fallen back in the export table. The Middle East accounts for 40 per cent of all arms imports in a market which is expanding again after almost a decade of decline following the end of the Cold War. Saudi Arabia alone bought £5.5 billion worth of foreign weapons in 1996, making it by far the world's biggest arms importer. Al Yamamah, a rolling oil-for-arms deal established by Thatcher, had by 1997 generated around £40 billion of business, mainly for UK aerospace industries.[2] Some half a million people are employed in two thousand arms factories in the UK. Each of them has a constituency MP who would protest at job losses.

One specific problem loomed for Cook straight away. What was the new government going to do about the sale to Indonesia of sixteen Hawk training aircraft, Alvis armoured cars and Tactica water cannon, worth a total of £160 million and signed in 1996 by the outgoing Tory administration. The Indonesian air force had by the time of the election already taken delivery of a previous consignment of forty BAe Hawks. Under the Tories, the UK had become Indonesia's largest supplier of arms. Exports had increased over the previous five years by 150 per cent, totalling £438 million in 1996 – 10 per cent of total British arms exports that year.

Cook had consistently said that he was against revoking the export licences for tactical reasons. He told a party meeting at the 1996 conference that there were no merits in 'reimbursing' the defence industry £1 billion in likely damages from a cancelled contract. This was a far cry from his views of two decades previously; but it was the political reality. Nevertheless, such was the emphasis on 'good news' after the election that little attempt was made to stress from the outset that the contracts would – reluctantly – be honoured. The impression built up that they were in the balance. The end result was not what Cook wanted, but it was hardly surprising. 'The legal advice we received on the Hawks was the worst possible. We couldn't say we would definitely be sued, nor could we say it was watertight,' said a minister. They concluded it was not worth the risk. It was always going to be an exercise in damage limitation, making clear that this was not a Labour government selling Indonesia the planes; that its hands were tied; and that allowing the contracts to go ahead did not imply a softening of the commitment to raise East Timor and the whole issue of rights violations with the Indonesian government, as Cook told Jose Ramos-Horta, the Timorese leader, in one of several meetings they had before, during and after the general election campaign.

It came down to an executive decision. The advice was that, to be able to revoke the export licence with legal impunity, the UK would have to show that there had been 'material' changes for the worse on the ground in Indonesia and East Timor since the time when the licences were granted. A change in British circumstances – the arrival of a new government – was irrelevant under international law. Compensation could, the lawyers said, be set at a sum greater than the whole Foreign Office budget. What particularly angered Labour MPs and pressure groups was a suggestion by ministers that there was no evidence the planes were being used in East Timor – this, after all, is what the Labour government had said in the late 1970s, an argument Cook had ridiculed then.

The announcement was delayed several times, in an attempt to pick a moment that would cause Cook least aggravation. It was agreed to make it coincide with publication of the new set of criteria for arms sales in general

– another piece of bad news for those looking for radical change. The backbench human rights group was led by Ann Clwyd, a frontbencher in the late 1980s who had been sacked by Blair for disappearing to Turkey to look at the plight of the Kurds without telling the Chief Whip – an absence which coincided with a session of Foreign Office questions she was supposed to attend as a shadow minister. Clwyd says that she had been excited by the mission statement and human rights speech, after which she went up to Cook and told him, half jokingly: 'I'm very pleased, but I'll be watching you.' She urged lobbyists to 'lay off him for a while'. But when speculation increased that the Hawks were to be allowed to go, she rose every day in the Commons to ask the government to make a verbal statement to the House. The announcement eventually came – in a written answer, a parliamentary device sometimes used to play down a decision. It was issued in the name of Tony Lloyd, the minister responsible for the arms trade. By good fortune, Cook would be flying to Bosnia that day, and so would be away from the Commons chamber. In the morning, however, he tried to explain the decisions to the most vocal group of Labour MPs against the arms trade, inviting Clwyd and her colleagues to a meeting where he told them it was 'not practical' – he did not say impossible – 'to backdate these new criteria to apply to decisions on licences already taken by the previous administration'. They responded by putting together an early day motion – a petition – attacking the decision. In all, 136 MPs, mainly Labour, backed it, in an impressive display of anger. Demonstrators assembled outside Downing Street carrying a banner bearing the slogan 'Ethical Foreign Policy RIP'.

Even some of Cook's friends were upset. Ken Purchase, his parliamentary private secretary, said: 'I was mortified. The government had the right to annul the contracts. If we had inherited twenty people on death row, we would have reversed that. You can never satisfy the demands of the arms lobby.' Human rights groups and NGOs say that the situation in East Timor had indeed deteriorated by the time of the announcement, and continued to do so subsequently.

The Hawks controversy overshadowed the announcement of the more fundamental review of the rules for selling arms. Lobbying on both sides had been intense. Defence contractors had long enjoyed a powerful alliance with more traditionally minded Labour MPs. Bob Ainsworth and Jim Cunningham, two MPs from Coventry, where Alvis is based, had been to see junior ministers. Another of the town's MPs, the businessman Geoffrey Robinson, who had become Paymaster-General, had direct access to Blair. The DTI, which is responsible for issuing the licences, was highly sceptical about changing the rules. The Ministry of Defence, especially its junior ministers, John Spellar, John Reid and Lord Gilbert, lobbied hard to minimize any change. Several key figures in the defence lobby were regular visitors to Downing Street.

Blair had striven to ensure that defence did not re-emerge as the 'problem' for Labour it had been in the 1980s. He listened to the likes of Lord Hollick, an important behind-the-scenes player in the Labour hierarchy, who had been a director of British Aerospace before being appointed an adviser to Margaret Beckett at the DTI. Hollick, made a Labour peer on Kinnock's recommendation in 1991, was managing director of the MAI group and chief executive of United News and Media; he played perhaps the most crucial role in building links between Labour and the business world, running a business unit at Millbank devoted to building links between Labour and the private sector. Sir David Marshall, chairman of the Society of British Aerospace Companies, was part of the Foreign Office team in the comprehensive spending review that was taking place in the government's first year. Bob Bauman, chairman of British Aerospace, and George Simpson, managing director of GEC, helped to establish the Institute for Public Policy Research, a Blairite think tank. These figures had been helping to fund Fabian Society conferences, and several IPPR activities, and these captains of industry were the kind of people Blair liked to invite around to Downing Street.

At the other end of the spectrum, Lloyd – who did most of the drafting of the arms policy statement – was being lobbied by NGOs. In May Saferworld, a campaigning group, and the Department of Peace Studies at Bradford University submitted a draft to civil servants at the Foreign Office's non-proliferation department, which was coordinating the work. They proposed that the criteria be tightened to stipulate that licences should not be granted for any equipment that might be used for internal repression, and that there should be a 'presumption' to refuse permits for exports to countries of 'concern' such as Indonesia, unless a legitimate defence requirement could clearly be demonstrated. Instead of the DTI having to prove that a particular country had used equipment against its own people in order to get a licence stopped, the onus would be on the purchaser country to prove it really needed the arms for defence against an external aggressor.[3]

Some of these ideas were adapted into a final Foreign Office draft that went to Downing Street. Officials there were not happy. They thought that the criteria were far too tight. John Holmes, Blair's principal private secretary and top civil servant, went through it with officials from Cook's private office for four hours, line by line, telling them to tone down various areas. On Friday 25 July, the last working day before the Monday announcement, they were still making serious changes to it. Cook and Blair met to go over it, but it was largely a one-way conversation. Blair wanted change to tone and substance. The preamble was beefed up, eventually saying: 'The government is committed to the maintenance of a strong defence industry which is a strategic part of our industrial base as well as of our defence effort.'[4] Without referring to the Hawks for Indonesia, it said that while the present government was 'not responsible for the decisions on export licences made by the previous administration', it did not consider it realistic or practical to revoke licences which were 'valid and in force' at the time of the election. In what Cook's team claimed was a concession, it said the criteria would constitute broad guidance and would not be applied mechanically. In other words desk officers, junior civil servants, would no longer simply tick off contracts. Ministerial discretion would be permitted.

Most of the work was concentrated on the section entitled 'Human Rights and Internal Repression'. This made clear that the government would 'take into account respect for human rights and fundamental freedoms in the recipient country' and would not issue a licence 'if there is a clearly identifiable risk that the proposed export might be used for internal repression'. The main difference from the previous set of rules that applied under the Conservatives was the substitution of the phrase 'might be used' for 'likely to be used'. When it came to defining what might be considered internal repression, Downing Street insisted on the caveat 'unless the end-use of the equipment is judged to be legitimate, such as protection of members of security forces from violence'.

'We inherited twenty thousand existing export licences. We took the view it was not practical to get in the business of revoking any of them. We didn't make the specific decision on any one of them,' said Cook later, by way of explanation. 'Inconsistency is inevitable to compromise, and compromise is inevitable to foreign policy. That is real life. But you know, as I said in my first speech on human rights, it's very easy to keep your hands clean by never going near anything that's difficult or complex, but you're not going to change anything by doing that. If you want to bring improvement then you've got to be prepared to tackle the problems.'[5]

Cook set off for the airport, leaving Lloyd to take the flak and answer for the government. He wanted his trip to the former Yugoslavia to confound the doubters and send a clear message about the new approach of the Labour government. He had his work cut out. The day before, he had given an interview to the *Sunday Times* suggesting that further aid to the mainly Muslim Bosnian government in Sarajevo would be in jeopardy unless it took stronger steps to stamp out Mafia-style corruption; the government there was furious. The Bosnian Serbs were outraged by his warning that NATO forces were on the look-out to snatch more indicted war criminals hiding inside Republika Srpska; a month earlier British soldiers, under international auspices, had killed one Serb war crimes suspect in the village of Prijedor and taken another away to the international war crimes tribunal in The Hague. The Croats were fuming at Britain's part in persuading the IMF (along with Germany and the United States) to withhold a £25 million credit 'because of the unsatisfactory state of democracy in Croatia'.

In Sarajevo, Banja Luka, Tuzla and Zagreb – the four main stopping points on his three-day visit – Cook did not pull his punches. For British diplomats used to the more conventional Hurd and Rifkind way of doing things – the smiles, the warm words and the occasional tut-tut behind closed doors – this was a novel experience. Cook took time between official meetings to give interviews to journalists from television channels and papers not in state pockets, and to hold discussions with opposition politicians. He scarcely concealed his disdain for the Bosnian Serb and Muslim leaderships and for President Tudjman of Croatia, clenching his teeth and frowning his inimitable frown, while warning them to carry out their international commitments.

In Sarajevo he accused the leaders of all three communities of connivance in corruption, and warned of further military action to bring suspects to justice. His message, shorn of any of the usual diplomatic finesse, was delivered after talks with President Alija Izetbegovic. From there he was driven fifteen miles across the green line to the Serb-held suburb of Lukavica to meet their local leader, Momcilo Krajisnik, who had refused to leave his own territory for fear of arrest. On the journey, British diplomats pointed out the home of Radovan Karadzic, the Bosnian Serb henchman wanted in The Hague to answer for war crimes. That hideout was so tantalizingly close, yet inaccessible – a reminder for Cook of how difficult it was becoming to achieve his aims. As Cook left Sarajevo, the British ambassador there, Charles Crawford, pointed out to him a report in the local government newspaper, *Dnevni Avaz*. Cook smiled as the envoy, translating as he went along, read that not only should he, Crawford, be expelled; as for the Foreign Secretary's warnings over corruption, 'If the accusations prove to be unjustified, we shall ask the foreign citizens who have been spreading such lies on the Bosnian government to leave our country without delay.'

The following day it was on to Croatia and a meeting with Tudjman at his residence in the hills overlooking Zagreb. 'We can't tell you what time the meeting will finish because it depends how long it takes for the president to walk out,' joked one official. Cook warned Tudjman that Croatia risked being disqualified from international financial assistance unless it began to implement the provisions of the Dayton Accord that had brought the war to an end and established the new political arrangements. He cited slow progress towards the return of refugees; little movement to break the state stranglehold over the media; failure to surrender indicted war criminals to the international tribunal; and reluctance to exercise control over the

Bosnian Croats. The talks ran to time and no one walked out; but the protagonists agreed to disagree on just about everything. All Cook got from Tudjman was a lecture on Croatian history back to the middle ages, a denial of human rights problems, a refusal to engage on the subject of repatriation of refugees and a claim that he had no influence over Bosnia's Croats. Cook was relying on international cooperation. 'If international coordination broke down, I certainly would lose some of my optimism,' Cook confided, as he was driven to the airport.[6]

Cook made little secret of his poor opinion of the leaders of what he calls 'little statelets', who define free speech as the right to assert their nationalism. What was new for British officials was not the private views of their Foreign Secretary, but his willingness to criticize his interlocutors in public. 'I want to have a foreign policy that embodies our values as a government, and the values on which we base our domestic policies are values of civil liberty, of democracy, of good governance, of justice. Those are not values that we should leave behind when we leave the country and check out our passports, those are values which should also inform our foreign policy,' he said. As for causing offence: 'First of all, you don't antagonize the country. You may have caused some irritation to the government of the country, but you don't antagonize the country. And indeed in a number of places I have been it is quite obvious that what I've been saying is very welcome throughout that country and one of the lessons I think that we need to absorb is that over recent history there has been a very positive, progressive movement of countries towards forms of democracy and good governance. We don't necessarily do the best for Britain if we over-identify ourselves with regimes that try and stand in the way of that progress, because when it happens people may remember that we were rather closely identified with the previous regime.'[7]

But was this candour to be applied across the board? What about China and Tibet? What about Russian corruption, as against Bosnian? Would Cook talk to them in the same way? He was putting his head above the parapet. He was fully aware of the consequences of failure, of the ridicule President Carter encountered as a naïve idealist confronted with the complex workings of the world. 'What's important is to succeed,' he said, as he left Zagreb behind him. 'The next important thing is to have tried.'

The trouble was, there were a lot of people back home – some in his own department – who did not want him to succeed. The Foreign Office had got used to doing things in time-honoured ways, and many saw little reason to change. A small group, mainly of older diplomats past and present, viewed with intense suspicion the arrival of a man remembered for his anti-nuclear, anti-Atlanticist views, and his hostility to the intelligence services. After three months in which he could do little wrong, stories started appearing in the papers. At first they were small, just little barbed remarks fed over lunch by officials and other MPs; and they were as much to do with his style of work and manner, as with his politics. Cook, some claimed, was not paying enough attention to the job.

From the moment he ordered keys to be found for the gates from Downing Street, Cook was determined to do things differently. When in opposition, the shadow Cabinet had been sent on a series of away-days and weekends at Templeton College Oxford to discuss how to cope in government. Those who had served under Wilson and Callaghan gave their advice. Gerald Kaufman's book, *How to be a Minister*, became required reading again. It is a witty guide to the dos and don'ts of government, one of the most important of which is: don't allow yourself to be taken over by the Sir Humphreys of this world. Cook resolved not to allow himself to become bogged down in the minutiae of office. For the Foreign Secretary, this is perhaps more difficult than for any other Cabinet minister, because of the time that has to be spent out of the country. 'The big problem', Cook complained, 'is that you spend about half your working days abroad, that's unavoidable. The trouble is that back home people expect you to do a full working week ... which is impossible when you're there for two and a half days.' He tried to cut down on the number of formal events, delegating them to junior ministers as much as possible. 'Robin tries to sort the political from the professional. He desperately doesn't want to become a Foreign Secretary who does only the work for the following day,' said a member of his team.

In the first few months of government, many ministers were struggling with their red boxes, taking them – as advised by their civil servants – to pore over documents to be signed until the early hours. Cook wanted to be different; and one of his predecessors had blazed the trail for him. 'The story goes that Ernest Bevin, on his first weekend, was left with five red boxes and a note saying: "Foreign Secretary, we thought you would like to do these five red boxes over the weekend." And on Monday, when the staff came in the private office, they found the five red boxes in the same place with a note in his handwriting: "A kind thought, but sadly erroneous." I'm happy to say that nobody's ever tried to present me with five red boxes, but ever since I heard that story I have recognized that you can be a successful Foreign Secretary if you focus on the big questions, not necessarily if you finish the paperwork.'[8]

He likened his job to that of a company chairman, rather than the chief executive. 'He's a good chairman,' says a senior official. 'Meetings don't drift. He's very good at summing things up and builds a consensus around his own position. Colleagues keep on telling me how impressed they are by the sheer amount of material he can absorb.' Cook admitted: 'I've been quite ruthless in cutting down the routine paperwork, which is what anybody at the top of a big business would want to do. It's also been valuable throughout the Foreign Office, because it has meant we have been delegating decisions. The job's become more rewarding for people further down the chain.'

For the first time, lower-ranking officials found themselves invited to important policy sessions. Even more astonishing, Cook would then ask them their frank opinion about whether a particular decision could work. As in opposition, he respected those who were fast off the blocks and were clear in their thinking. He was intolerant of lazy adherence to past practice. One paper he received was part of the Foreign Office's submission to the Whitehall defence review. He banged off a memo to his private office saying it had clearly been drafted by someone who saw a bear around every corner and a spy in every bath. It was, needless to say, thoroughly rewritten. The pontificators got short shrift. Some officials with high opinions of themselves were not used to snappy put-downs, and there was resentment from those used to the old cosy way of receiving insincere praise for memorandums that would be filed away for a rainy day.

His days, which usually began with breakfast in the canteen, would be apportioned to the last minute. Other meals – when he was not at official banquets – would consist of sandwiches munched at his desk, often in the middle of meetings. (His eating habits did not endear him to some of the more fainthearted.) He did not enjoy being interrupted, but as his meetings tended to over-run it was often difficult for his advisers to catch him in between even for a split second. Time-keeping and speech-writing provided the biggest headaches. First drafts of speeches would be submitted by officials and then invariably deconstructed by their boss. To make life more difficult, he would sometimes only get round to looking at the final draft the evening before he was due to make the speech. He paid particular attention to speeches in the Commons, jealously guarding his reputation as the Chamber's foremost orator. He never had enough time. He was rarely seen in the Commons corridors, tea room or bars, just talking to fellow MPs. Ken Purchase, his PPS, said of his boss: 'Working for him is like being handcuffed to a ghost, tugging and pulling but never sure where he is.'

Cook agreed to an arrangement giving him two nights a week free, although one of them was intended for paperwork. Officials say that when he did go through his boxes, he did not – unlike Rifkind – skim read. He would even look at annexes. One weekend in three was also earmarked as his own time. Horses and racing were his one relief. At one point he considered asking the Household Cavalry if he could occasionally help with their early morning exercise in nearby Carlton Gardens; but he realized he would not be able to do it regularly enough. So he took up jogging around St James's Park, a strange hobby for someone so uninterested in sport in his youth. He tried to time his foreign trips to coincide with big races – the Breeders' Cup in America, the Melbourne Cup in Australia, and meetings at Happy Valley in Hong Kong. In the Philippines in August he asked for a Saturday afternoon free to go to the Manila Jockey Club, where he astonished his hosts by tipping an unfancied horse named Good is Good. The head of the Jockey Club went along with him, for politeness' sake, only to find that the horse won.

At British courses, Cook would keep the social chit-chat to a minimum, preferring to stand at the rails going through the form book, sometimes with his elder son Christopher. In July he went to Ascot for the King George VI and Queen Elizabeth Diamond Stakes. He and Chris avoided the champagne and society chat, and instead walked the course to see whether the going had changed.

'The office will have to get used to Robin, not the other way round,' said one of Cook's advisers. It did not take long for most, although by no means all, to do just that. By the summer Cook felt that his private office was working well. They learnt quickly to deal with his manner, which they felt was more than compensated for by his mental energy and his openness. 'There are no airs about him. What you see is what you get,' says one official. Many younger members of the Foreign Office were extremely enthusiastic about the prospect of a Labour government, having felt under-valued and humiliated by Tory xenophobia, especially Malcolm Rifkind's ill-fated 'home truths' tour of European capitals a few months before the election. Cook would, at the very least, encourage fresh thinking and shake some of the cobwebs away.

'I said after my first fortnight that I wasn't quite clear whether I had a Rolls-Royce of a support staff which was looking after me exceptionally well, or whether I'd been kidnapped and taken into custody,' said Cook. 'The dividing line between these two concepts is actually pretty fine. Now I'm in charge of my private office. It is not the other way round. On the whole I have found officials in here very committed, very intelligent, and I haven't detected at any stage any resistance to the policy changes I have made. There is no *maquis* somewhere in the underground trying to resist the policy that I'm putting through.'

He was being somewhat optimistic. Here, after all, was a politician who had been around for twenty-five years, who through his forensic skill and less-than-diplomatic personal approach had made enemies among rivals in his own party, senior Tories wounded by his attacks over the years, disgruntled diplomats who did not like his way of working, and figures in the intelligence services who resented his many activities, notably in the ABC,

Agee–Hosenball and Zircon cases. One friend says that he was aware from the mid-1980s that smears were being prepared for whenever Cook would make it into government. One of the more absurd ideas floated in the security services was to hint at doubts over his sexuality, to get back at him for his campaigning to lower the age of consent for gay men. That idea was quickly abandoned; but the hostility was not. There were some who were gunning for him. 'Robin's problem', said a friend, 'was that he left himself vulnerable to attack.'

12

Two People Apart

After the election campaign and the exertions of a frantic first three months of office, Cook was looking forward to his holiday. He and Margaret had arranged shortly after the election to take a three-week break in America – so busy were they that they had worked out in advance the times they would see each other that year. The first week was to be spent at a lodge in Vermont, where they would hike, rest and just talk quietly on their own. They would then move on to Montana, to a ranch where they could indulge in their love of horse-riding in the remote heartlands of the midwest.

Margaret finished work early on Friday 1 August to catch an early afternoon shuttle from Edinburgh to London. The Foreign Secretary's two official cars were waiting for her as she got off the plane. Robin was in one with David Mathieson – they had planned to go through some remaining paperwork in the couple of hours before the Cooks' flight to Boston – and Margaret joined them for the short drive to Terminal Four. The bags she had packed for them both had been checked through. It was during that ten-minute drive that Alastair Campbell telephoned the Foreign Secretary. While he took the call Margaret and Mathieson talked about holiday destinations, paying little attention to Cook's deadly serious, monosyllabic mutters down the phone.

The Cooks' younger son Peter had arranged to meet his parents at Terminal Four, in a café in the departure lounge. Living close by at Slough, he could make it over to Heathrow to wish them both bon voyage without being away from his desk too long. After waiting for a while, Peter was approached by an official who asked him to follow him to the VIP lounge in the secure part of the terminal. Robin, meanwhile, had ordered his bodyguard and the catering staff to wait outside the lounge. There, according to Margaret, he told her: 'The holiday's off. The *News of the World* has got the story, and I can't see how the marriage can continue.'

What Campbell had told Cook was that the paper would make the details of its revelations known by the following morning, Saturday, leaving them little over twelve hours to sort it out. Campbell had been phoned on Friday morning by the *News of the World*, who agreed not to contact Cook himself, Margaret, Gaynor or the children, provided a statement was issued in response to the story. Campbell told Cook that, for what it was worth, clarity in news management was the only way they were going to get out of it. Cook interpreted 'clarity' as meaning he should make a choice one way or the other and told Campbell that he knew he could not go on with the holiday with Margaret, being pursued by photographers and reporters. Nor could he ditch Gaynor. Campbell was not surprised by the response.

Cook had gone through the scenario in his mind before. He and Margaret had tried to patch up their marriage – sometimes he even thought it might still work – but he quickly concluded he had only one option. Did he panic? His friends say he could not face confronting the choice, so tried to forget about it for as long as he could. They deny he was 'bounced' into it, saying that he had known for some time that he would rather be with Gaynor.

Margaret broke down in tears. She had known for some time that there was a possibility that one of the tabloids would reveal details of her husband's long-standing affair with Gaynor Regan. But she had assumed that affair was over. Not only did she think she and Robin had got on much better since the election, she never thought he would have the time in government to resume the liaison.

By the time Peter arrived, Margaret had collected herself. She told Robin that he had better break the news to his son himself. Peter was dumbstruck. He had had no idea what had been going on. As he consoled his mother, Cook talked on the phone again to Campbell and to Blair. He was visibly relieved when told that he had the Prime Minister's support and that his job was safe. Cook agreed to issue a statement the following evening, once the first edition of the paper had made the story public. He and Campbell toyed with the idea of making the announcement in Scotland, but decided it would be best that he stay in London. Cook wanted to contact his most trusted aide, Jim Devine, but he was out of reach in Ireland.

By now it was late evening and no one knew where the family should go. Mathieson had gone to meet Gaynor and taken her to a 'safe house'. She too had been preparing to go on holiday, to France with a girlfriend, Mary Warner, who had previously worked part-time in Cook's office. But their holiday also had to be cancelled; the prospect of being dogged by the press pack made it pointless. The hideout chosen for her was the north London home of Anna Healy and her husband John Cruddace, an adviser to Blair on trade union relations. Their attempts to keep her out of the public eye nearly went wrong when their two-and-a-half-year-old went with his father to the corner shop and, on recognizing Regan's picture in the papers, blurted out: 'That's auntie Gaynor.'

Margaret and Peter agreed to go back to Carlton Gardens. There, estranged husband and distraught wife sat up over a bottle of whisky until late in the night trying to absorb what had happened.

Next morning, the news management operation went into full swing. Cook discussed the wording of statements with Campbell, who was on his way to a family holiday in Italy, and his deputy, Tim Allan. Margaret and Peter, who had left Carlton Gardens early, flew back to Edinburgh, where they were met by Christopher. The three of them went to the supermarket to stock up with provisions for what they knew was going to be a siege by journalists. Margaret called a few close friends to prepare them ahead of the television news. They then cooked a meal and sat around, waiting for the announcement. Robin appeared on the steps of the Foreign Office and, to the accompaniment of flashing camera lights, announced that he was leaving his wife for his secretary. Margaret had agreed to issue a statement through her employers, West Lothian NHS Trust: 'Whatever my husband's private life may have been, he has always been a very good Member of Parliament and is a very good Foreign Secretary. These are the only matters of concern to the public.' Blair's office said: 'The Prime Minister is very sorry for Robin and Margaret and he feels for all concerned. He sees this as a personal tragedy for those involved which does not affect Robin Cook's capability as a truly outstanding foreign secretary.' Bristow Muldoon, the young and affable chairman of Cook's constituency, said: 'We are sad for Robin and his wife that their marriage has ended. However, the fact remains that Robin Cook has been a first-class MP, both as a constituency MP and as a leading national figure. Livingston constituency party continues to fully support Robin and looks forward to him representing the constituency for many years to come.'

Some colleagues at Westminster tried to get in touch with Cook as soon as they had seen the news. Peter Hain paged him that night. Cook phoned him back and they discussed whether it would be a good idea for friendly MPs to use their contacts in the media to rally support for him. They decided against it.

After the statement on the news, Margaret and the boys then watched the evening movie, the James Bond film, *A View to a Kill*. They scoffed a box of expensive chocolates and drowned their sorrows with some good bottles of wine. The next afternoon they sat in front of *Butch Cassidy and the Sundance Kid*, laughing at the appositeness to their situation of the film's ending, when the two heroes find themselves surrounded. For the first few days, with journalists dug in outside the front garden, Margaret stayed inside. The boys would slip out the back door, unbeknown to the photographers, and drive off to buy provisions. Inside the house, they would sit around, talking things through and watching films. Christopher joked that the racing column he had written for Robin for the fateful Saturday had proved one of their most successful, but no one had noticed. After a few days the reporters disappeared, and the trio went a few times to see plays at the Edinburgh Festival. Margaret then went to stay for a short while with her mother in the west country.

'Labour Minister and his secret love. Cook: my marriage is over,' screamed The *News of the World*'s front-page headline over its 'world exclusive' on Sunday, 3 August. The story revealed how Cook had led a double life, in opposition and in government, spending nights with Regan at his London flat in Sutherland Street, while at weekends he would return to his wife. The lovers had gone to extraordinary lengths to keep the affair secret. To avoid alerting his Special Branch bodyguards to the presence of anyone else inside his flat, she would let herself in and sit in the dark until he arrived later; they would order meals from pizza delivery firms. In the mornings he would empty the bin in a skip around the corner, then feed the meter where her car was parked before being picked up and taken to his office. She would go to the Commons shortly thereafter.

The newspaper claimed it had got the story by chance. A freelance photographer, Andy Tyndall, saw Cook walking down the street with a big bag of rubbish, and thought it would make an amusing picture. He decided to come back with his camera, but poor weather put him off. He told a colleague about it, who came along. They hung around once or twice, and saw Cook go through the procedure each morning, including the day of his trip to Bosnia. It was when a woman came out of the flat an hour and a half after he had left that they realized they were on to something.

For all the effort Cook and Regan had put into keeping their affair from becoming public knowledge, it was an open secret among a wide group in the Labour party. That nobody had let it go further testified to the remarkable discipline of party workers and MPs alike before the election. Anna Healy talked to Cook about it from an early stage; but no one else dared broach the subject. 'With Robin it's not easy even for friends just to walk in through the door,' said one. There had been several warnings of trouble ahead. As far back as the start of 1996, Cook would tell late-night or break-fast television crews wanting to interview him about the Scott Report to meet him at a hotel in Sloane Square, where a room in the lobby had been made available. Suspicions were raised. 'During the week he was the only member of the shadow Cabinet that you couldn't phone direct. You could only reach him by pager. It was virtually impossible to get a number off him,' said one party official. Once or twice in his early days at the Foreign Office, the ever-industrious switchboard operators at Downing Street were asked by Cook's own officials to intervene by paging him with the message to 'call No. 10'. His diary, which was distributed to a couple of dozen officials from private office to news department, would include several appointments on weeknights allocated to 'constituency secretary'. Mixed in with the intricate planning necessary to conceal the relationship was an air of fatalism that at some point the press would probably be able to stand up the story. Labour party officials knew that a hotel porter had tipped off a tabloid about Cook being seen early in the morning with 'a woman with long hair' in summer 1996; but it was not clear whether they had enough to go on.

Gaynor was born on 2 February 1957, the only child of Joan and Alan Wellings. Her father, who trained as an engineer, ran his own printing business. The family moved several times, to Coventry and then to the Cotswold village of Upper Tysoe, near Stratford-upon-Avon. Gaynor went first to Nottingham University, but did not enjoy it there and started her English degree again at Hull. There she met her future first husband, Stephen Regan, at her freshers' ball. They studied together in the Brynmor Jones Library, where the poet Philip Larkin was librarian, and Stephen later dedicated a book on Larkin to her. He was from a working-class Durham background and was passionately committed to the Labour party. After graduating in 1979, she moved to London and decided on a nursing career. But she gave it up after six months to join Stephen travelling in Canada. They stayed there two years before moving to Oxford, where he had got a job teaching at Ruskin College. In 1982 they married. They lived in Charlbury and went to local Labour party meetings. She did various secretarial jobs, first with a top medical specialist, then with Sir Michael Kaser at the Russian department at St Antony's College, from where she moved to become personal assistant to Sir Claus Moser, Warden of Wadham College. From there she applied successfully for a job in Cook's office, after which she lived in London during the week. Distance put paid to the marriage: Stephen and Gaynor separated in 1994, but have remained friends.

Cook and Regan share many characteristics. They are both often awkward at first encounters, not as socially adept as others, but intensely loyal to a close inner circle of friends, who in turn are extremely loyal to them. She, like him, has had to overcome shyness – he has simply had more experience at it. They are both graduates in English literature and both share broadly the same political philosophy. They share similar interests in classical music, the theatre and fine art. Perhaps the thing that riles Cook the most is the portrayal of her as po-faced and characterless. Cook says of her: 'She can be uncannily intuitive as to what I'm thinking before I even know it myself. We are both only children. But she likes to keep herself very private and I respect, indeed admire, that. She is very intelligent. She was critical of some of my campaigns, like Matrix Churchill. A lot of judgmental stuff has been dumped on her. She is really not just a secretary, as the press describe her.'[1]

For a year, since first becoming aware that the press were in pursuit of the story, the two of them had been living in fear of a media circus. Tony Blair and everyone else who knew about the affair hoped that – with so much mileage having been gained from press disclosures of Tory financial and personal 'sleaze' – nothing would come out until after the election. But they all assumed that in Cook's case the media frenzy would not last long. After all, he had never preached on standards of personal morality (attempts to draw a comparison with his ethical foreign policy had always been specious) – indeed, he had gone out of his way throughout his career to espouse libertarian views on sexual morality. The *News of the World* claims it thought long and hard about whether to run the story. Labour and Tory ministers alike had warned repeatedly that privacy laws might be the only way to stem an over-zealous press that delved into celebrities' private lives even where no public interest could be justifiably claimed. But the newspaper concluded that Cook's position merited publication of the story.

In the absence of Blair and Campbell, Mandelson had been entrusted with coordinating and presenting policy that August – invariably a dangerous month, when newspapers are craving for the tiniest of crumbs to fill otherwise news-free pages. He was determined to divert journalists' attention from the Cook saga. It had not been an easy few days for the government. After three months of eulogies across the media, without the barest hint of criticism of the new administration, the first cracks had begun to appear. John Redwood had made inroads by drawing attention to Lord Simon's share portfolio, and the suicide of MP Gordon McMaster had turned a spotlight on endemic corruption in some Scottish constituencies. Mandelson, reverting to his time-honoured method of briefing a select group of trusted reporters, let it be known that investigations had begun into claims that Chris Patten, the former Governor of Hong Kong, had passed classified material about negotiations on the colony's future to the journalist Jonathan Dimbleby. (Those investigations were quietly dropped in December.) He also gave impetus to a second diversionary story given to a Sunday newspaper, that the royal yacht *Britannia*, due to be retired, might be reprieved after all, with ministers moving towards the option of a privately funded refit. The headlines the next day, Monday, were not that bad, leading one Downing Street spin doctor to proclaim 'a fantastic operation'. There was relief that Cook had got away relatively lightly.

Cook decided to brave it out by turning up for work on Monday morning. Those officials who were still there (most had gone on holiday) kept out of his way. But with nothing in his diary for three weeks, he found himself, for the first time since taking office, with time on his hands. He would sit in his room with a box of biscuits and talk to those aides and colleagues who were still around – more candidly than they had ever known. 'It was the first time I ever saw him open up,' said an official. 'He would just sit and chat.' He did not see Gaynor all week, and her absence compounded his depression. 'Of all Robin's emotions, guilt is one of the strongest,' says a friend. 'He finds it hard to deal with.' By Tuesday the editorial writers and columnists had injected some venom into their writing. After reading them, he threw the papers on the table. One friend recalls: 'He was thinking of throwing it in. His pride was damaged, and he said to me: "Tell me what you think. Am I taking this properly, or am I just depressed?"' We had to take a lot on the chin. We had convinced ourselves for years that nothing was going to happen. It was handled hour by hour. Only by about the Thursday were we confident that he really was going to ride it out.' That Saturday, one of Cook's advisers drove Regan from Anna Healy's house into Carlton Gardens. She was to stay there officially for the first time.

Few separations involving politicians have been subjected to such a glare of publicity as this one. So where did it go wrong? Some might argue that, in modern times, for a marriage to last two decades is a success in itself. The split spawned a bout of soul-searching about the damage done to marriages by distance, and this was certainly the most obvious explanation. For twenty-three of the twenty-eight years of their marriage the Cooks effectively lived apart – physically and emotionally. The Commons, with its late nights and febrile atmosphere, has torn asunder many a married couple who in other circumstances would have sailed, or muddled, through. 'We all knew they were leading separate lives,' says a friend. 'His home was London.' Spouses living in far-flung parts of the UK were not often seen at Westminster, but at conferences and the odd other occasion most would put in an appearance. Not Margaret. Apart from a few of the Scots, most MPs knew nothing about her. She did not have a key for Robin's London flat, although she says she asked a few times. Once when she stayed there she wrote down the phone number which was written on the handset.

For all his interest in health as a political issue, Robin did not pay much attention to Margaret's work. In front of friends, he would jokingly call her 'the blood doctor'. Her career took off after the birth of the boys. She began work as a consultant haematologist at the Bangour hospital in Livingston in 1976, but says Cook pressed her to change jobs: 'He tried to persuade me to go into psychology, the acceptable face of medicine.' She was largely disdainful of politicians – although, she insists, not of serious politics – and when other MPs or journalists called at weekends could give them short shrift. When he first became an MP she occasionally went to functions in

Edinburgh, but she lost interest. 'She never helped with his politics,' says one political friend of Cook. 'Even though she said she agreed with what we were doing, I remember at the 1983 election it was a battle to get her involved in a promotion of a health policy in her very own hospital.' Livingston's medical services were a hot political issue: the Bangour hospital was replaced by the ultra-modern St Johns in 1989, but an additional wing took another five years to be opened.

It was the boys and horses that drew Margaret and Robin together. But their brief weekends at home were intense and could often become fraught. Even their hobbies became a potential problem. They did little entertaining – in fact, very few people Cook terms friends and colleagues can recall being invited to his house. 'We both had a strong work ethic in common,' Margaret says. 'We didn't keep open house. He was driven mercilessly, and I suppose I was too.' One source of tension was money. For almost all their married life Margaret earned more than her husband. Moreover, he showed little interest in saving, and enjoyed spending money on dinners in restaurants, good-quality malt whiskies and endless trips around the country. Their shared passion for horses was an expensive pastime.

Friday nights would often revolve around constituency functions, Sunday nights he would sometimes take the sleeper back to London. So Saturday night was the focal point of the family weekend. She would cook, and then they would play board games. They had dozens of them. Colditz, Articulate and Totopoly were favourites. 'Sometimes I would opt out and do crochet because I couldn't take the ruthlessness of the playing,' she says. The disdain was understated. They did not argue in front of the boys. She remembers one particularly difficult Christmas evening playing Monopoly. As for chess: 'He would sit for ages, pondering his next move. I was more impetuous and would get bored. In spite of that I would usually beat him and he would go silent.' The same applied to horse riding: within a few years of their both starting as novices, she was by far the stronger rider. She believes that is why he turned his attention to being an amateur tipster.

Early holidays were taken in the New Forest, where they first met Clive Hollick and his wife, Sue. The Hollicks bought out the woman who had rented them their first cottage there, and for a few years the Cooks went to stay with them each summer. Once the boys had gone to university, Robin and Margaret began to take trips abroad, some of them quite adventurous: in 1993 they went to Canada to do a spot of white-water rafting and grizzly bear watching. At home in the summer, the family would go for picnics. Robin would often lark around with the boys at castles and other monuments, shooting cap pistols at each other. 'We would scare the tourists off with our shoot-outs,' recalls Peter. 'We would also chase each other with truncheons made of heavily-rolled sheets of newspaper. This, I suppose, you could call interactive history.' His father was not the practical type. 'The only DIY he attempted was to put up a Christmas tree, a process which one year took five hours. Once he put egg cups in the oven and melted them.'

The other axes in the family were very strong – the boys got on well with each other, and each had a close relationship with each parent. This experience of a somewhat closed community made the very public separation desperately difficult for the boys to take. Despite the shock and acrimony, they tried hard not to take sides afterwards. As for Gaynor, they felt little animosity and tried to come to terms with her being their father's partner – which would have been easier had they met her before seeing her in the newspapers. They fastidiously kept out of the limelight, seeking comfort in a shared view that most of the blame lay with the media. Peter, younger but taller than Chris, is the more introverted of the two, more political – a committed supporter of the Campaign Against the Arms Trade, he refused to consider applying for a job with British Aerospace after graduating in electrical engineering from Newcastle University; he now works for the telecommunications firm Cellnet in Slough. The more gregarious Chris, who completed his law degree at Aberdeen, works as a solicitor in Edinburgh specializing in personal injury damages.

Both parents always agreed to conceal their problems from the boys, and neither son can remember any serious argument between their mother and father in front of them. But alone, the parents stumbled through several crises. Margaret recalls how in 1987, just before the general election, he told her he was close to Celia Henderson, a riding instructor at a local stable. 'He told me he had had a whole string before her. The boys were in the house, so I couldn't lose my temper. But I made up my mind that the next time I would leave him,' Margaret says. That friendship ended during the campaign, and, according to one close political friend, Cook was so distraught that he considered giving up politics then and there. But Margaret says that soon after the election her suspicions were aroused again. Henderson was a family friend, and yet, she says, 'I was aghast at the way Robin seemed so relaxed in her house and in her company. You know when someone is particularly familiar with a place.'

Mary Kaldor, an old friend from the disarmament campaigns of the 1970s, was one of those in whom he confided. Cook would sometimes stay with her and her husband at their home in Brighton around Labour conferences. Margaret was never with him – indeed, she was virtually never seen at any political function. Kaldor recalls that as early as around 1988 Cook said he did not think he could stay with his wife. In late 1996 she went to talk to him in his Commons office about Bosnia; but 'all he wanted to do was to talk about his marriage'. But he would never give his London home number even to Kaldor.

Margaret Cook says she was aware of her husband's relationship with a secretary from 1995. But she said nothing, hoping it would blow over. Why? Here, after all, was a woman who was an intellectual match for her husband, who knew her own mind and was used to speaking it. 'He knew that I'd never lose my temper in front of the boys,' she says. 'I suppose I had my head in the sand.' In August 1996, a week before they were due to set off for northern Spain on a walking and riding holiday, he told her about Regan. 'We were in the kitchen. He said: "Margaret, I've got something to tell you. I've had another affair. I didn't mean it to go on that long, I thought I'd better tell you." I told him what I thought of him.' Once again she played the stoic and they went on holiday as planned. 'It all nearly fell apart. I was on autopilot. We were staying in a self-catering place in the middle of the Picos de Europa. It was too quiet. The last night, in the middle of Rioja country, he said, for the umpteenth time, he would stop seeing her.'

By then, though, they might as well have been living apart. She was extremely fond of the family home, their three-bedroomed seventeenth-century mill in Clermiston, to the west of Edinburgh city, which they had moved into shortly after Peter's birth in 1974. The most impressive bit of it was the big, bay-windowed sitting room, which used to contain two millstones worked by donkeys, and now looked out on to their large garden with its mature trees. Their next-door neighbours lived in what had been the old farmhouse. The mill was conveniently located for both Margaret's hospital and Robin's constituency meetings, but he wanted to live in a Georgian building in the New Town, the more fashionable part of north Edinburgh. 'He thought this was a bit suburban,' she says. 'We used to argue about it.' He was coming back each weekend to a hermetically sealed environment. He might have talked politics, especially when the boys were around, but during his battles with Brown and Mandelson, amid his doubts about policy directions, leadership contests and Blair, his only listening board and solace was in London. So keen was he to see Regan that she would pick him up from the airport on his return from Edinburgh whenever she could.

The Cooks had another row just before Christmas 1996 when he said the relationship with his secretary had carried on. 'The boys never suspected anything. He promised he would tell them after Christmas, but didn't,' says Margaret. 'I think he was trying to get me to leave him. He said to me: "Do you not think our paths have diverged?"' One of Cook's closest friends told him that Christmas that he had to 'deal with the problem once and for all,' warning him: 'Unless you do, you'll be mauled.' Nothing more was said.

Immediately after the election, friends say, Margaret had a new lease of life. 'Before that she could be irritable if you phoned. She suddenly became much more vivacious.' Shortly afterwards, she found out that her husband had failed to tell her that she had also been invited to the Festival Hall celebrations – he had gone with Regan and the rest of his inner team – but she brushed it off. That, she says, was only one of several invitations that did not get to her. In 1995 she had gone with her husband to a royal banquet at Windsor Castle, sitting between Prince Charles and the Duke of Edinburgh and opposite the Queen. However, an even larger gathering the following week at Buckingham Palace, to which she had also been invited, she heard about only later.

A week into his new job, Cook spent his first day off with Margaret at the Badminton horse trials. They talked a lot, and agreed to work out their diaries for the rest of the year, to give them as much time as possible together on holiday, at equestrian events and on official trips. He invited her for the Hong Kong handover at the end of June, and to India in October. She booked her leave well in advance. He issued a minute for the office, setting out the foreign visits on which she would accompany him.

On her way to Hong Kong she stayed overnight in Carlton Gardens, the first time she had been there. Cook's office realized only the day before that they had forgotten to arrange a flight down for her from Edinburgh to London. She told them she might as well come down in the evening, only to be informed that her husband was planning to take the whole day off. She knew nothing of this, and said: 'He must be getting himself a horse.' In their brief time in Hong Kong it seemed to those with them that they were making a real effort. After their return, when he was in London and she in Edinburgh, he would call her every evening. On 20 July she went down to Kent for her first trip to Chevening, the Foreign Secretary's official residence, basking in 3,500 acres of sculptured landscape with its lake, its unrivalled library and its deafening tranquillity. Chris and Peter were also there, as was the family friend John McCririck and his wife Jenny, universally known as 'the Booby'. McCririck remembers it as a 'magical evening'. Margaret told him she had never been to the United States, and joked that now she would be flying tourist again, after the first-class luxury of the official plane to Hong Kong. The Cooks agreed to host a terrific New Year's bash at Chevening. 'They seemed very happy,' says McCririck. 'He looked in love with her.' Cook even referred light-heartedly to what it was like to be a happily married man. The following day they were guests at Highgrove with Prince Charles. Margaret was, briefly, enjoying her new life as wife of a secretary of state.

Margaret says she was genuinely shocked at the events that took place two weeks later: not the newspaper revelations – they had all been bracing themselves for that for a year – but Robin's choice of Gaynor over her. Those who know them both well were also taken aback by his decision. But, at the same time, they were surprised that the marriage had not ended earlier. Why did Margaret, a charming, smart, self-reliant woman, put up with it for so long? The boys had long since flown the nest; and yet neither partner summoned up the courage to make a break until the situation was forced upon him. She holds to the belief that, in spite of his decision in the airport VIP lounge, he remained in two minds for some time. When they both went back to Carlton Gardens that terrible Friday evening, to talk late into the night, she says: 'He wanted me to plead with him to keep me. I couldn't do that.' The following Friday he returned to their home in Edinburgh, partly to arrange his belongings, partly to talk. They were both desperately sad. She began putting her thoughts on paper.

Her first letter to a newspaper blamed the breakdown of her marriage on NHS cash shortages which had increased the workload of consultants like herself. 'The vicious financial stringencies imposed on the health service by the last government have prevented rational approaches to staffing and many consultants, myself included, have carried excessive workloads with little hope of alleviation,' she wrote, with the help of Jim Devine. Then she penned a letter to the *Scotsman* on her own. This one was prompted by an article about politicians losing touch because of overwork. It did not mention her husband or his lover, but its message was clear:

Perhaps the overdriven workaholic personality is selectively attached to politics. The perceived necessity to compete ensures that the individual, once on the conveyor belt, has no rest. Ambition and single-mindedness prevent the leavening effect of leisure and time to stand and stare. Finer feelings and natural emotions become blunted. Public recognition affords some solace: praise, adulation and acclaim become manna on which the starved soul feeds. He/she is likely to become strongly attracted to any person who regularly and unstintingly supplies it, to the severe detriment of other relationships.

The letter suggested that Labour women MPs might change things. 'I believe women are less susceptible to the overdriven psyche. Probably by nature less aggressively competitive, those who have raised children and looked after elderly relations also learn that important things cannot be done in a perpetual hurry.'

After that letter appeared, she says, Cook rang her and said he wanted to see her. 'He said I had been right in my letter. I got a terrible feeling that he wanted to make it up to me, but I didn't wait to be asked.'

She and the sons received a host of letters. The McCrircks offered their support and asked the boys to look after their mother. She even got a letter of commiseration from Prince Charles. One letter did not go down so well. It came from Tony Blair a few days after the break-up. She paraphrases it thus: 'Dear Margaret, I am so sorry that the press continues to harass you. There's not much more one can say in the circumstances but Cherie and I are thinking about you.' She fired off a reply: perhaps the Prime Minister might also have been sad about her ruined marriage, rather than just the press coverage? She demanded a meeting with Mandelson. Quick as a flash, the phone rang, and there was Mandelson on his mobile phone from a train. 'He kept losing contact, said Mr Blair was very upset for us, and didn't mean to sound cold. I told him the letter had been insensitive and that he should come up. I wanted to see if he came running, and he did. Within a couple of days he was up. He called me and came round.' This was a tricky assignment for Mandelson. He knew further revelations would damage the government. He tried to assure Margaret that no insult had been intended from Blair's letter, and told her to get in touch if ever she was unhappy in the future. 'I made him hot water with lemon,' she says. 'He laid on the charm – I remember we talked about horses.'

Gradually, Margaret Cook put things back together. Jenny McCririck invited her to join her in the United States, where she had been with her husband at the Breeders' Cup, and the two women went horse riding in Phoenix, Arizona. The McCriricks were among those who tried desperately to remain even-handed and to minimize the acrimony between the estranged Cooks. Margaret also went on holiday with a neighbour in October (the time she had earmarked for going to India with her husband), to the Galapagos Islands and Ecuador, where they were caught up in civil unrest. She rode her horse even more keenly, and would often be seen arriving at the hospital still dressed in her riding kit. She saw a lot of the boys, but it would take them a long time to get her off the subject of their father and the break-up of the marriage. Eventually she started socializing, more vigorously than she had ever done while with Robin. She began to write newspaper articles – about why the pharmaceuticals industry should be nationalized, about marriage in general and about herself. In a letter to *The Times* on 26 August, she wrote: 'Virtue does have its own reward. Does any woman know a greater delight and solace than two excellent sons?'

Cook was desperate to ensure that his sons did not shun him. Whatever else had gone wrong, he prided himself on his relations with his boys. He had dinner with Chris within a fortnight of the break-up, and went with him to Goodwood races that month. He would see Peter, who lived so much closer to London, at least as often. Slowly he began to immerse himself in work again, and – as his other friends and MPs came back from their holidays – sought their support. There was no sanctimoniousness among those who knew him, only genuine shock. Of all MPs, Cook, they thought, would be the last to leave his wife for his younger secretary. Perhaps, they thought, he was more like them than they had thought. Ken Purchase, his PPS, told him straight: 'Yet another hero has been found to have feet of clay.'

13

The Queen is Not Unhappy

As Cook was preparing for his first major multi-nation trip, a fresh problem presented itself. On 24 August, the *Observer* published an interview with Clare Short, largely devoted to the crisis in the British dependency of Montserrat which had been ravaged by a series of volcanic eruptions. The island's chief minister, David Brandt, had expressed disappointment at the level of aid earmarked by the UK for his island. Short, keen to ensure that her international development department's tiny budget was not entirely consumed by the crisis, said of the Montserratians: 'They'll be wanting golden elephants next.' Her remarks caused a furore. The Tories called on her to apologize to the island's eleven thousand people. They – and others – demanded that she revise a long-planned trip to Africa and Asia, to talk about long-term development ideas, and go to see the situation for herself. She refused and said she would send her deputy, George Foulkes. Two days later, Cook announced the formation of a Montserrat Action Group to coordinate practical assistance across Whitehall. This would involve six departments, including Short's DfID, but be led by Liz Symons, the Foreign Office junior minister. 'Our assistance strategy needs to be delivered speedily and effectively, but requires cooperation across Whitehall,' Cook said in a statement, issued through Downing Street. Short, who was being summarily ridiculed in the media, saw the intervention of her erstwhile friend as unnecessary and malign.

It was only the latest in a series of snubs felt by Short, a woman who has always worn her heart on her sleeve. A year before the election, she complained of 'dark forces' around Blair, manipulating the media message against anyone who said anything remotely left-wing or controversial. She spoke of a 'conspiracy to stop politicians talking honestly, so you get robots who just clone what they are told to say out of press releases'. In 1996 Blair had shunted her off from shadow transport to overseas development (as it was then called) to show his anger at her refusal to buckle down. However, this demotion held the seeds of her re-establishment at a senior level: for the Labour foreign policy document released earlier that summer had repeated a long-held pledge not only to increase a foreign aid budget that had been eroded by the Conservatives, but to hive off the Overseas Development Administration from the Foreign Office and restore it to the status of a fully fledged government department, headed by a minister of Cabinet rank. With more shadow ministers than the government payroll would allow, there was widespread speculation just before the election that Short would not get the equal status she believed the job deserved. Jonathan Powell suggested there was no need to chop and change the Foreign Office. But Short called their bluff by threatening to resign if the promise was reneged upon; and a couple of days before the election, Blair decided to adhere to the original plan. Short got her seat in Cabinet.

The creation of the DfID led to bitter turf wars among officials. It was to take over UN functions from the health and environment departments, all ODA functions, and the £70 million 'know-how fund' for eastern Europe from the Foreign Office. Relations between the two permanent secretaries, John Vereker and Sir John Coles, were, according to ministers in both departments, particularly strained. But Cook had consistently supported the idea of a separate department, and – for the first few months in government – he and Short worked well together. There was, after all, no reason why they should not, sharing as they did the same kind of passion for a realignment of priorities in foreign relations. But then, in an interview with the *Independent on Sunday* at the end of August, she implicated Cook as one of those to blame for whipping up what she said was an off-the-record remark the week before. 'I've been here a few times and this is the pattern. It is not to do with the truth. It's to do with finding a scapegoat, but I am shocked that complete misinformation can go so far. It was from either/or both Number 10 and the Foreign Office press departments, and it unleashed this vitriol.' Allegations against her, she said, had been spread by 'vile and dishonest' spin doctors: 'Behind the scenes this is being fed by people who don't want my department to succeed. It's not just me, but I'm the whipping girl for people who cannot bear the idea of an independent department with an aid budget which is committed to development and not to Britain's short-term interest. They are out to destroy the department.'[1] It was later suggested that she had been 'saved' from the sack by the distraction of the death of the Princess of Wales.[2]

For two left-wingers who had felt put upon by the press in collusion with some in their own party, the animosity was unnecessary; but Short – who more than most of her colleagues emphasizes the personal as much as the political – tried to get her own back on Cook by conspicuously praising Gordon Brown whenever she could. She even travelled with the Chancellor later in the year to meetings with the World Bank and others in a trumpeted mission to cut the debt burden for poorer countries.

When Short gave the second of her interviews, Cook was already in the Far East: four countries in five days of garlands, motorcades, meetings, press conferences and onward flights. His hosts treated their guest with some wariness. Here was a man who had shown already a penchant for preaching universal values, pitted against leaders who advanced the concept of 'Asian values' – their justification for curtailing democracy in the alleged interests of the people and of prosperity. The trip had been carefully tailored for the UK domestic audience. Each stop had a story of its own. In Malaysia, Cook's initiative in involving MI6 in an offensive against the drugs trade, especially in Burma, the world's biggest opium producer, led the BBC *Nine O'clock News*. Less pleasing was a threat by Prime Minister Mahathir Mohammed that Malaysia and other ASEAN countries would boycott the following year's EU–Asia summit in London unless Burma was invited. Mahathir further suggested that the 1948 UN Declaration on Human Rights be redrafted as it had been drawn up by 'superpowers which did not understand the needs of poor countries'.

The Indonesia leg was always going to be the most fraught part of the tour. The pro-government *Indonesian Observer* marked Cook's arrival by harking back to Britain's colonial past: 'His psyche may not be different from that of a man who has just been deprived of valuable real estate but is too proud to acknowledge it.'[3] Cook's first act on arrival was to telephone Bishop Carlos Belo, the bishop of East Timor and a Nobel Peace Prize winner, to offer support and hear the latest on the situation in his country. Yet he shied away at the last minute from what would have been a more significant gesture. Mukhtar Pakpahan, a trade unionist and former lawyer facing charges of subversion for criticizing the government, had been confined to a hospital bed for the past six months with a lung tumour, as he awaited the resumption of his trial. Cook had an on-off appointment to meet him, but did not show. Officials explained that there simply was not time to fit it in; but they failed to tell Pakpahan that the visit was cancelled. They said, however, that Cook did plead his case with his Indonesian opposite number, Ali Alatas.

Even though the Hawk jets were being allowed through, Alatas was not well disposed towards Cook. Ever since the establishment of ASEAN in 1967, Indonesia has been a powerful proponent of its guiding principle of non-interference. Alatas told Cook that arms exports were a buyer's market. His country saw no conditionality in such sales. 'If this becomes the general policy of the UK and it turns out that certain types of equipment are not available to Indonesia, we will have to look elsewhere. We are already doing so.' Cook was not to be fobbed off, but was careful to dress up his human rights proposals as a 'partnership'. He proposed sending a team of EU ambassadors to East Timor for the first time, but he made clear this would not confer legitimacy on Indonesian sovereignty there, which the EU has never recognized. He also announced that Britain would send police to advise their Indonesian counterparts on modern policing methods, and would give computers and books to human rights and legal aid groups. Ali Alatas said he had no objection to this; he did not feel his state would be undermined by the donation of two thousand pounds' worth of treatises by the likes of John Locke, John Stuart Mill and Karl Popper, along with works of political science published by the University of Minnesota – all in English.

From Indonesia, it was on to Manila and Singapore, and back home in time for the TUC conference. On the way back, Cook pronounced himself highly satisfied with the trip: 'I don't think there's been any week of my life in which I have had more publicity than during the week in which I went around the countries of South East Asia or Indonesia, Philippines, Singapore, Malaysia, and we proved then that although you may be out of the country you are certainly not out of the loop.' Moreover, he believed he had demonstrated that he could fight hard for principles without the need to 'kow-tow or row' with his hosts. To Cook and his advisers, it was a model trip for the new regime, and just the right tonic to set him back on course.

While foreign policy, he believed, was becoming more interwoven with domestic policy, Cook was aware that the image of the Foreign Office remained woefully behind the times. On 19 September, therefore, its august doors were opened to a thousand invited guests – sixth-formers, school careers advisers and representatives of community groups – not just to stroll around and admire the splendour of the Gilbert Scott building, but to learn that British diplomacy might need them. To all but the most cynical, it was a refreshing sight to see officials (told not to dress in pin-stripes) trying to explain what their work entailed to young people who would not have imagined they had a place there. The immediate aim was to attract more women and ethnic minority applicants to the department. By the time of the election, only nine of Britain's 154 ambassadors were women (although the figure was slowly rising), while only 3.3 per cent of UK-based staff came from ethnic minorities – and of those, not one occupied the rank of head of department, let alone ambassador.

'If I'm going to represent Britain I need a Foreign Office that is representative of the whole of modern Britain,' Cook declared as he welcomed the guests. They were standing in the Durbar Court, a vast Victorian atrium encrusted with marble and mosaics and adorned with a bust of Clive of India and other great administrators of the subcontinent. This, in years gone by, was the physical heart of the vanished India Office, named after the *durbar* – a formal reception held by maharajahs or British governors to mark a great occasion of state. On this day the venerable room had taken on all the attributes of a late twentieth-century trade fair, with an Internet site and stalls explaining policy on immigration and human rights, export promotion, the EU presidency, environment, science and energy, drugs and international crime. Two live video conferences were laid on by satellite: first with the High Commissioner and his staff in Singapore, then with Yekaterinburg – the Russian Urals town known variously as the place where Tsar Nicholas II and his family were assassinated and the birthplace of Boris Yeltsin. Cook then took groups up the stairs into his office. As the visitors prepared to depart, he told them: 'This is not a stuffy hidebound place, full of men in pin-stripe suits sitting as if with umbrellas up their spines . . . I hope we shook some of your stereotypes, and that some of you will apply to work here.'

As the autumn wore on, it brought the advent of the conference season – over the years, a time of particular activity for Cook. Having tried with varying success to persuade Cabinet members to stand down from the NEC, Blair was quietly pushing for Mandelson to win the place that Brown had vacated. His challengers were Peter Hain and Ken Livingstone, the former leader of the GLC and still one of the darlings of the left. In opposition, August had always been Cook's month, allowing him to mount a campaign of some sort during the August lull while other colleagues were abroad. This year he had indeed been in London, but not by design. Having announced his candidature for re-election to the NEC in the early summer, he had become so worried about a backlash over his personal life that for weeks after the August events he regretted standing; he also feared that his lack of involvement on domestic issues might count against him, and he was uncomfortable at accusations that, after the decision on the Hawks, the espousal of ethics in foreign policy could be seen by activists as no more than a rhetorical flourish.

As delegates began to arrive in Brighton for the conference, the *Guardian* reported in its front-page splash on 26 September that 'in a symbolic show of determination', the government had 'blocked two arms contracts with Indonesia in the first test of Foreign Secretary Robin Cook's ethical foreign policy governing exports to oppressive regimes'. Cook had phoned Michael White, the paper's political editor, from New York where he was attending the United Nations General Assembly. The applications, worth 'up to £1 million', were two orders for sniper rifles and one for armoured troop carriers.

'It certainly does demonstrate that we have put in place tougher criteria. Those criteria are biting and they're delivering the policy that we promised,' Cook said. 'I briefed officials of the Indonesian government on our change in criteria, but we also confirmed our continuing commercial relations. I don't see this decision spreading in any way into the wider commercial and diplomatic relationship between us.' The report said that both the DTI and the MoD had gone along with the decision – there had seemed no need to refer it on to Downing Street. Downing Street was furious. Jonathan Powell let it be known to Cook's office that he was 'extremely pissed off'. John Holmes then fired off two official memoranda, copied to a reasonably wide circulation, to John Grant, Cook's new principal private secretary, who had taken over from Ehrman in July, expressing irritation and demanding to see all documents relating to the decision. The Prime Minister's office was angry both at the decision itself and at the way Cook had announced it, circumventing the usual central command through Alastair Campbell. In Blair's view, this was just the sort of 'gesture politics' that he so deplored. But, Cook's friends insist, the Foreign Secretary knew what he was doing. The Labour leadership was keen to snuff out any rebellion or contentious debate in the first conference held under a Labour government for two decades. One of the resolutions giving cause for concern called for a total embargo on arms sales to Indonesia. Cook, his allies say, 'wanted to make a point to show that (a) the new guidelines were biting, and (b) his radical credentials in the party were still intact. This was high stakes politics.'

In his speech to the conference, Cook said Britain was giving a new lead in promoting the ethical dimension to foreign policy. He said he had agreed with Lionel Jospin, the French Prime Minister, that the two countries should sponsor a European code of conduct to regulate the arms trade. But there was a curious last-minute insertion to the speech: 'Britain has one of the largest arms industries in Europe. We have a duty to the four hundred thousand people who work in our defence industries to [ensure they] continue to have the opportunity to work.'[4]

Cook's colleagues had noticed that around this time relations with Downing Street had become distinctly frosty. Blair tended to regard the conference season as an unwelcome distraction. He had come to expect, with some irritation, that Brown and Cook, in their different ways, would each play to their respective supporters. While their policy statements would be strictly within the loyalty code, the words 'comrade' and even 'socialism' would occasionally rear their heads, although not on the main conference floor. Cook had already marked out his ground when he addressed the TUC on 10 September. His speech followed one by Adair Turner, director-general of the CBI, a man who sees eye to eye with Blair on most issues. Turner made clear that the employers' organization was opposed to government plans to reintroduce a law recognizing union jurisdiction at the workplace if a majority of employees voted in favour. The issue was highly sensitive, with many in the party furious at hints that Blair would agree to water down the proposals. In a pointedly fraternal address, Cook said the link between unions and the Labour party was not tactical but a 'strategic bond' that would endure. He urged trade unionists – few of whom in the previous six months had managed to get over the threshold of Downing Street – to help communicate the government's message. As for Turner's warning, he said: 'All I would ask is that it is also recognized that tensions can arise within a workforce when they feel that their legitimate aspirations are being ignored and are not being listened to. You cannot ask a workforce to bring their innovation, initiative and creativity to their work station but then say to the same workforce, "We are not going to listen to you when you want to talk about the conditions of work in the workplace." It is an issue of democracy.'

He then touched on another theme close to his heart: the constitution. Comparing the House of Lords to the cast of a Gilbert and Sullivan opera, he told delegates:

> By the time we meet again next year, we will be on the verge of putting into practice our commitment to clear that medieval lumber of parliament and to make it absolutely established in both Houses of Parliament that the people who take part in passing the laws of our country should earn their seat by the process of democracy, not by the right of birth.[5]

Downing Street admitted that the speech had not been cleared in advance and that it did not appreciate what it saw as pressure to include a commitment to abolish voting rights for hereditary peers in the Queen's Speech for the 1998/9 session. (There had been some disappointment among radical constitutionalists in the party that Blair had not inserted the pledge in his first legislative programme on taking office.) 'The interpretation being put on the Foreign Secretary's speech, that there was a clear commitment for the next Queen's Speech, is not accurate. That is not what he said,' a spokesman for Blair insisted.

The conference at Brighton produced a curiously muted week, with few speeches from the rostrum that could be seen as pure Blairite. Mandelson was despondent, counting on one hand the number of true believers there were in Cabinet. Brown had on the first day delivered a typically double-headed speech, pledging full employment as if to demonstrate his roots. Nor did the NEC elections provide much comfort for the modernizers.

Cook's concern about a decline in his personal popularity proved unfounded: he was re-elected on to the NEC in first place, with an impressive tally of votes. Doubts about his standing with the rank and file, even after the upheaval in his personal life, could be cast aside. Next in the popularity stakes came David Blunkett, followed by Mo Mowlam and Dennis Skinner. To the consternation of the Blair camp, Mandelson was pipped by Livingstone. The official spin was that Mandelson had done as well as anyone could be expected to when standing for the first time; nevertheless, the result provided Blair with further confirmation – were any needed – that the party lagged well behind the leadership in his modernization project. The best that could be said was that the outcome was of largely symbolic significance. The NEC had already agreed to a new set of rules, set out in the document *Partnership in Power*, which from the following year would change the procedure for its elections. In future, MPs would be elected to the NEC by the parliamentary party, not the constituency parties, and those places would be reserved for backbenchers.

Whenever *Tribune* holds a rally, Brown and Cook have tried to be there. Both had made speeches at the paper's sixtieth anniversary party the previous March, at which Cook had got into trouble for 'predicting' a landslide victory in the general election. At the traditional conference rally Cook and Brown appeared on the same platform, though naturally enough they were kept apart by Peter Hain, Tony Banks, the newly appointed sports minister, and Mark Seddon, *Tribune*'s editor and the host for the event. For the broadcasters next day the only speech of note was Banks's irreverent run around Westminster, in which he likened William Hague, the new Conservative leader, to a foetus. The first to speak had been Brown. Putting on the comradely hat that he reserved for such occasions, he spent an inordinate amount of time on issues bordering Cook's empire. He and Clare Short, he told the activists, were fighting hard at international fora to eradicate world poverty and cut the debt burden for developing countries. Cook, his body half turned away from the speaker, was trying to conceal a scowl and scribbling furiously on his notepaper. 'I've heard that speech before,' he whispered drily to Seddon. This was Brown the socialist, as opposed to Brown the purveyor of hard economic choices. As soon as he finished speaking and accepted the applause, Brown swept off, his entourage in tow. Cook, having smiled weakly through Banks's contribution, was the last to speak. In his turn, he dwelt on issues that were more in Brown's empire, such as the need to combat 'poverty wages' and to rebuild the NHS: 'Some things are too precious for the market place. Health care is one.' He then added, with more than a twist of bitterness: 'I can say, with no fear of retribution, that it was a landslide. The left never gets things wrong, we're just before our time.'

A few days after the conference, Cook set off for what he expected to be an enjoyable week in the Indian subcontinent, where he was to take part in the celebrations commemorating the fiftieth anniversary of independence. He would be the first Labour Foreign Secretary to accompany the Queen on a state visit since David Owen in Portugal in 1978. The minister is tradition-ally required to stay in the background, keep two steps behind the monarch, and give advice when required. Nobody thought of sending a press officer or political adviser with Cook; in the past there had been no need for such a figure. For the Queen it was an important occasion, rich in symbolism and sensitivity between the former colonial power and its largest colony. Her last visit had been as long ago as 1961.

The region was particularly sensitive for Labour politicians, too. Fringe meetings at Labour conferences on Kashmir, whose sovereignty has been disputed by India and Pakistan since the end of British rule, had always been highly charged. In 1995 Cook had got himself into hot water over a speech he made in Brent when he told Indian community leaders that 'Kashmir is part of the Indian state'; a qualification intended to reinforce long-standing support for a negotiated settlement was drowned out by applause. Cook was furious, as he had been told that the meeting would not broach the issue; in the event he was forced to discuss it after it had dominated proceedings. The NEC decided that it had to clarify party policy on the question, which loomed large in some thirty marginal seats, containing many of the 450,000 British voters of Pakistani origin. The 1995 NEC statement on Kashmir, which Cook knows by heart, says:

A solution is for the parties directly involved to find. However, Britain must accept its responsibility as the former imperial power in a dispute that dates from the arrangements for independence, and recognise that it is under an obligation to seek a solution that is based on our commit-ment to peace, democracy, human rights and mutual tolerance. Labour in government will be prepared to use its close relationship with India and Pakistan to provide good offices to assist in a negotiated solution to this tragic dispute.

To prevent misunderstandings, on the eve of the NEC meeting that was to adopt this text Cook sent an aide to the London residence of the Indian High Commissioner. One or two minor changes were made as a result, but Labour officials believed the statement would defuse the issue.

The pre-election document *New Labour, New Life for Britain*, said: 'Labour in government would be well-placed to help find a solution to the conflict in Kashmir, a solution that is acceptable to all the peoples of the region – Muslims, Hindus and Buddhists'. The difference from the NEC text was marginal, but hinted that the government would get involved only if asked. John Major, in the subcontinent at the start of the year, had used roughly the same language. After the election, some Foreign Office experts saw the reference to 'the former imperial power', however well intentioned the wording, as insensitive. They were also less sanguine about Indian intentions, fearing that, with successive governments there in precarious positions, India was spoiling for a fight. There was also the sensitive legacy of the Amritsar massacre, in which 379 unarmed protesters were shot by British troops in 1919. The Queen had refused to apologize for it on behalf of the British people.

Violence in Kashmir had been particularly intense on the eve of the trip. In all, twenty thousand people have died in an insurgency against the Indian security forces there that has lasted since 1989. On the first full day of the Queen's visit, 7 October, Cook had a private meeting with Nawaz Sharif, the Pakistani Prime Minister, at which he said the UK would, if requested to do so, use its 'good offices' to find a just solution for Kashmir. He thought nothing of the remark, which was seen as a pro forma repetition of the existing line, while making clear that the UK stood ready to help. After all, John Major, visiting the region that January, had said roughly the same thing. On the following day, addressing a joint session of both houses of the Pakistani parliament, the Queen urged the two countries to 'take stock and renew efforts to end historic disagreements'. The oblique reference to the disputed territory was inserted on Foreign Office advice. Initial reaction in the British, Indian and Pakistani media to the first leg of the trip was muted.

As the Queen was spending the weekend resting at an up-country retreat, it had long been agreed that at this point, on the Friday, Cook would return to the UK to do constituency and other work. It was at this point that the visit started to go wrong; his decision briefly to return home from the subcontinent would backfire on two fronts, and the hiatus became known in the press as the 'lost weekend'.

The first press release issued by the Pakistanis about the Nawaz Sharif meeting was relatively innocuous. The second one, released two days later, was more provocative, suggesting that the British were urging intervention. By this time Cook had flown back to Britain, and it was difficult to counter the Pakistanis' new line. Cook had been accompanied at the meeting by John Grant, his top civil servant, the British High Commissioner to Pakistan and a second secretary from the embassy taking notes. Without a 'spin doctor' on the ground, it was virtually impossible to get his point across. By the time he arrived in India for the second leg of the trip late on Sunday 12 October, the sparks were flying.

Cook had already had one bad experience of diplomats in the subcontinent. On a visit in November 1996 as opposition spokesman, while staying at the British residence in Islamabad, he had been woken at 4 a.m. by a telephone call. It was from Jo Moore, a party press officer. 'The government's fallen, Robin,' she told him. He jumped out of his socks, thinking she meant John Major. She explained it was the Pakistani government. Within minutes the *Today* programme put in a bid for an on-the-spot telephone interview. Cook, like most politicians, never knowingly turns down the programme. So he rang around the High Commission to check the facts. The furthest he got was the duty clerk, who did not know anything. Cook then burst into the room of Andrew Hood, the researcher accompanying him, in his pyjamas, fulminating. The High Commissioner, once he got up, was coy. He had said the night before over dinner that he was absolutely confident the government was not going to fall. His complacency left a mark on the shadow Foreign Secretary.

The Prime Minister of India in October 1997, Inder Kumar Gujral, was head of a thirteen-party coalition. Aged seventy-seven, he had been a supporter of Mahatma Gandhi's 'quit India' campaign, and was gaoled briefly by the British authorities in the early 1940s. He believed he had achieved a diplomatic coup by persuading President Clinton to reject any idea of foreign mediation in the Kashmir dispute. Gujral belonged to that section of Indian society that had no nostalgic affection for the British, but rather a deep suspicion of them; he was expecting a hint of contrition from his visitors and wanted the anniversary to draw a line under the past. He took a particularly hawkish line on Kashmir. As Cook flew back in on the Sunday, and the Queen left her country retreat, Gujral was quoted as saying of the British government: 'A third-rate power has presumed to say that they have a historical responsibility to solve the Kashmir issue.' The Indian media went to town. The visit was in serious crisis. The following morning Gujral backed off, saying his remarks were without foundation. Cook accepted this, only for the visitors to receive several symbolic snubs. It seemed as if Gujral was determined to embarrass his guests, perhaps as an act of historical retribution. The Band of the Royal Marines accompanying the Queen were told to keep away from the opening of a British exhibition at India's National Museum. All British diplomats, except Sir David Gore-Booth, the High Commissioner, had their invitations to a state banquet withdrawn. And more trouble was in store. On 14 October, as the party was visiting Amritsar, Prince Philip ruffled feathers in characteristic fashion when he took issue over a sign that said two thousand 'martyrs' had died in a massacre at the spot. The following day the hosts cancelled a reply to a toast the Queen was due to give at a banquet in Madras. 'I don't call that a speech, so I can't see what the fuss is all about,' said Gore-Booth. Even as the Foreign Secretary's party departed two days later, there were arguments on the tarmac between officials of the two governments.

Early years in Bellshill

Robin Cook (*far left*)
with fellow pupils in
the final-year class at
the Royal High,
Edinburgh, 1964

Graduation from the
University of Edinburgh, 1968

In the constituency: the young MP in Edinburgh Central in the mid 1970s

Days at the races: (*above*) at Kelso, and (*below*) with Channel Four Racing pundit John McCririck at Brighton racecourse on the eve of the Labour party conference, September 1997

With Margaret, three-week-old Peter and eighteen-month-old Christopher, June 1974

With Gaynor at the Easter Banquet at the Mansion House, London, on 23 April 1998 – their first public engagement together since their marriage earlier that month

The Foreign Secretary in action (1): (*above*) launching a new era in foreign policy less than two weeks after taking office in May 1997, and (*below*)with US Secretary of State Madeleine Albright at the Globe Theatre, May 1998

The Foreign Secretary in action (2): (*above left*) at the Golden Temple of Amritsar and (*above right*) at the Patterson Arran Bakery in October 1997; and (*below*) mobbed by right-wing protesters at Har Homa, March 1998

The new Secretary of State for Foreign and Commonwealth Affairs
on his first day in office, 2 May 1997

The Queen had not seen anything like it. Sir Robert Fellowes, her private secretary, gave a discreet briefing to accompanying journalists in an attempt to play down the sovereign's role in the diplomatic bust-up. 'The old technical position is that the Queen is here on the advice of ministers in Britain. She does not go out on a limb,' he told them. As soon as it realized what might be inferred from his words, the news department at the Foreign Office in London hurriedly rang around journalists, suggesting Fellowes' remarks had been 'misinterpreted'. The first editions of the papers were faxed to Fellowes at 4.30 a.m. in Madras on Friday and Cook, back in London, spoke to Fellowes on a scrambler line. Buckingham Palace then took the unprecedented step of issuing a press release at 5.52 a.m., London time: 'We have seen media reports from London suggesting that the Queen is unhappy with the government's handling of arrangements for the State visit to India. That is not the case. The Queen has been entirely satisfied with the advice from the Foreign Secretary and his officials in the preparations leading up to the visit and during the visit itself.'[6]

Two hours later Cook was on the *Today* programme, dismissing the furore as a 'storm in a toast cup'. Had the Queen been put up to issuing a statement? he was asked. 'If you're saying Her Majesty can be browbeaten into making such a statement, you are underestimating Her Majesty.' He put some of the blame on the Foreign Office, which had organized the visit well before the election: 'It might have been helpful if they had arranged this trip at some moment other than the fiftieth anniversary so that we could have focused on looking forward to the exciting relationship between India and Britain in the twenty-first century. That is where we want to anchor our future relations with India, as two equal, independent countries with mutual respect for each other and very strong mutually beneficial trade.'

Downing Street went on to emergency spin patrol to protect both the Palace and Cook. Blair asked for a 'major effort of communication to explain more widely the thus-far unreported success stories of the visit'. In media terms it had been an unmitigated disaster, immortalized by a photograph of Cook wearing oversized sunglasses and a white trilby lent by Gore-Booth. The 'silly hat syndrome' had caught out many a politician before him, notably Major at the Khyber Pass. It would not have taken a genius of a civil servant or adviser to spot the pitfalls – however trivial such a concern might seem. Cook's aides privately blamed Gore-Booth for some of the presentational and diplomatic mishaps; and the trip confirmed his resolve to rid the Foreign Office of the stereotypical Eton-educated, pinstriped mandarin. What most frustrated Cook, though, were the priorities of the media. He complained that the trade fair he had attended in Delhi – the biggest ever staged by Britain in India – had not received a second of airtime. Nobody wanted to know that bilateral trade between Britain and

India had more than doubled. As for the Kashmir question itself, the only way Cook believes he could have avoided discussing it was if he had refused to meet Nawaz Sharif – and that never was an option.

Malcolm Rifkind – who was assuming for himself a media role as Cook critic-in-residence – expressed sympathy of sorts, arguing that the most successful visits could often be those that provoked little media interest. 'The problem that Foreign Secretaries have was beautifully summed up by Harold Macmillan who says in his memoirs: "Foreign Secretaries are always in a cruel dilemma, their speeches hover between the cliché and the indiscretion. They are either dull or dangerous."' For several days after returning at the end of the trip, Cook was out of sorts. He said little to anyone. What was particularly upsetting for him was that, perhaps for the first time, his judgement as a politician was being openly called into question. He could understand and deal with people who disagreed with him, or who were angry at a particular position he adopted, but he was not used to being portrayed as bungling. Cook would later feel vindicated for taking a more active role in the subcontinent when India dramatically raised tensions by conducting its first nuclear tests, and Pakistan quickly followed suit.

Cook was not the only senior figure getting into trouble. The autumn was also proving tricky for Gordon Brown. Several Cabinet colleagues were angry at his attempt to bounce them into a further round of personal pay restraint, phasing in their previously arranged £16,000 pay rise, to set an example to public sector workers. Blair's aides were becoming increasingly annoyed at Brown's self-aggrandizement and empire-building. There was nothing subtle about this. Perhaps its most striking public expression was the two-part fly-on-the-wall documentary about him, in opposition and government, that Brown had agreed to on a request from old chums at Scottish television. The films, which had taken nearly a year to make and were shown around conference time, portrayed his advisers as a clique who ruled the roost over civil servants and expressed pride in distorting and manipulating the media.

Then, on Friday 25 September, the *Financial Times* published a front-page story. The government, said Robert Peston, the paper's political editor, 'is on the point of adopting a much more positive approach to European economic and monetary union, with a statement shortly that sterling is likely to join at an early opportunity after the 1999 launch'. It went on: 'Senior members of the Cabinet are openly canvassing the prospect of sterling participation around the turn of the century, possibly before the next general election. The changed approach to EMU stems in part from a growing convergence of views between Robin Cook, the Foreign Secretary, and Gordon Brown, the Chancellor, who had previously been seen at loggerheads.'

The markets exploded, seeing the report as an authoritative leak from the Treasury to prepare the ground for an imminent government announcement. Gilts and shares soared; the pound plummeted. The FTSE share index recorded its biggest one-day points gain for ten years. Sterling fell to a four-month low against the German mark – exactly what exporters wanted. At the Treasury and among other pro-Europeans in government, there was delight. There had been hints of movement in the offing. After the conspicuously opportunist shift towards the British bulldog outlook at the election, to keep Murdoch and other tabloids on board, the government had succeeded in shunting EMU off the agenda. The issue had not been discussed once by Cabinet – not that in the early months anything contentious was broached when all senior ministers were present. But, with a decision due in early 1998 on which countries would be eligible to join a single currency at its inception the following January, ministers were aware that the silence could not last much longer. An announcement was due by the end of the year.

Brown had been saying privately over the summer that membership in the first wave was still an outside possibility for the UK, and that if the timetable was too tight, efforts should be made to facilitate entry as soon as possible after. Similar messages had come from Mandelson – who had to balance his ardent pro-Europeanism (he was a vice-chairman of the cross-party European Movement) with his good relations with the Murdoch family. Others in government were ardently in support of EMU – Lord Simon, for example, who said of John Major's 'wait and see' fudge in 1996: 'You cannot be half pregnant. There isn't an option of sitting on the fence, both ears to the ground, waiting for the iron to enter our soul.'

Blair, a thoroughly modern European with culinary, cultural and travel tastes to match, loathed the little-England mentality so often presented by the Tories, and in principle was in favour of EMU; but on the politics of British entry he was decidedly cautious. Opinion among Cabinet members varied, but the issue was never the fault line it was under the Conservative administration. In opposition, Cook had made much of highlighting his more sceptical position, although he too had shifted by suggesting that if all went smoothly membership would be unavoidable by the time notes and coins were converted in 2002. In government, he was under strict instructions to keep 'on message'; but even so, his reservations were perceptible. On 8 June, after the election of Jospin as French Prime Minister and the Bundesbank's decision to rule out plans to revalue German gold reserves, he said on *Breakfast with Frost*: 'I think one would have to say that the last week has raised some very significant questions in the minds of politicians on the continent as well as commentators within Britain.' Britain would carry out a 'hard-headed assessment', he said, repeating the required mantra; but 'at the moment we think it unlikely that that assessment would point to us joining.' As for easing the convergence criteria, as suggested by Jospin: 'The debate at the moment seems to be in danger of polarizing between a softer euro which would not be workable and a hard euro which would not be popular.'

On 19 September, as Jacques Santer appealed to the Labour government to demonstrate its *communautaire* credentials by agreeing to join in the first wave, Cook said on BBC radio: 'Tony Blair, Gordon Brown and myself have all said it is unlikely that Britain will be joining, partly because we are a new government with a big agenda to do.' As for later: 'We have always said that if it goes ahead and if it's a success, then in the longer term, it would be diffi- cult for Britain to stay out.'

The suggestion that Cook had been brought onside thus gave the *FT* story greater credibility. His agreement to an accelerated entry into EMU was not a prerequisite for Brown or Blair, but it would help smooth the path among more sceptical Labour MPs. What had actually happened was that Peston had met David Clark, one of Cook's special advisers, and put to him the proposition that surely Cook accepted a more positive approach to a single currency and that some form of statement could be expected shortly. Clark said that was the case. When the story came out Cook was still in New York. He was annoyed, but in public affected a nonchalant response. After checking in with Downing Street to agree on the line, he issued a carefully worded rebuttal, to accompany the other denials being made. 'I think I can authoritatively state that there will be no such announcement in the immediate future. The position on a single currency which I have stated in recent days is exactly the position I've been stating over the last year.'[7] In reality, the positions of Foreign Secretary and Chancellor were not too far apart. Brown saw the glass as half full, Cook as half empty. Cook fervently believed that the deflationary pressures inherent in the Maastricht criteria had led to a sharp rise in unemployment in continental Europe; and that those criteria could, and should, have been devised differently. But he accepted from around 1996 that a single currency was a virtual certainty and that Britain had to devise a strategy of dealing with it.

As Downing Street rowed back from open displays of enthusiasm for EMU, Blair had several informal chats with Brown. Cook was kept at a distance, although he did meet Blair a couple of weeks later, on 16 October, to discuss the need for an official statement as soon as the Commons returned for its autumn session. The following day Brown gave an interview to *The Times* in which he said he was on the verge of ruling out first wave entry for the UK in the course of the parliament – potentially until 2002. The line had been meticulously agreed with Blair. Unbeknown to Downing Street, Charlie Whelan, who was drinking in the Red Lion pub across the road on

Whitehall, was phoning journalists to brief them on the interview. As quickly as they had shot up on the Friday, on the Monday morning the markets tumbled – just as Brown was inaugurating a new share-dealing system at the London Stock Exchange. Behind him, live on television, the new screen was pockmarked with an increasing number of red squares, denoting 'sell'.

This could have been a temptation to *schadenfreude*; but Cook, having experienced his own difficulties in the previous two months, made a point of keeping his counsel; Mandelson even thanked him later for not indulging in any Brown-baiting over EMU. Mandelson and others, however, were furious at the bungling, the indiscretions and the policy lurches, and at the following Thursday's Cabinet, several senior figures expressed unhappiness at the way the issue had been handled, with Prescott specifically criticizing Brown. Such displays of candour were rare at the weekly sessions, at which discussion was formal and disagreements not aired in public. The real decisions invariably took place elsewhere, and on EMU did not generally involve Cook – so much so that when Sir John Kerr arrived as the new permanent secretary in November and went through the files he could find virtually no written Foreign Office submission on the issue. Asked why Brown had not bothered to brief Cook on EMU, one of his advisers suggested: 'That was for Blair to do.'

To Cook's disappointment, the single currency furore overshadowed his three days with Blair hosting the Commonwealth heads of government summit in Edinburgh, beginning on 25 October. The occasion had the Blair imprint all over it, with the traditional pageantry toned down and the presentation geared to the projection of a more modern image. Thoroughly unlike summits in the Tory era, this one had working groups on subjects such as AIDS, press freedom, landmines and women's rights. Blair's attention was focused mainly on getting Brown's statement on EMU right for the following Monday, the first day back after the parliamentary recess. Cook was consulted as the drafts were being written, but no more so than other members of the Blair entourage, such as Lord Irvine, who was faxed the details just as quickly. Within hours of the end of the Edinburgh summit, Brown sought to put an end to the controversy by setting out the reasons why it was almost (although not completely) certain that the UK would not be in a position to join EMU before 2002, but added: 'We are the first British government to declare for the principle of monetary union, the first to state that there is no overriding constitutional bar to membership.' The wording was not a million miles away from what Cook had said before the election – no to entry in the first wave, but very difficult to stay out when EMU was fully operational.

Having tried to keep the Foreign Office out of the debate from the beginning of the election campaign, the Treasury was eager to preserve its hegemony on EMU. The day after Brown's statement it was the Foreign Office's turn for an hour's ministerial questions. The first question on the order paper, from Conservative Warren Hawkins, was to the point: 'What is Her Majesty's Government's policy on joining the arrangements for a single currency on 1 January 1999?' John Grant, Cook's principal private secretary, had a few days earlier received a memo from the Treasury requesting that the Foreign Secretary should simply refer all future inquiries to the Treasury. Not even in the Tory government, when EMU was even more contentious and Kenneth Clarke, the Chancellor, had at least as much to say on it, was such a tactic tried. Cook ignored the request, but was happy to repeat what he saw as the official line: 'As the Chancellor of the Exchequer made clear in his statement yesterday, British membership of a single currency in 1999 could not meet the five economic tests that the Government have set out. The Government will therefore be notifying our European partners that we shall not seek membership of the single currency on 1 January 1999.' Subsequent questions from backbenchers and from the shadow Foreign Secretary Michael Howard elicited the same bland response, each time referring back to Brown's statement. But Cook made no mention of the government's 'support in principle', speaking only of whether entry would be in Britain's economic interest, and the stipulation that any Cabinet decision in favour of joining would be put to a referendum. The last question on the subject, from Dennis Skinner, was music to Cook's ears: 'Is my Right Honourable friend aware that I am pleased that the government will not apply to join the exchange rate mechanism [to peg sterling to the euro]? After what happened on 16 September 1992, that would be like a dog returning to its vomit.' Cook replied, with a wry smile: 'I think that my Honourable Friend will wish me to clarify to the House that it was not our vomit, but that of the Conservatives. He puts his finger on one of the reasons why we are in office and they are out of office.'[8]

The turf war over the issue was not yet at an end. Brown's attempts to persuade his EU counterparts that Britain had the right to a place in 'Euro-X', the club of finance ministers open only to those countries joining EMU, fell on deaf ears. Cook was kept in the dark. Brown's frosty reception on the continent was seen in the Foreign Office as the inevitable consequence of playing to the domestic gallery without bringing in the diplomatic expertise of British diplomats in the EU capitals. 'The Treasury was never much good with foreigners,' quipped one Foreign Office minister. Treasury officials would counter with: 'The Foreign Office cannot be trusted.' The personal antipathy between Cook and Brown was as pronounced as ever. Questioned by the *Daily Telegraph*, Cook spoke of a 'very good relationship' with Blair; as for Brown, theirs was 'a perfectly healthy working relationship'.[9]

Within the Foreign Office, however, things began to look up. Part of the improvement was due to the arrival on 13 November of a new permanent secretary, Sir John Kerr, in place of Sir John Coles. He was seen as a less fusty proponent of the mandarin art, an alumnus (like Donald Dewar) of Glasgow Academy who knew his way around Whitehall, including – vitally – the Treasury. There he had handled the privatization of British Aerospace and become principal private secretary to successive Chancellors in the early 1980s. As head of chancery at the Washington embassy he accompanied Margaret Thatcher at her 1984 and 1986 Camp David meetings with Ronald Reagan, and as European Community assistant under-secretary helped Thatcher draft her 1988 Bruges speech that laid the foundations of Euro-scepticism, before becoming ambassador to the EC. Thatcher described him as 'the man with the golden pen' after the 1992 EC summit in Edinburgh when he scaled down demands from Jacques Delors, the Commission president at the time, for an increase in funding and introduced a re-scaling of budget payments. His reward was the top foreign posting – as ambassador to Washington. Kerr is a blunt talker, like his secretary of state. He is also more modern in his attitudes. At the height of Gaynor Regan's personal difficulties, Kerr and his wife tried to support her. She and Cook were guests at their home, and also for a long lunch at the Garrick Club just before Christmas.

Another appointment, at a lower level, was also making life easier for Cook. He wanted a high-flyer to change the way speech-writing was approached. The Office trawled through the files and suggested Mathew Gould. What intrigued Cook was not his education (traditional Foreign Office: St Paul's School and Peterhouse, Cambridge), nor, particularly, his age (just twenty-six), although it was impressive – but his shared hobby. Gould, like him, had been an ardent debater at university, winning the freshers' debate at the Cambridge Union. During his visit to the Philippines, Cook's office had a chat with Gould and asked him, as a test, to write his speech to a local business association. Impressed with that, Cook invited him to his room in Manila's Shangri-la hotel to offer him a job. Within a week Gould was drafting the Foreign Secretary's annual address to the UN General Assembly, and shortly thereafter joined him in London. The job was heavily upgraded, in keeping with Cook's passion for speeches. Gould's predecessors would submit drafts to the Foreign Secretary's private office, who would pass back his thoughts in a formal memo. Now Gould sits with his boss, sometimes at the residence, as they chew over particular passages together. It is all very direct.

Cook and Kerr were about to embark on the most taxing six months facing the Foreign Office for a long time. Britain's presidency of the EU would coincide with the major EMU decisions, but also with attempts to kick-start the enlargement to central Europe that had been put off at the Amsterdam summit. Cook used several speeches to outline an agenda he had pushed hard in opposition – switching the tone of European decision-making away from an 'obsession with institutions' and making it more relevant to ordinary people. On that, he and Blair and the rest of the Cabinet were at one. 'Britain has a mission as president to give Europe back to the people,' Cook said in a speech to the Irish Institute of European Affairs in Dublin in November. Jobs, crime and the environment were three areas in which the EU could be a real factor in the daily lives of people. A couple of months earlier in Hamburg he had made a similar point: 'If I have a concern about the EU it is that the image it provides is of summits and top politicians discussing matters that are of obsessional interest to them. We need to escape the jargon and the obsession that surround these institutional debates.'

The official launch of the British presidency took place at 11.20 a.m. exactly on 5 December when a Eurostar train glided into platform 24 at Waterloo, children's artwork gleaming prettily on its nose and on the side of the carriage nearest to where Blair and Cook were waiting. 'Our presidency is an opportunity to demonstrate that Britain now has a strong voice in Europe, that the indecision, vacillation and frankly sometimes anti-Europeanism of the past have gone,' said Blair. Labour's fixation with presentation and modernity was, however, not to everyone's liking. The logo for the presidency, a collection of abstract and brightly coloured shapes, had a star representing Britain at the centre of the firmament and Italy resembling a pepperoni pizza. The Italians took umbrage at the depiction. Several ambassadors were offended by having to sit quietly on the set as they listened to these speeches. 'Not all of us wanted to be extras in a New Labour film,' said one.[10]

While Cook's attention was firmly focused on the EU presidency and other foreign issues, a domestic subject was threatening to tear the party apart. Blair had signalled that reforming the welfare state would be one of his top priorities and that he would not shirk tough choices. The plan was for an all-embracing public relations offensive to convince voters and traditional party supporters of the need to tackle the growing social security bill and refashion the provision of benefits. However, Labour in opposition had committed itself to supporting a cut, planned by the Conservatives, of £11 a week in lone parent benefit. The pledge had many MPs in uproar. A junior Scottish minister, Malcolm Chisholm, resigned in protest. When the Social Security Bill's second reading came to the vote on 10 December, party whips made clear that any rebellion or unpermitted absence would be met with stiff punishment. Of the Cabinet, Prescott was in Kyoto where the summit on global warming had dragged on interminably; Meacher was away.

Cook was in London, but had a dinner planned with the Spanish foreign minister, Abel Matutes, and the issue they were to discuss, Gibraltar, was serious and had remained unresolved between them since the Madrid NATO summit in July. Spain had reacted furiously to a threat by Cook to veto full Spanish membership of NATO if it did not cede control of Gibraltar airspace. The issue was about to come to a head at a further meeting of the alliance. The social security vote was due to take place before 10 p.m.; in fact, the division bell sounded not long before midnight. Cook's dinner at Carlton Gardens just happened to be a long-drawn-out affair. Should it ever come to the left of the party asking where he was the night they went for lone parents, Cook would be able to say he was elsewhere, on urgent government business.

14

Retribution Time

Cook had not had a proper rest for a year and a half by the time he and Gaynor went off to Chevening for a two-week Christmas break. There they walked, talked and read, rarely leaving the grounds. Gaynor's elderly parents Alan and Joan, who by then were living in an old people's home in Kenilworth, joined them there for some of the holiday. Peter and Chris had seen their father the weekend before Christmas but spent the rest of the time with their mother, and Cook's mother Christina, at the Old Mill. Alan Regan had already proved himself a match with the horses. To Cook's amusement, Alan had beaten the rest of them at their first outing at Warwick in November, winning £69 on a dual forecast. He had a simple formula – back any horse that had been favourite in its previous outing but had done badly; it would be keen next time out to make amends. Cook got on well with his new set of in-laws. Another visitor to the Kent countryside was US Secretary of State Madeleine Albright, who spent a night there on the way to staying with her daughter and son-in-law, who was working for a City bank.

Before his return to London, Cook had one urgent question to resolve. Would he try to become Scotland's first First Minister? He had long harboured the ambition, but time was running out. Eighteen years after being denied devolution, Scotland's voters had, in a referendum on 11 September, approved by more than two to one government proposals to set up a separate parliament with strong legislative powers. Cook had always wanted to keep his options open until the last moment. Asked by the *Scotsman* back in November 1995 whether he was interested in standing for the parliament, he had said: 'Yes, I would consider it. At the present stage I am unable to say that is definitely what I would do.' As for becoming its leader, he developed what would become a stock response: 'It would be extremely presumptuous of me to express any view.'[1] The decision would ultimately depend on the timetable for the establishment of the Scottish parliament, his job satisfaction at the Foreign Office and his prospects afterwards. Yet why would anyone give up one of the great offices of state to become the biggest fish in a small pond?

The Scotland question had given Blair a considerable headache. When he took over from Smith he was uncomfortable with the policy commitment to establish a parliament for Scotland and a weaker assembly for Wales immediately after the election. He wanted a specific mandate, a specific referendum endorsing devolution and the right of a Scottish parliament to alter income tax levels. Early in 1997 Blair discussed the issue secretly with Robertson, Brown and Dewar, who agreed. A month before the change leaked out in the newspapers, Cook still did not know about it – though when it came to presenting the decision to a hostile Scottish party, he gave the impression of having been involved in making it.

Blair's U-turn infuriated many in Scotland and led to considerable hostility on his subsequent trips north of the border. Relations were particularly bad between members of the Scottish executive and the shadow Scottish secretary, George Robertson. After the election, Robertson was moved to defence, a job to which he was well suited, and Donald Dewar took charge of Scotland. There was no sense of demotion for Dewar in this move; he had been upset when his good friend Smith had moved him in 1992 from shadow Scottish secretary, a post he had occupied for nine years, to social security, and Blair's reward for running a tight ship as Chief Whip was to give him back the job he always wanted. Dewar had been an ardent devolutionist since his early thirties, and from day one of government he immersed himself in the minutiae of the white paper setting up the parliament. The document he presented to the Commons in July was greeted with wide acclaim. Although his views were to the right of the mainstream of the Scottish party, it became the conventional wisdom that the First Minister's job was his for the asking.

Yet in those first few months of the government, Dewar was not altogether sure that he should put himself forward. He wondered whether his age – he was approaching sixty – might be an impediment. But he had little time to think about his own position before the devolution campaign got going. Cook, for his part, was too preoccupied with foreign policy and the collapse of his marriage to make a decision. When Blair asked in August what his intentions were, he replied he could not say. Cook was kept at a distance from the referendum campaign, a decision he understood. Although he had embraced devolution in 1983 with all the enthusiasm of a late convert, the leadership did not want to become bogged down by questions about his position in 1979. Brian Wilson, another former opponent of devolution and now a junior Scottish office minister, was similarly omitted from the campaign. Cook tried to help – doing a pro-devolution photo-call supporting his friend Devine – but the papers the following morning were only interested in a picture of Gordon Brown and Sean Connery in front of the Forth Bridge.

The referendum outcome was seen as another success for Dewar. But still he did not announce his plans, believing that to be presumptuous. If he had, the speculation would have ended; as it was, though Cook had still not given the matter too much thought, when pressed he would not rule out the chance of a fiefdom of his own north of the border. Dewar told a close friend of his concern at what he saw as Cook's machinations. The Foreign Secretary had accepted an offer to address the opening conference of a new Blairite organization in Scotland, Scottish Labour Forum, on 1 November. Cook put a lot of work into his speech to the SLF. Without saying anything particularly controversial, he was testing the water for a possible challenge. He laid out a six-point agenda, setting out what he believed should be the priorities of a new Scottish parliament. Because of the proportional voting system, the parliament would naturally be a coalition, and would adopt a different tone and working methods, far away from a House of Commons encumbered with overbearing tradition and an adversarial mentality; the new parliament would be 'enjoyable' and 'inclusive'; it would focus on an agenda of environment, poverty and housing issues, as well as 'supply-side' responsibilities in areas such as education and training. This would be a forward-looking Scotland, not the 'backward-looking Scotland of the kaleyard, tartanry and the broadsword'. He received a long standing ovation.

Dewar's relations with Cook had not been warm since they had clashed over the poll tax in the late 1980s. But Dewar is not one for unnecessary arguments, and expressed his gratitude to Cook for intervening in one aspect of the devolution bill. Foreign Office mandarins had been resisting a plan to grant diplomatic representation for the Scottish executive in Brussels, and Cook made sure they relented.

To many in the Labour Party, the issue was just about signed and sealed, even though Dewar was curiously still resisting calls to declare his hand formally. Then came a story in *Scotland on Sunday* on 14 December. 'Donald Dewar is set to stand aside in the battle for the historic post of First Minister in a Scottish parliament, leaving the way open for Foreign Secretary Robin Cook.' The two, it said, had met to discuss the issue on 3 December in London, and Dewar had concluded he was too old for the job. The occasion was likened to the famous dinner conversation between Blair and Brown in 1994 at the Granita restaurant in Islington, at which Brown agreed to stand aside for the party leadership. The story quoted a 'Cook ally' as confirming a meeting, and saying: 'If Robin Cook can't be British Prime Minister, then he might as well be Prime Minister of Scotland. But he has not yet made up his mind.' Another 'Cook ally' added: 'Donald told Robin that he doesn't want to do it. If he stands, he wouldn't mind being Speaker, but he believes it should go to a younger man. Cook is now very interested.'

Jim Devine, Cook's agent and close friend, admits that he was approached at a Labour party dinner in Glasgow that Thursday by the journalist concerned, who asked him to confirm that Cook and Dewar had met and that Cook had not ruled out seeking the job. The rest, Devine says, was 'top spin'. Some of Cook's friends believe that his enemies manufactured the story as a pre-emptive strike. But by whom? Dewar is almost unique in senior Labour circles for his old-fashioned refusal to leak stories. In the Cook camp, the finger was pointed once again at the Brown team. 'Robin talked to Donald a lot. We were all a bit miffed that the thing went into circulation and then, of all things, for him to be blamed for it. He didn't actually talk to anybody about the meeting with Donald. It was in the papers before anybody else around him knew he'd had the meeting,' said a friend of Cook. Dewar confirms that they had met several times, as all Cabinet ministers do, to coordinate several areas of policy. According to Dewar's friends, their only agreement was that each would inform the other if he chose to stand. It was taken as read that they could not stand against each other.

Throughout December the rumours refused to go away. On Boxing Day, *The Times* weighed in, suggesting that while Dewar was likely to go for the job, Cook had still not made up his mind. That morning he was on the radio, ostensibly to talk about horses. He could not resist keeping the story going, and again refused to rule himself out. 'There was perhaps an element of vanity,' says a ministerial colleague. 'He could not close down a temptation.' His aides were pressing him to stay, with the exception of Devine – a long-time member of the Scottish executive – who wanted him back north of the border. Michael Howard, the shadow Foreign Secretary, called on Cook to make up his mind or be branded 'a lame duck Foreign Secretary'. Britain would not be taken seriously as holder of the EU presidency, Howard said. 'He should act now to end the speculation.'

By this point several key figures in the party were urging Cook to declare his hand. Blair was not happy about the dodging and weaving. 'We'd all asked him to settle it earlier,' recalls a senior official. 'He said the stories were nothing to do with him. This was all a bit annoying. There was something about Robin that he always felt the need to be slightly out of kilter with the rest of us.' People around him were deeply suspicious of Cook's motives for the job. They pointed out that he was not one of those Scottish MPs who had built his reputation in Scotland: on the contrary, he had worked almost entirely on a UK level. He would go to a Burns supper each year – and would recite 'Tam o'Shanter' by heart – but that was about the end of his patriotic identification. Blair's colleagues feared that Cook wanted the Scottish job as a rival power base and a springboard for an alternative, more interventionist economic policy the likes of which had been rejected by the Labour party in recent years.

By the time Cook applied himself seriously to the question, several factors were working against him. One was time: his original plan had been to complete the six months of the EU presidency and then take stock, but the closing date for nominations to the party to become a candidate for the Scottish parliament had been moved forward from July to March 1998, only halfway through the presidency. Dewar's stock, too, had risen considerably after the white paper and referendum; and – the crunch factor – Blair told Cook that he did not want him to take the job. The Prime Minister made this clear during a phone conversation with the Foreign Secretary over the Christmas break. If Cook had decided to go right to the wire and insisted on putting himself forward for the Scottish job, Blair would have faced a terrible quandary. Dewar was the safe and reliable choice. Now he told Cook that if he threw his hat in the ring he would have to stand down as Foreign Secretary straight away – even though the Scottish elections would not be for another eighteen months – because he did not want Britain's EU presidency disrupted.

Cook knew already what Blair thought. During the EU summit in Luxembourg a few weeks earlier, Blair overheard a fellow prime minister telling Cook: 'I hear we'll be visiting you in Scotland soon.' Blair replied: 'There's no way I'm letting him go.' Indeed, it seemed incredible to Downing Street that he – that anyone – would want to give up one of the great offices of state. Cook had, shortly after taking office, implicitly acknowledged the curiosity of his position. 'To be the Foreign Secretary of Great Britain is a very important opportunity. If you can't get a sense of awe out of that – if you want something bigger and better – then maybe you ought to get out of the job,' he said.[2]

Brown, absolutely determined to keep Cook away from the Scottish job, marshalled his forces. On 3 January, the *Scotsman* said Dewar was 'on the brink' of declaring his candidature. Brown, it said, was urging him to do so, as were a host of others. It named George Robertson, Alistair Darling, George Foulkes and Brian Wilson. The following day *Scotland on Sunday*, under the headline, 'Brown's team go to war against Cook', said Brown's supporters in Scotland had been putting pressure on Dewar. It quoted 'a senior source' as saying: 'This is a put-up job to try and back Donald into a corner so that he has no choice but to take it.'[3]

The case was stacked against him; but, like a student in an essay crisis,

Cook postponed decisive action to the last minute. The night before he was due to return to London, Sunday, 4 January 1998, Cook sat down and wrote on a large piece of paper the pros and cons of a move to Scotland. His mind by then was virtually made up. As he had told David Frost earlier that day, 'I've got some way to go before I'm bored with the job. There will be time enough to think about the future at another time, but I'm very happy at my job.'

On his first full day back at the office Cook was due to appear before the all-party Commons foreign affairs select committee. He knew what he would be asked, and rang Dewar in advance. The question came from his NEC colleague Diane Abbott. He replied: 'I am staying as Foreign Secretary, I am not applying for any other job in Scotland or anywhere else we have discussed.' Everyone in the Scottish parliament would find it a 'very rich and exciting job. But for better or worse, I am happy to be in a job I enjoy very much and I am not in the market for looking for a new job. I think it would be a fundamental human right of the committee to continue to see me for many years to come.' He noted that the longest stint as Foreign Secretary this century was Lord Grey's eleven years. He would not make that, he said, but wouldn't mind a crack at Sir Geoffrey Howe's postwar record of six years. His choice of term was significant, leaving open the prospect of succeeding Dewar in 2003. It would not be any easier then, though. So why, asked friends and critics alike, did he not kill the possibility at the outset? Or, if he had wanted to take the risk, why did he not do so as early as June, when his stock was high, and Dewar was racked with self-doubt.

The answer lies partly in his working habits: as with his homework and his speeches, he never likes to be rushed into making decisions before he absolutely has to. Cook's indecision on Scotland followed the same pattern as his hesitation during the 1994 Labour party leadership contest – and his reluctance to decide what to do about his marriage until forced to. 'It was typical Robin,' says an MP friend. 'Again, it comes down to self-confidence. He tortures himself about decisions. People say he's a schemer. But a good schemer moves quickly and doesn't share his thoughts. There are others around the place who are like that, but not Robin.'

Although the chances of success were slim, part of him did hanker after Scotland, not because he has any great affinity for internal Scottish politics (unlike Brown and others, he had not used the Scottish executive as a route to power), but because he sees the Scottish mentality and body politic as closer than the English to his thinking on welfare and the role of the state. And there was the sense that after the Foreign Office there would be nowhere else for him to go. Having failed to take on Smith in 1992 and Blair in 1994, he was slowly resigning himself to the fact that he would never get the top job in London – or, probably, the chancellorship he had so long coveted. He was playing less and less of a role in influencing all aspects of domestic policy, including the constitution. In any case, he had ruled himself out of many jobs, Home Secretary among them, by declaring five years earlier that, after devolution, jobs relating mainly to England could not be held by a Scot. Trade and industry was what he had originally wanted, but that would now seem like a demotion.

Back in the previous September, Cook had told his constituency party: 'I've always said it would be a great honour to stand for the Scottish parliament,' he said. 'I've never made any commitment or ruled anything out. But you can be sure, you'll be the first to know.' He had planned to announce his decision to them on 10 January. Now, though, it was clear that if he waited until the end of the week his announcement would be misinterpreted. A bigger problem was looming.

His early optimism that Margaret had accepted her fate gracefully had faded away. She had told him in September, in one of their fraught telephone conversations, that she had done a television interview for Linda McDougall, a current affairs reporter and wife of the indefatigably independent MP for Grimsby, Austin Mitchell. McDougall had approached Margaret soon after the split, when her emotions were at their rawest. Margaret assured her estranged husband there was nothing much in that to worry about, although she was concerned that McDougall might use some personal recollections she had given her of their marriage for a book chronicling the role of spouses to parliamentarians. McDougall showed her a copy of the section of the book referring to her. Margaret pleaded with her to change it, saying that her remarks – over dinner on the night of the Princess of Wales's death, at the Witchery, a smart restaurant by the castle – had not been intended for publication. Margaret said McDougall agreed to tone them down, but did not. Cook and his aides prepared themselves for a rocky weekend, but assumed Margaret would confine herself to 'general stuff about egos'. What happened over the next three weeks far exceeded their worst fears.

In fact, Margaret had started putting her thoughts down on paper immediately after the break-up. The long-term plan was for a book of her own. In the meantime, she started writing occasional articles for the *Scotsman*. Cook's friends are convinced that since its takeover by the Barclay brothers and their installation of Andrew Neil as editor-in-chief, the *Scotsman* has taken against him. The mutual antagonism between Cook and Neil goes back several years to a row live on air. Margaret had also become friends with Will Peakin, editor of the Scottish edition of the *Sunday Times*. She started writing an occasional diary for them and began to enjoy the limelight. Her mood was bitter, her aim often below the belt, her style sometimes witty. In her first piece she noted the number of Christmas cards sold in shops that bore a picture of a robin. 'It is strange that such an aggressive little creature has come to symbolize the season of goodwill.'

McDougall wrote only eight pages on Margaret Cook in a book of more than two hundred. These were reproduced in *The Times* on Saturday 10 January, and previewed in the paper the day before. They cast the errant spouse in a desperately bad light. Margaret alleged that he had had more than one affair. She described him as spendthrift – he was 'pretty chaotic' with money – and said she knew from the start at university that he had a 'super-shiny ego'. After their friends and family had waved them off on their honeymoon train from Bristol to London, Robin had pulled out papers from his briefcase and said he 'had work to do'. Once, when she was on the phone at home dealing with an emergency at the hospital, her husband tried to get her to put it down so that he could dictate his weekly racing column. Robin, she was quoted as saying, wanted 'love and support, adoration really, but he was too busy to return it'.

That Friday, 9 January, Cook was in Carlton Gardens with Regan, trying to work out how to deal with the disclosures. He opened up the final edition of the *Evening Standard*, which bore the headline 'Wife tells of "Cook's lovers"', and threw it down in despair. Regan managed a wry smile. He feared this might be the end of him. Two days of frenetic activity followed, with only one aim in mind. On Saturday Cook called Margaret and told her how serious the situation was. Mandelson played a major part that weekend. He too phoned Margaret, urging her to 'clarify' her remarks. She asked Mandelson whether her husband's job was on the line, and Mandelson said it was not. That, she says, was when she realized the power Mandelson wielded. She agreed to 'put a lid on it'. A statement was issued in which she said her reported remark referred to 'love affairs' before they were married. Cook phoned friends he had not spoken to for many months, even years, to seek their advice. He asked them to rack their brains to pinpoint anything that might in the future be deemed damaging. He was particularly anxious that weekend that more former relationships might be revealed. His fears were realized when the *Sunday Mirror* linked him with Celia Henderson. In a statement published the following Monday she said: 'I have seen reports about myself. I do not intend to give any comment whatsoever about this matter, nor do my family.'[4] No other identities were ventured.

Blair, who was in Japan, gave wholehearted public backing to Cook. 'On the international stage he has made a huge reputation for himself. I mean that guy is doing a tremendous job for Britain. You go to these international forums and he is a key player. They listen to him. It's just part of life. You get used in politics to these sort of things coming along.' But Blair and his aides did not appreciate the Foreign Secretary's difficulties overshadowing the

Prime Minister's visit. Campbell gave his own on-the-record account to travelling journalists of what had happened in the VIP lounge at Heathrow the previous August.

On the Sunday, Cook was due in Scotland on constituency business: a surgery at 4 p.m. followed by a general committee meeting of his local party. As soon as he and Regan landed they were hounded by photographers at the airport. The pictures of them trying to get away made for terrible television. His aides realized their mistake: they should have insisted that a government car be waiting on the tarmac to take them directly from the plane. When they arrived at the Caledonian Hotel, where they had taken to staying, they were shattered. Peter Hastie had been watching the McDougall documentary for them; it had offered no new damaging revelations. Cook resolved to clarify matters that evening. As soon as he returned to the hotel after completing his constituency business, he called television crews into a room off the lobby: here, at nine o'clock, he issued a statement saying he intended to divorce his wife. She first saw it on the news. No one had thought to inform her in advance.

For Gaynor, it was difficult to come out into the limelight. In Scotland she hardly knew her way around at all. Her first appearance as Cook's partner, at a constituency meeting in September, was tense. She, Devine and Hastie sat in a corner, sipping white wine and eating peanuts as Cook fended off accusations by activists of a government sell-out over the imposition of tuition fees for students. Cook did not introduce her formally to the meeting. Some of those present were not too happy with what had happened. Joe Thomas, the local provost and a former miner, had been a party member for more than thirty years. He suggested that his local MP had paid the price for an error of judgement. Margaret, he said, was an exceptional person and he hoped the two would get back together again.

By January 1998, after eight difficult months in opposition with ministers running rings round them, the depleted ranks of Tories were finally getting the knack of harassing the government. Cook was a perfect target. There were many in the Conservative party with particularly bitter memories of how he had torn them apart at the dispatch box. There were some in the Foreign Office who had not come to terms with the changes he wanted to introduce. There were others with personal grievances. There were newspaper editors who thought he was too clever by half. Put these elements together – as officials in Conservative Central Office were beginning to do – and you create a potent mix. Malcolm Rifkind in particular resented Cook's claim to be giving the Foreign Office a new lease of life; and he especially resented the treatment of a former member of his staff.

Anne Bullen has certain views about the world. She is happy to call herself a 'true blue girl', with her pearls, twin-sets, neat hair-do and clipped voice. A spinster, she has lived in her tidy sixth-floor flat in an upmarket tower block on London's Fulham Road for twenty-five years. Her parents lived in Oxfordshire in the neighbouring village to Douglas and Judy Hurd. At the age of twenty-four she went to work for De La Rue, the company that makes banknotes: a true Establishment outfit, it holds regular dinners for ambassadors in London, at which the Foreign Office is represented. Anne rose to become personal assistant to Peter Orchard, of whom she was extremely fond. When he died in January 1993 and his successor requested changes, she decided to leave. She had been there thirty-two years. In early July that year she met Sir Robin Butler, the outgoing Cabinet Secretary, at Wimbledon, where the company traditionally has a marquee to play host to the great and the good. A month later she received a message saying Douglas Hurd needed a diary secretary. The post carried the title of assistant private secretary to the Foreign Secretary and the not insignificant salary of £24,000. Orchard's successor at De La Rue was the Earl of Limerick, who had been a junior trade minister in the Heath government when Hurd was working in Downing Street. He and Hurd had remained friends.

Hurd used an order in council, an executive device, to get Bullen's appointment through a suspicious Whitehall, fiercely protective of its established procedures. She began work for him on 7 November 1993, on a three-year contract. When Hurd left office in June 1995, she continued with Rifkind, his successor, who in 1996 extended her contract by one year.

Bullen first met Cook in autumn 1994. He had just been appointed shadow Foreign Secretary, and had come in for one of the briefings for the opposition held regularly under Privy Council rules. She found him 'perfectly civil', but spoke to her friends afterwards about his 'rough edges'. During the 1997 election campaign, when civil servants compiled their briefs in preparation for either of the main parties taking power, she told her colleagues in the private office and the 'engine room' (the next-door room occupied by secretaries) that she would stay on until her contract ran out as she was intrigued to see what 'this man' was like. 'It's a tough old job. Unless you're a tough girl you won't last the course,' she would say.

Life with her new boss did not start well. When Cook arrived on 2 May, he went straight through to his office with Coles and other aides, and did not emerge until 10 p.m. Bullen did not appreciate not knowing what was going on. She tried in subsequent days to get him to do the diary. She then tried to persuade him to go to Carlton Gardens to look at his new residence. (He was still staying at Sutherland Street.) He finally relented, but told her: 'You're beginning to sound like an estate agent.' Cook did not like people telling him what to do, nor did he appreciate the restrictions that some of his staff assumed, unquestioningly, went with the job. Not only would he sometimes steal off to the canteen directly through his own door, rather than through the private office; on other occasions in the first few weeks he would give his detectives the slip and make his way either to the Commons to see colleagues or to Sutherland Street. He would later phone to say where he was.

Bullen realized early on what was going on between her boss and Gaynor. She took her cue from the written diary, with its references to appointments with the 'constituency secretary' two or three times a week and advice from others not to put in any engagements after that. After a small party at Carlton Gardens, one senior civil servant asked a special adviser if rumours of the affair were true. He pretended not to hear, but was told, within Bullen's earshot, 'everyone in the Labour party knows about it'.

When in opposition, Cook had been used to seeing Gaynor day in, day out; now she was confined during the day to his parliamentary office in the Commons. Even so, he would try to see her as much as possible; on the way to the airport when leaving for overseas trips, he would choose to travel with her rather than with Ehrman, his principal private secretary, who would follow in a second car. At the same time he was finding Bullen an unhelpful influence on the private office. According to Cook's aides, on one occasion when John Monks, general secretary of the TUC, phoned for him, she told the Foreign Secretary 'some union man' was on the line. She also caused several Cabinet members to raise their eyebrows. At their Templeton courses, the fledgling ministers had all been told not to allow themselves to be taken hostage by difficult civil servants. Other ministers had problems with their press offices. Cook's was his diary secretary, and he wanted her out.

On 21 May, Ehrman called Bullen in and said Cook wanted to bring Gaynor in as his diary secretary. She said she understood that, noting that Howe and Hurd had brought their own people in. She agreed to work until the end of June to see her replacement in. A week later, Cook apologized for not telling her himself earlier. She told him she believed Gaynor 'understands you better than I do'. On 30 May Coles told her the plan had changed: Gaynor did not want the job after all. Bullen told him she thought that was a good thing. 'I think she's a little bit more than a constituency secretary,' she told him. Coles looked up, but said nothing. It was known around the Office that the job of diary secretary required top security clearance that included detailed investigation of applicants' private lives. In Regan's case, this would inevitably have revealed her relationship with Cook. As the listing of his engagements in his diary and his hotel interviews with journalists showed, Cook's attempts to cover his tracks were decidedly half-hearted. A certain fatalism had taken hold. He had baulked at confronting the issue himself, and it was as if he wanted someone else to do it for him.

The new diary secretary was Lynn Rossiter. She had spent the previous five years travelling the world as cover for secretaries in far-flung embassies before returning to King Charles Street. She had been back four weeks, working for a deputy under-secretary, when her name was put forward by the personnel department. She was approached on a Tuesday, interviewed separately by Cook and Ehrman on the Thursday, offered the job on the Friday and started work the following Tuesday, 17 June. A thoroughly modern and informal civil servant from West Cornforth, a former mining village in County Durham, she could not have been more different from Bullen. She has learnt to deal with Cook's foibles, cajoling him to be more punctual with appointments, learning which requests he deems important and which not. The position of gatekeeper is crucial. Gordon Brown brought in Sue Nye, who ran his office in opposition. Tony Blair has Anji Hunter, who has been his eyes and ears for so long. The problem in Cook's case was not his need to get rid of Bullen, but the conflict of interest surrounding Regan. To make matters worse, nobody had reckoned on Bullen's thirst for revenge. When she left, no one thought there was anything amiss. Cook went to her leaving party, made a short speech of thanks and presented her with a silver dish on behalf of colleagues. Any slight she may have felt at the manner of her removal (she had always reckoned on staying until November) appeared to have dissipated.

The first hint of a story came at lunchtime on 25 July when Francis Wheen, a *Guardian* columnist and *Private Eye* contributor, received an e-mail claiming that Cook had wanted to move Regan to his private office. 'Robin has been advised (very gently) by the FO that Gaynor would fail the security check since the standard vetting procedures have turned up, under routine investigation of her flat, an intimate relationship with ... the strait-laced presbyterian Foreign Secretary himself,' the message said. It then gave the address of his Sutherland Street flat, plus details of his travel plans and his conversations with members of the private office. The message ended with a complaint that Cook was neglecting his duties: 'He objects strongly to the FO's fixation with him having to meet ambassadors all the time.' The man responsible for the tip-off tried to preserve his anonymity by using a bogus e-mail address. When Wheen tracked him down, he discovered he was a financial consultant working in the City. The man said he had been encouraged to leak the information by 'well-placed friends in Whitehall'.

A few hours after Wheen received this message, the *News of the World* photographers began their stake-out. 'I was puzzled when the e-mails started arriving,' says Wheen. 'They had a lot of stuff indicating an inside job. The man hadn't expected I would get hold of him, and was very nervous. He said he was put up to it by friends in Whitehall. He said he had passed on the information to one or two Tory MPs.' Wheen aired his suspicions in the first issue of *Private Eye* after the *News of the World* story was published. 'Was the discovery of Robin Cook's extra-marital fling a cock-up or conspiracy?' it asked in its colour section.

Having seen Cook survive the first knock in August, the Conservatives had been seeking to get the story of Bullen's departure up and running soon after. Malcolm Rifkind tried to point journalists in Bullen's direction in early September. But it was not easy. The Blair honeymoon was still strong. It took Margaret Cook's 'revelations' in January to open the door. On the morning of 21 January, at around ten-thirty, Bullen was sitting in her apartment when she received a call from the *Mail on Sunday*. A piece had appeared in the same paper's Black Dog column the previous Sunday alluding to the Regan-for-secretary episode. As she put down the phone, she was shell-shocked; the paper, she says, offered her money for giving full details of her departure and Cook's attempts to put Regan in her place, on the record. She told them she was not sure, and suggested they call again later. On 25 January the *Mail on Sunday* wrote that Bullen had been asked to vacate her job for Regan, but that the plan had fallen down over security clearance.

The next two weeks were to be the worst yet of Cook's career. One allegation followed another. He and his aides were floundering, their every response fuelling further attacks. Several in his own party, seeing him on the political floor, wanted to exact revenge for previous slights. Labour MPs began to peel off, volunteering their disapproval of Cook to journalists. Gordon Brown had only recently experienced troubles of his own – the re-airing of old grievances against Blair for elbowing him out in the 1994 leadership contest – but he had emerged relatively unscathed. Why the difference in their treatment? 'Gordon had much more money in the goodwill bank,' said a friend of Cook. 'Robin never schmoozed and never believed he would have to call in favours.'

Michael Howard, scenting his first strike as shadow Foreign Secretary, started peppering the Foreign Office with parliamentary questions. Even before the Bullen saga, these had forced Cook to reveal that Regan had accompanied him on two official journeys – to Edinburgh for the Commonwealth heads of government meeting, on an RAF plane, and in November for an emergency meeting with Albright on Iraq. At this point the Tories were making hay with accusations of spendthrift ministers taking spouses and partners on official trips. Downing Street ordered that Regan be taken off such expeditions for the time being to avoid further trouble.

Cook tried to ride out the storm. On Monday night his office issued a statement admitting part of the allegation:

After the decision was taken to replace Miss Bullen, Gaynor Regan was, for a short time, considered for the post. Having worked for several years as Mr Cook's personal assistant in opposition, she was an obvious candidate. But, having considered the possibility, both she and Mr Cook decided not to pursue it. Any suggestion that her appointment was blocked by a third party is completely untrue.

But on Tuesday the *Mirror* published three new claims about Bullen, though not sourced directly to her: that Cook did not bother to tell her that she had to go in favour of Regan; that he had kept Princess Diana waiting for ten minutes when she went to see him about landmines in June; and that he had flown home in the middle of the Kashmir crisis, a round trip of eight thousand miles, to spend the weekend with his 'mistress'.

By then Cook was being hounded in Brussels. An early morning press conference with Yevgeny Primakov, the Russian foreign minister, turned into a humiliating barrage of questions about his private life. Immediately afterwards he phoned Downing Street for help on coping with the onslaught. Campbell had just emerged from the 9 a.m. daily media strategy conference chaired by Mandelson. Cook told him that 'he felt humiliated by being asked questions in front of Primakov', recalls a leading official. 'He said he couldn't go through with another press conference without tackling the issue. "I am thinking of saying something." Alastair said "fine", but told him to stress that the woman was appointed by the Conservatives and would have found the atmosphere inimical. "Say it was just one of those things and brush it off," Alastair told him. We felt reasonably confident it would die down if we struck the right tone. In any case, we had material on Bullen. But Robin went against the flavour of the advice.'

The question came up an hour or so later during a press conference with the Albanian foreign minister. Cook responded: 'Anne Bullen was not a career diplomatic servant. She was a personal appointment by a previous Conservative foreign minister and on a fixed term contract which expired last November. After my appointment as Foreign Secretary I reluctantly came to the conclusion that I could not extend her contract because she was impossible to work with. One option after I decided to close her contract would have been to appoint Gaynor Regan, who had been my diary secretary for four years. I quickly decided not to pursue that and asked the permanent secretary to appoint a diary secretary through the normal procedures.' The phrase 'impossible to work with' led to headlines accusing Cook of 'slagging off' his secretary, and gave television reporters a way into a tricky story they had so far steered around.

The man on whom Cook relies most heavily for advice, Jim Devine, was once again unable to help. He had been admitted to hospital for an operation, and by the time he was back on the scene it was too late. Devine, an affable political fixer and trade unionist with his own power base in Scotland, has been very close to Cook since the early 1980s. Now, having been on the party executive since 1983, he was being talked about as a potential general secretary of the Labour party. When Cook's crisis was at its peak, Devine joked that he was forced to call upon both his skills – his political acumen and his training as a behavioural psychologist. David Mathieson, his political adviser in London, spends most weekends in Segovia with his partner who works for the British Council. When he returned on the Monday evening he started briefing journalists that Bullen was a 'card-carrying Tory'. Again, according to Downing Street, that was not the best way of pouring cold water on the story – even if Bullen herself makes no secret of her political allegiances. The spinning went from bad to worse. Cook compared himself with Bill Clinton, whose tenure of office was in the balance over the Monica Lewinsky accusations. 'It is important that he continues with his duties, as I do myself,' Cook said.[5]

On Wednesday, in reaction to suggestions that Diana had been snubbed, he released the text of the Princess's letter to him, dated 11 June. It read: 'Dear Mr Cook, I so much appreciated you giving up your precious time this morning to brief me on the government's position on the various issues concerning anti-personnel landmines. There is so much to be done beyond a ban itself, in the fields of clearance and victim's care support, and it was kind of you to say that my initiatives were helpful . . . Once again my sincere thanks for finding time in your diary to see me this morning,' ending with a handwritten 'yours sincerely Diana' in her usual style. Nobody in Cook's office realized that, even if the letter was completely sincere, someone out there in the press was likely to construe it otherwise. 'Those of us who saw the chemistry between Robin and Diana would never have imagined the letter could have been taken the way it was,' says an aide.

Then there was the so-called 'lost weekend', courtesy of the *Daily Mail*. The irony here is that Cook had never seen anything untoward about flying back in the middle of his tour of Pakistan and India. He had toyed with the idea of using the three days to travel to the Middle East, but saw little merit in condensing a visit to the region into such a short space of time. He considered going again on 4 November, to take in Israel, Gaza, Egypt, and possibly Syria and Saudi Arabia; but the Luxembourg European jobs summit got in the way. 'Scheduling difficulties' were cited. Indeed, his reluctance to visit the region in 1997 had caused some consternation in the Foreign Office. 'It took us a long time to engage Robin in the region,' said one official. With the benefit of hindsight, the Middle East would have been a good place to be that October.

Cook arrived back at Heathrow early on Friday 10 October. The trip, according to the *Mail*, cost £3,510.[6] He met Regan in London, from where they flew up to Edinburgh. His itinerary there began with a photo-call at Oxfam to launch its annual fast for good causes; then he went to the Paterson Arran biscuit factory, which had been given an order to supply biscuits to the Foreign Office. Cook told the employees that he had first come across their biscuits in the Foreign Office canteen. 'I was astonished to discover they are made here in Livingston. So I arranged for a visit here to the bakery. I like the ginger cookies – I can testify from personal experience how good they are,' he joked.[7] At 1 p.m. he met twenty-two leaders of small and medium-sized businesses from the Lothian region to support their bid for a local training and enterprise council. At 4 p.m. he conducted a surgery at Dedridge, one of the small towns in the constituency, which lasted more than three hours. He and Regan then took the last commercial flight back to London at 8.40 p.m. The next day, Saturday, he spent with Regan, and with his son Peter – he had tried to see both sons as often as possible since the split-up – and early the following day, Sunday, he left for New Delhi, thinking nothing had gone amiss. The *Edinburgh Evening News* ran a piece that Monday entitled 'From Dedridge to Delhi'. Cook's office said that it had been agreed in July that his presence was not required over the Queen's weekend break. But still, an impression had been made. Buckingham Palace was prevailed upon by Downing Street to issue a statement denying that the Queen had felt snubbed. 'This is wholly inaccurate, mischievous and wrong. We issued a statement while in India expressing our satisfaction. It was agreed well in advance that the Foreign Secretary would not accompany the Queen outside the capital cities.'

Cook had always set great store by his party and constituency work. It was a somewhat old-fashioned view, but he held it deeply. He would be exacting in preparing speeches, even to thirty activists at his local general committee. 'I'm a party animal. It gives me sustenance. I breathe it.' He tried in his early months in office not to cut down too much on party work. During his long trip to the UN General Assembly, he contemplated taking Concorde to return for less than a day to chair the NEC's pre-conference meeting. He would try to get to his constituency once every three weekends. Although Hastie and Regan would attend his surgeries, he would meticulously take down in longhand each case history; and he had kept abreast of the minutiae of housing policy ever since his days as convenor on Edinburgh Corporation. Here was a Foreign Secretary, sitting in a dilapidated room, not having to refer to his staff when asked by downtrodden constituents for advice on their entitlements to particular social security benefits or their place on the local council flat waiting list.

He would take up even the most bizarre cases affecting constituents. Shortly before the general election, he discreetly tried to help two local unemployed men who were in trouble with the law. William Kane, aged fifty-five, and his brother-in-law William O'Byrne, fifty-three, were arrested on 12 January 1997 at the Loganlea miners' Welfare and Charity Club in Addiewell on charges of breach of the peace and assaulting police officers who had arrived to check on late drinking in the early hours of the morning. Cook visited the two in police cells shortly after their arrest. Kane, a former miner, and O'Byrne, who works in the building trade, were old chums and had canvassed for him during election campaigns. Kane was steward and O'Byrne president of the club, which Cook used sometimes for social events and constituency surgeries. When he took office he asked Hastey to keep him informed about their impending trial and even took a break from preparations to greet visiting dignitaries for the funeral of the Princess of Wales to fax a character reference to lawyers acting for the two. In the end they were both fined, and Cook had to coax Kane into paying up. The two would hardly, by metropolitan middle-class standards, be regarded as New Labour models; and it would be hard to find other Cabinet ministers who would have taken such an interest in their plight.

By the end of January it was open season on Cook. Tory spin doctors tried to interest journalists in a supposed story that when Cook was in Edinburgh with Regan he had once stayed at the Moat House Hotel 'in a reinforced bed made for the King of Tonga'. The interminable Bullen controversy led to bitter exchanges between Hague and Blair at Prime Minister's questions. Blair agreed that if Cook had sacked a civil servant and sought to replace her with a close friend at public expense, that would have been wrong. 'That is not, however, what happened. As the Right Honourable gentleman knows, the particular person was not a career civil servant. She was appointed personally by a former Conservative Foreign Secretary. When her contract came to an end she was replaced by a career civil servant.' Hague said Cook's behaviour was 'certainly secretive, clearly open to misinterpretation, probably unwise, and possibly worse', at which point Blair lost his temper.

The fact that the Right Honourable gentleman engages in that type of question shows how completely useless and pathetic the Conservative opposition are. Since he appears to be suggesting that the sleaze and scandal that enveloped the previous Conservative government are the same under the present government, let me tell him what people objected to. They objected to cash for questions for Conservative MPs. They objected to money in brown envelopes for Conservatives who became ministers. They objected to money coming from Chinese drug dealers.[8]

Campbell followed this up by accusing the tabloid newspapers involved of 'bunging money' to Bullen, 'to make her talk'. He went to the nub of the government's fury: 'The Prime Minister does not get involved in these attacks on personal lives. Can you imagine Neil Kinnock or John Smith or Tony Blair attacking the Tories over the break-up of Douglas Hurd's marriage?'

Regan was taking the publicity extremely badly. She was a virtual prisoner in Carlton Gardens, likely to be hounded if she tried to leave. She urged Cook to clarify her status as soon as possible, so that the press would stop hounding them. The following morning, 29 January, Cook was quoted in the *Sun* as saying: 'Gaynor has transformed my life. I have experienced more happiness in the last few months than I can remember. Gaynor is resigned to the prospect of a honeymoon in Brussels. I have to ask my diary secretary to find a free weekend.' Purchase popped his head round the door of Cook's office to go through the press cuttings. He pointed out cheerily that Shirley Bassey's court case had knocked the row over Gaynor off the front pages. That too was about the sacking of a secretary. The remark was a bit too close to the bone, and did not get the laughs intended.

With the media management at rock bottom, Mathieson and Hastie asked Devine to call Cook from hospital to talk things through. Other aides did not have the same kind of authority to talk to him frankly, or to criticize him – something Cook does not take to kindly. His relationship with his three special advisers is much more formal than is the case with other ministers. Brown, for example, turns almost constantly to Charlie Whelan for advice on the press and to Ed Balls on policy. Cook's advisers have to book in time to see him, or catch him between meetings. And yet at that point he needed hands-on advice. 'For the first time in his life Robin has had a challenge in politics that he doesn't fully understand,' said a friend. 'Probably his strongest emotion is guilt, made worse by knowing that Gaynor is being harmed.' Some in the Scottish party wonder whether Cook would have suffered so many knocks in his first year in government if Devine had been with him in London.

What bothered Blair's entourage was the way some of the practical decisions had been taken. In previous years Cook had brushed aside repeated requests by those close to him to resolve his marital dilemma before the press got to it – which they knew it would inevitably do. When it did, the first phase the previous August had gone as well as could have been expected; but the events of January were badly mismanaged. 'What was so frustrating was that Robin had at his disposal people with huge experience of these things, of dealing with press trivia. He could have just said, "I'm in trouble, please help,"' says a senior official. Ken Purchase, Derek Fatchett and other loyalists agreed, and told Cook as much. 'When in trouble we kept on digging and digging,' said a colleague. 'We had no strategy of dealing with it.'

Devine did his best to repair the damage. He invited reporters to Livingston to give them his interpretation of events surrounding the 'lost weekend' and of Cook's character: 'As a person who has been close to Robin for the past twenty years, professionally and politically, and as his agent since 1993, I am appalled at the scurrilous and petty charges which the member for our constituency is receiving. The primary function of an MP is to represent his constituents. He was unavailable to attend a surgery the week before, and would have been unavailable to attend the following week, and the Robin Cook I know would not have spent four days anywhere twiddling his thumbs.' Devine told them that during the last general election research showed that one in three constituents had a personal or indirect dealing with Cook. 'This was reflected in the result where his majority increased by 50 per cent.'

As Cook was leaving the weekly Cabinet meeting that day, Gordon Brown approached him for a quick chat. He was taken aback – the two had long ago agreed in the interest of Cabinet harmony to keep their contacts to a bare minimum. Brown agreed to pop into Cook's Commons office that evening. Purchase had arranged for Cook to gather about thirty allies in the parliamentary party to discuss what had happened. The group had met consistently in opposition and included, apart from Purchase, Fatchett and Hain, others such as Tony Lloyd, Jean Corston, Angela Eagle, Roger Berry, Richard Burden and Dick Caborn. As they were leaving at around 7 p.m. they were startled to see Brown arrive. Brown, Cook, Mathieson and Denis Turner, a Midlands MP, had some small talk about Scottish temperance before the two long-time adversaries were left alone.

They got a fair way down a bottle of malt whisky and agreed to call a truce. Both had been stung by controversy, and both had more to gain from being on reasonable terms. Brown told him to 'hang in there', and that 'we may have had our differences in the past but sit tight, these things are temporary'. There would be no briefing against each other. The story was characteristically spun to the *Sunday Telegraph* three days later as 'strong Brown helps prop up weak Cook', but Cook was not in a position to complain. 'Gordon Brown is spearheading a concerted Cabinet effort to shore up the position of Robin Cook, his long-standing rival, amid growing fears that damaging claims about the Foreign Secretary's conduct are jeopardising the government's credibility,' the paper said in its front-page report.[9]

Cook had no way of gauging the long-term sincerity of the gesture, but there was no denying its importance. A certain collective psychosis had taken root in opposition, with animosities exacerbated by a sense of powerlessness and frustration. Highly ambitious and intelligent individuals had too much time on their hands and not enough responsibility. The ingrained instincts of internecine rivalry continued into government; but by the end of the first year, with many of them having already encountered crises of one sort or another in office, the first signs were emerging of a desire by the combatants to work together.

Cook was not yet, however, in the clear. Margaret was furious at his remarks in Thursday's *Sun* that he had never been happier. She contacted the Sunday papers to accuse him of a 'cruel slight'. She had not poured oil on to the Bullen business, and this was the thanks she got. 'The last month I have been supporting him and doing the loyal wife bit and that's his response.' Cook went apoplectic at her latest intervention, and told her as much on the phone. They agreed she would put out a corrective statement. 'The stories in the press with regard to the Foreign Secretary are trivial and should be laid to rest so that he can get on with his job which he does well. We have reached an amicable settlement with regard to the divorce and now wish to look to the future and not the past.'

Gordon Brown's first practical expression of new-found solidarity was to encourage his closest friend in parliament, Nick Brown, the Chief Whip who was at the centre of the furore over the Chancellor's unfulfilled ambitions, to rally support behind Cook. The Tories had called a half-hour debate for 4 February, the first available slot, to have a go at Cook. The device, an adjournment debate, had to be tabled in the name of a backbencher. The hapless Oliver Letwin was shouted down by an army of Labour backbenchers who had been marshalled by the Chief Whip to destroy the debate. Michael Howard did his best, accusing Cook of a 'scandalous abuse of ministerial power' and claiming that his treatment of Bullen rendered the Foreign Secretary 'unfit for public office. The only honourable course open to him is to resign.' Cook had made himself scarce, in Kuwait, and the case for the defence was made by Derek Fatchett, his deputy, who stole the show. He repudiated attempts to equate the Tory 'cash for questions' scandal and other financial improprieties with the Bullen episode. 'The opposition is playing games and obsessed with trivia . . . Their only message is that the Tories were sleazy so let's see that Labour is sleazy as well. But the public can tell the difference.' In his coup de grace, Fatchett revealed that the chairman of the Diplomatic Service trade union, Ric Girdlestone, had written to Hurd on 25 November 1993 saying he was 'at a loss to understand' why a career civil servant had not been given the job of diary secretary; three internal candidates for the job had been rejected. Hurd had replied: 'The diary secretary position in my private office has always been a difficult one to fill. The job requires a mix of skills, including experience as a personal assistant and considerable maturity, which few

DS9s [the rank required] possess.' Fatchett said this showed that Bullen's appointment was unique and 'caused controversy among staff in the Foreign Office. I have no doubt that there were suggestions of personal and political influence.'[10] Bullen's own admission of how she got the job bears that out.

That debate was seen as one step too far even by Labour MPs not usually well disposed towards Cook. 'The PLP is very inclined to support any colleague who is set upon by a combination of Tory politicians, the Tory press, and civil servants,' said one Cabinet minister. The saga finally died down when journalists turned their attention to Lord Irvine and his penchant for extravagant wallpaper. Ironically, it was an intervention by the Lord Chancellor himself that provided the last spot of trouble in this particular saga for Cook. Irvine suggested, in an interview with the *New Statesman*, that the media should have been prevented from revealing Cook's private life by privacy legislation of the kind that would follow incorporation of the European Convention on Human Rights into UK law. He was firmly stamped on by the spin doctors.

Blair at this point was in Washington, rendering support to Clinton over his troubled private life. Blair had pointedly not taken Cook (or Brown, for that matter, although the reasons for the Chancellor's going would have been less obvious). Instead he invited Jack Straw, whose handling of his own crisis over Christmas (his son's purchase of soft drugs in front of a reporter) had been privately commended by the Prime Minister. Blair tried to reconcile his own more prescriptive views about the nuclear family and personal morality with the reality of the high divorce rate among MPs and society at large. 'People have got to make a choice,' he said. 'It depends what people want. If they want a government that's going to look after their interests and be able to handle their affairs on a world stage then they've got it. They're going to have to make a choice in the end whether they are going to allow difficulties in someone's personal life to intrude on things that, in the end, are the things they were elected to achieve. I just think the public have a slightly different sense of priorities from the media.'

There were two sides to Blair's defence of Cook. He believed strongly that, unless anybody had broken the law or done something palpably wrong, a marriage break-up was a personal tragedy that did not impinge on the ethical standards of any politician. Affairs with secretaries were nothing new. How many Conservatives had left their wives and married their secretaries without being the target of brickbats? Nor was bringing in a secretary of one's own to manage the extraordinarily difficult diary pressures on senior ministers anything new. Hurd did it. Howe did it before him. The problem for Cook came in the merging of the two issues.

Bullen categorically denies that she was responsible for the original

News of the World disclosure. 'Someone was making that look like me', she says. A few months after the revelations, she was suddenly taken off the list of guests for the Foreign Office Christmas carol concert in December 1997, on the orders of Cook's private office who are convinced someone in the Foreign Office did it. For six months or more after leaving the Office, Bullen had still to find herself a job, notwithstanding a CV which named Rifkind and Coles as referees.

She would later express surprise at the furore caused by the January disclosures about the way she was asked to leave. She does not deny that during that frantic fortnight Conservative Central Office had 'kept me cheerful', with key figures offering her advice on how to deal with the press. She now says she had never meant Cook any harm, had never had bad feelings against him, and had never wanted him forced out of his job. 'It was completely stupid. I should never have spoken to the press,' she says. If anyone from Cook's camp had got in touch with her when the saga reached the newspapers, she would have cooperated and distanced herself from the remarks. 'If only someone had come to the rescue.'

15

The Relaunch

After all the bad publicity, in early 1998 those around Cook were convinced it was time to overhaul the image. One of the criticisms that stung him most, and appeared least justified, was that he was not dedicating enough time to the job. In the middle of the month, after talking it through with his son Chris, he phoned his old friend Harry Reid at the *Herald* in Glasgow and gave him just over a week's notice that he was giving up his racing column. His enthusiasm for the sport seemed to have rebounded on him in the volley of revelations from Margaret. Diary columns had started to poke fun, for example when he tipped a horse called Celibate at Ascot. The column had long stopped paying – since the election Cook had decided to forfeit the £100 per week (which he had always divided equally with his son) because the rule book for ministerial behaviour was unclear on the issue. For Chris, who had been doing most of the work since the election, giving up the column was a blow. He considered asking Reid if he could do it under his own byline, but realized that the paper wanted a famous name. It chose Alex Salmond, the SNP leader, whose first column, on 21 February – to Chris's delight – failed to pick a winner.

Devine, meanwhile, urged Cook to meet him and Mathieson for a strategy session. There was much to be done. Cook had all but forgotten the elementary lessons of keeping his friends and allies on board – something the ever-vigilant Brown would not fail to do. One of Cook's closest MP friends recalls how, in the midst of the Bullen saga, he saw him 'walking around the Members' Lobby in the Commons for the first time since he became Foreign Secretary. He was blinking in the light like a hare. I've hardly seen him since the election. I never imagined a man I thought too astute for his own good would get into this position. It was flabbergasting.' The same MP says that two years earlier he had invited Cook to address his constituency's annual general meeting. His speech went down well enough, but not his manner. 'In the middle of the mayor's reception he went off to the corner to file his racing column. People were quite upset. He seemed completely impervious.' Why, his friends wondered, had he not learned to flatter his colleagues? Forget your scruples, just do it a bit, they urged; after all, everyone else does. 'He leads a compartmentalized life. He's not one for small talk. He gives the impression of a man always in a hurry. He's got more like that as work has expanded.' His lack of time was exacerbated by a perfectionism that, in the short term, paid dividends. Another colleague described him as having 'all the characteristics of an ultra-intellectual – his constituency is the mind, not the heart.' Part of his oratorical skill had always been the put-down (invariably supported by hard evidence), preceded with a sigh of deliberation that had become his hallmark. But that style did not translate well into ordinary conversation. Many a backbencher has complained of feeling deflated after being given short shrift by him in the corridor for not exactly knowing their facts. One senior party official, having attempted to discuss the poll tax with Cook, said of him: 'Robin wasn't the kind of person you would just phone up and have a cup of tea with. People felt intimidated by him.' He had always believed that success would come through merit alone. When it did not, he was at a loss. His friends had long come to terms with some of his more distinctive character traits. Even they sometimes felt belittled, but his wit, intelligence and personal loyalty usually saved the day. What they had not anticipated were the several lapses in judgement of his first year in government. 'For all Robin's command of his political subjects, his own personal instincts failed him when boxed into a corner,' said one. 'At those points he stopped taking advice.'

His friends did try to help – some in the most direct way possible. At a Burns supper in Glasgow, one speaker, Anne Lorne Gillies, an SNP candidate from the Western Isles, mocked Cook's 'ugliness' and his 'way with women'. Amid all the laughter, George Foulkes became so angry he tried to heckle, shouting: 'This is disgraceful!' But only a few in the room heard him.

Devine suggested Cook had no choice but to adapt to the more superficial, image-conscious world. He urged him to focus more on what seemed the trivial concerns of the modern media, and less on the finer points of a particular speech or policy. But it went against the grain. Cook's politics were those of the discussion forum, the negotiating table, the library: 'He's a very political person in an apolitical society,' Devine said. Another friend put it more bluntly: 'The aim now is to avoid the David Mellor syndrome.' In other words, he had to ensure that his reputation was refocused away from the personal, back on to the professional.

Almost immediately he was presented with the perfect opportunity to re-establish his credentials. For months the Iraqi President Saddam Hussein had defied the international community by playing cat and mouse with UNSCOM, the UN team trying to inspect his potential for building and storing biological and chemical weapons. The Western allies had been here so many times before. Cook's first Iraqi crisis had come in November, when Saddam had expelled the UNSCOM team in protest at its dominance by Americans. The foreign ministers of the P5, the five permanent members of the UN Security Council, met in emergency session at 2 a.m. on 20 November. The aim was to agree a united front to step up the pressure. No single country had called the meeting, so there was no host. 'Well, shall I take the initiative and begin?' asked Cook. 'What a good idea. And why don't you act as chairman and read the final communiqué afterwards?' said Yevgeny Primakov, his Russian counterpart. Cook turned to John Grant, his principal private secretary, tapped his glass and said: 'I might as well call the meeting to order.' Saddam backed down. Cook's handling of the issue was praised in Cabinet.

By January, Saddam was defying them again, and this time the stakes were higher. Clinton dispatched aircraft carriers and large contingents of troops to Kuwait and other parts of the region. The rhetoric became ever sharper. Many diplomats could not see a way out of a war; some, especially on the left, suspected Clinton of talking up the hostilities to get himself off the hook in his worst domestic political crisis yet, over allegations of sexual misconduct by Monica Lewinsky, a young White House intern. But Blair was staunch in his support for the US leader. Cook was in a desperately uncomfortable position. In the 1980s he had been vocal in criticism of the Conservative government for arming Iraq against fundamentalist Iran. That war led to the hideous chemical weapons attack on Alabjah. In the 1990–1 Gulf War he was prevailed upon by Kinnock to keep his criticisms to himself. In August 1996 Cook was forced to adapt his views to the New Labour template, defending a further round of US air strikes on Iraq. But he chose his words carefully, speaking of 'appropriate and not disproportionate' action.

This time around Cook was vociferous in making the case – on human rights as much as political grounds – for a tough line against Iraq. 'You are dealing', he said,

with one of the few world leaders who has personally killed people. Saddam is the clearest example of a leader who is also a terrorist. He used mustard gas repeatedly and used cyanide gas and nerve agents when he bombed Kurdish towns and killed thousands – mainly women and children. These are weapons not of military use but of terror. Here is the link between our opposition to Iraq and an ethical base to foreign policy. We have taken a very strong line against nuclear, chemical and biological weapons. It would be totally inconsistent with that if we were to allow Saddam to remain in possession of weapons of mass destruction.[1]

Yet the government was finding it hard to get its message across. It issued satellite photographs of Saddam's presidential palaces, which he insisted were 'no go' areas for the inspectors, one of which was described as being the size of Paris.

Cook showed no signs of flagging in his opposition to the Iraqi leader's obduracy. In a debate in the Commons on 17 February he warned Saddam that any retaliation against air strikes, especially using chemical or biological weapons, would meet a 'proportionate response'. The tabloids portrayed him as threatening to use nuclear weapons. Some twenty-three Labour left-wingers rebelled against a motion backing efforts to reach a diplomatic solution but supporting the resolve to 'use all necessary means' to achieve Iraqi compliance with Security Council resolutions. Tony Benn warned MPs that in voting with the government they 'will be consciously and deliberately accepting the responsibility for the deaths of innocent people if the war begins, as I fear it will'. He accused Cook of 'cloaking himself with the garment of the world community. I must tell him, he hasn't got it.'[2]

Cook was stung by suggestions of hypocrisy, based on comparisons with his early days in Parliament as an anti-militarist. To emphasize the point, the *Scotsman* reproduced a photograph of him at a 1970s CND march. Some in his own constituency – considerably further to the left than many in England – accused him of sabre-rattling. At the same time, he was having increasing misgivings about what he feared was enthusiasm among some in Washington, notably the Vice-President Al Gore and the Defense Secretary William Cohen, for going to war come what may. Derek Fatchett was put in charge of a committee of representatives from Downing Street, the Foreign Office and the Ministry of Defence, which met at nine-thirty each morning during the crisis for about half an hour to coordinate the government's 'message'. But there certainly was a difference in emphasis between Cook and some officials close to Blair, notably Campbell and Powell. In the Commons, Cook was asked whether a fresh Security Council resolution was required before air strikes. He replied that it was desirable and that Britain was working to that end. However, Downing Street had worked from the assumption that Resolution 687, which ended the Gulf War, was sufficient because Saddam was in persistent breach of his commitment under the terms set out by that resolution to destroy weapons of mass destruction and allow verification.

Throughout the crisis, Cook spoke to Albright at least once a day. In fact, they had been doing that for months. Some in Whitehall joked that he talked to her more than he did to his Cabinet colleagues. He had installed a black box hotline a few days after taking office, a secure line on which the pair could speak to each other directly. The first time he tried it, though, he got put through to the wrong number.[3] This communication took on elements of the bizarre on the afternoon of 20 February. Kofi Annan, the UN Secretary-General, was preparing for a make-or-break trip to Baghdad, which Cook was desperately hoping would succeed. Others in Washington or London saw it as unfortunate, offering Saddam an exit route enabling him to avoid air strikes. Cook was having lunch with his mother in the County Hotel on Dalkeith High Street – opposite her home in an old people's housing complex – when a call came in from Albright on the mobile phone of one of his bodyguards. Cook could not hear her because of the noise generated by a French women's rugby team, who had come to support France against Scotland at Murrayfield the next day. So the Foreign Secretary was forced to stand out on the street, one hand in his ear, discussing the latest developments in a serious international crisis with the US Secretary of State. He described it as 'pure Monty Python'.[4]

Cook was hugely relieved when Kofi Annan delivered the deal. He told friends afterwards of his pride in Britain's having kept 'the wheels on the ground'. The following week, Blair once again praised him for his role in the crisis. Another who spoke warmly, to perhaps universal surprise, was Clare Short. She had long been perhaps the strongest opponent of this kind of brinkmanship foreign policy, although in government she had kept studiously to the collective Cabinet line. Relations between her and Cook had gone from bad to worse since the 'golden elephants' affair. She had taken to calling him Robin Redbox, and was not talking to him directly. Moreover, she had formed a curious alliance with Gordon Brown, which only added spice to the animosity. The hostility intensified after a speech Cook gave in London on 4 February to the chief ministers of the remaining British dependent territories, in which he hinted strongly at the grant of full British passports to 160,000 people in the colonies and confirmed the intention to create a new department, the UK Overseas Territories Ministry, headed by Liz Symons. Cook wanted to grant citizenship to inhabitants of all the dependent territories – the Falklands and Gibraltar already have it – so as not to discriminate against black Caribbeans. A draft of Cook's speech was sent to Short and Straw, and both immediately lodged objections. Short protested that the dependencies came under her department, and Cook could not just annex them without taking notice of her. Straw protested that Cook's passport promise threatened to reopen the question of UK citizenship. To their astonishment, Cook ignored their suggestions. Downing Street told the three to 'sort it out among yourselves'.

In the view of George Foulkes, Short's deputy, this fight was helping no one. He had had a long chat with Cook while the two were at an EU–Americas meeting in the Bahamas in February. Cook had told him how low he felt. Foulkes suspected that staffers in both offices, and senior civil servants, were fomenting the trouble. In a speech in February, John Vereker, Short's permanent secretary, extolled the DfID's good relations with the Treasury, DTI and other departments but pointedly omitted to mention the Foreign Office. Cook, partly on Foulkes' advice, wrote Short a note saying how much he appreciated her support over Iraq in Cabinet. On 2 March the two met in the Foreign Office for their first chat for seven months. They agreed to draw a line under the argument and concluded that they could once again become natural allies – as long as they talked directly to each other.

Since the argument with Downing Street in September, Cook had avoided making arms sales an issue. The odd licence had been rejected, but without fanfare. The Foreign Office and No. 10 were approaching the issue from opposite directions, the former wanting to make clear the new rules were biting while the latter sought to reassure the defence industry that it was business as usual. It was clear by now which approach was winning. The Foreign Office tried to act tough by stealth. It hoped the criteria, and the publicity, would deter countries with dubious records from seeking contracts with UK companies. One official said approaches from Algeria, the Philippines and Bahrain had been deterred. 'We try to do as much as we can without alerting Downing Street. Every time you draw attention to any of this you get a memo.' They had learnt the hard way. But even these more discreet efforts were running against a stronger tide. John Spellar, the junior defence minister, told the Commons in November that defence exporters were facing serious delays in winning export licences as civil servants grappled with new guidelines. Downing Street stepped in, calling for more effort to be expended on clearing the backlog of licences and less on the trumpeting of the new ethical policy. Trade unions and companies also complained about posturing. Notice was taken. *Jane's Defence Weekly* reported that 1997 had been a vintage year for arms exports, worth £5.5 billion. George Robertson congratulated the defence industry in March on a 10 per cent increase in exports year-on-year, an 'outstanding performance'. All but one of seventy-three applications from Turkey had been approved in the ten months since the election. The Defence Export Sales Organization predicted that over the next five years Britain would secure contracts worth £23.7 billion – holding its position as the world's second largest supplier after the United

States and ahead of France. As for Indonesia, sales were going swimmingly. The DTI disclosed that in the year from March 1997 forty-eight licences had been issued, and only two refused. The chief executive of Alvis, the armoured car manufacturer in Coventry which was involved in £15 million worth of contracts to Indonesia, said he was relaxed. He told *Engineer* magazine: 'We have high hopes of doing further business with Indonesia.'

Old habits were dying hard. Such statistics as were given had to be prised out of Whitehall by a series of Commons questions from backbenchers. The defence industry was succeeding in its efforts to release as little information as possible. The DTI's six-monthly report, listing in general terms the value of arms sales, was delayed. The department claimed a computer logjam. A new annual report was also expected. This would set out the total value of defence exports to each country, list by country of destination the number of items delivered in each equipment category, and give details of all export licences granted and refused. Cook was hoping that the foreign affairs, defence and trade and industry select committees would be charged with scrutinizing it.

Over the winter, British and French civil servants had been working on the draft European code of conduct that had been announced by Cook at the 1997 party conference. The aim was to replace the eight existing EU common criteria for defence exports, agreed in 1991, with a clearer and tougher code. The first section provided detailed criteria to guide governments in decisions on granting licences. The second section involved a consultative process by which any EU country that declined to grant a particular licence must make its reasons for doing so open to the rest. If any country then wanted to undercut it would have to consult the country that turned down the order. The consultation element was toned down by the French. The actual criteria themselves were virtually a copy of the British ones of July 1997, and there was little evidence to show that loopholes – such as those allowing for the sale of 'protection' equipment for security forces – had been put there at French insistence.

The most telling reaction came from the defence industry, which remained silent – signifying its contentment with the outcome. The anti-weapons lobby was anything but content. Four groups – Saferworld, Basis, Oxfam and Amnesty International – issued a strongly worded press release pointing up the caveats to the agreement that rendered it, in their view, spineless.[5] Others weighed in. Letters were sent to newspapers from three Nobel Peace Prize laureates calling on the code to go further; the Archbishop of Liverpool joined the clamour, along with leading Muslim and Jewish figures.[6] The most high-profile case was made by three former senior officers, led by General Sir Michael Rose, who had headed British forces in Bosnia. Writing in the *Daily Telegraph* on 16 February, they said the code was unlikely to prevent another 'arms to Iraq' scandal: 'Unless the code includes explicit and restrictive criteria governing exports, tough consultation mechanisms and provisions for parliamentary accountability, it may simply legitimise business as usual.' There was also criticism of the economics. Three trade union bosses, John Edmonds of the GMB, Bill Morris of the TGWU and Ken Cameron of the firemen's union, took the government to task over the notion that arms exports were necessarily good for British jobs. 'The opportunity of the forthcoming green paper on defence diversification must be seized to enable our highly skilled defence-related workforce to use their talents in jobs that benefit everyone,' they wrote in the *Financial Times* on 18 February. 'A tough code of conduct, therefore, should not be a case of moral gain and economic loss. If it is coupled with a coherent programme of diversification, jobs as well as lives will be saved.' The final document, agreed at the end of May, was virtually identical to the draft. The discreet lobbying by the arms companies had prevailed.

The government's consultation paper on defence diversification confirmed the worst fears of those looking for change. The aim, said Robertson, was to use defence laboratories and intellectual property rights commercially for civil use. 'We are talking about defence diversification not defence conversion. We are not in the business of running down defence production facilities and converting them to civilian use. We believe in a strong defence industry, as an important national asset and as a major driver of economic growth and exports.'[7]

Cook was stung by the criticism and invited the NGOs in to tell them he had been upset by their press release. 'Politically this puts me in a difficult position,' he said. They stood their ground, telling him that he could have gone further. They pointed out that several EU governments – the Belgians, Swedes, Italians and Dutch – would lobby hard to strengthen the code before it was finally agreed. He told them that simply getting the French on board was no mean feat. He asked them to compare it with what existed before, rather than simply with what they would all like it to say.

Therein lay the crux of the dilemma. The more these interest groups – the people he had always listened to and respected – criticized him, the more he felt his authority within the Cabinet was undermined. Many on the left still held out hope that he was trying to do things differently. Blair's priorities, though, reflected somewhat different preoccupations. In November he had set out what he called his 'five guiding light principles' for foreign policy in the Prime Minister's annual Mansion House speech on international affairs. These were:

1 a strong European policy, ending the 'isolation of the last twenty years';
2 a stronger transatlantic alliance;
3 strong defence, noting that any cut in the defence budget would not reduce capacity;
4 free trade, with Britain at the forefront of moves against protectionism; and
5 what he called 'transnational issues' such as environment, drugs, terrorism, crime, human rights and international development.

It was only when it was pointed out by journalists that there was no mention of anything to do with ethics that a late addition was made: 'Human rights may sometimes seem an abstraction in the comfort of the West, but when they are ignored, human misery and political instability all too easily follow. The same is true if we ignore the ethical dimension of the trade in arms.'[8]

After the misunderstandings and difficulties that had followed in the wake of Cook's mission statement and human rights speech, attempts were made to redefine exactly what the Foreign Secretary had meant. Cook insisted that he had never actually used the phrase 'ethical foreign policy', although it was only when the policy started running into trouble that he disowned the phrase. The Foreign Office preferred to talk about an 'ethical dimension' and 'priorities', and about 'incremental change'. British embassies were going out of their way to make better contacts with human rights groups; visiting ministers would emphasize the issue to their counterparts more clearly. This had already been demonstrated in Latin America, where Tony Lloyd had gone to some trouble to make clear Britain's support for a human rights commissioner who was facing constant death threats.

Progress towards some of these aims could be achieved bilaterally, but increasingly, Cook argued, it was international institutions that could deliver change. Cook believed the agreement with Iraq had not only deterred war but restored a moral and political legitimacy to the UN, much of which had been lost in recent years. 'We have shown real, productive leadership in the UN. We were instrumental in gaining Kofi Annan a set of bottom lines which he took to Baghdad – we managed to get all five permanent members to agree on the same bottom line.'[9]

Blair had not wanted ethics in foreign policy to be defined narrowly in terms of the arms trade. Memos were exchanged early in 1998 discussing how the concept could be broadened to take into account issues of more immediate concern to citizens, such as the right to clean air (environment), the right to live in drug-free communities (crime) and the right to secure frontiers (defence). The emphasis was to be shifted to areas such as international crime and money laundering – 'drugs and thugs' as it became known in the jargon. The first clear example of this reorientation came in an initiative launched at the EU–Asia summit in London at the start of April to improve international police coordination in the battle against child pornography. 'This is what diplomacy should be about – not cocktail parties and negotiations on obscure subjects, but forging practical cooperation in areas that the British people really care about,' wrote Cook.[10]

Part of the problem lay in the image of the Foreign Office. The first steps had been taken to address that with the mission statement and open day. The whole approach to recruitment was changing, although that would take time. The Foreign Office had become the first Whitehall department to appoint an ethnic minorities liaison officer, Linbert Spencer. Plans were also afoot to make the building more approachable to the public. Mathieson was asked to look into turning the little-known entrance on Whitehall into a visitors' centre. The initial idea was to bring in banks of computer screens giving access to the Foreign Office website, and a small cinema showing a fifteen-minute video about the department and foreign policy in general. One of Cook's first concerns on taking up the job was with the Foreign Office's inability to do more to promote British cultural exports. He asked Fatchett to set up a working group with the culture and heritage department and the DTI, and from that emerged Panel 2,000, dubbed in the media the Committee of Cool. Fatchett saw that initiative as far more policy-driven than presentation-driven. But the ministers all did their bit for image, clearing out old paraphernalia from their offices. Gone from Cook's majestic room were all the old books and *Hansard*s from his 1860 walnut bookcase, which instead was filled with a Design Council display of modern British gadgets.[11] The Cool Britannia fad, with its exhibition of style on Horse Guards Parade, was a central part of a broader government message.

The way ideas were fed into Whitehall was also ripe for change. Cook felt that foreign policy-making had lost flair and imagination. The Royal Institute of International Affairs, generally known as Chatham House, was regarded by Cook and others in the department as having seen better days, now providing a social forum for retired diplomats and ivory-tower academics rather than people more directly involved in the creation and implementation of policy. NGOs, which had in the past gone directly to the press in frustration that their ideas were not being taken on board by the Foreign Office, would now find a ready audience. Cook served notice as soon as he got in that he wanted a think tank along the lines of the foundations run on behalf of political parties in Germany. When it finally emerged ten months later, the Foreign Policy Centre was only a shell, with two benefactors (Paul Hamlyn and Bob Gavron), one full-time employee, a board of management of the great and the good of Labour thinking and fund-raising, and one all-important patron: the Prime Minister. The aim of the centre was to create ad hoc groups of specialists who would produce pithy policy suggestions, each to run to no more than ten sheets of A4 paper, for Cook's red box. Launching the centre on 3 March, Cook joked (with Lord Simon in the room) that no offshore funds had been provided for the centre which, with its skeleton staff, could hardly be seen as a rival to a Foreign Office of two and a half thousand officials. As for press coverage of his policy initiatives, he quipped: 'I don't expect uncritical and sycophantic articles, but I do yearn for them.'

Another area of new British thinking was a push to create a permanent international criminal court with powers to order the arrest, prosecution and punishment of those charged with grave abuses of human rights. But here too Cook was having to temper his ardour. 'I am fairly hopeful there will be an ICC – the question is how strong. I want it to have the power of jurisdiction – but how broad that power should be is open to reasonable debate. One has to balance having a court with jurisdiction over other states with not letting member states off their primary duty to maintain law and order and take a tough line with criminals.'[12]

Cook's aides had prided themselves on a hitherto unsung achievement in his foreign policy – China. A visit there in January, overshadowed in the media back home by his private life, had seen human rights constructively discussed and the host government agreeing to a first visit by a UN High Commissioner for Refugees, a post now held by Mary Robinson, the former President of Ireland. China also agreed to a visit by EU ambassadors to Tibet. Cook's first visit to Beijing had been in May 1995, two years before the Hong Kong handover, when relations between China and Britain were extremely sour. He resolved then that his aim would be to maintain Britain's stance on human rights while emphasizing distance from the approach of Chris Patten, the then Governor.

Two and a half years later, towards the end of 1997, Cook decided to employ entirely new tactics with China. In 1998 Britain would, for the first time since 1989, not sign up to the annual resolution in June of the UN Commission on Human Rights condemning China's record. This ritual, he believed, appealed to China's wounded pride and set back efforts to improve the situation. Not only would Britain not sign, but Cook resolved to use his chairmanship of the general affairs council of EU foreign ministers to seek to alter EU policy accordingly.

Cook was convinced that, whatever initial criticism it might attract, his policy of engagement would bear fruit. The new Prime Minister in Beijing, Zhu Rong Ji, was being portrayed in London as 'China's Gorbachev' – a man who was moving slowly in the right direction in the face of internal resistance:

It's very important to keep China in perspective. The Chinese record gives rise to very serious concern, but there is movement. I was in Beijing in 1995 and I went back again in January – and there has been significant movement since then. We want a dialogue on this. We want the troika in Tibet to do their own programme. We want some releases from a long list of dissidents who are in jail. But I do think engagement produces some goods.[13]

Just before his January visit to China, Cook found himself 'too busy' to meet one of the country's most prominent dissidents, Wei Jingsheng. Wei, who was extradited to the US in 1997 after spending eighteen years in jail for anti-state activities, had arrived in the UK to give a lecture to St Antony's College, Oxford. Cook's people had been wary of him, suspecting that he was being 'run' by right-wing US Republicans. However, in the public eye Wei was likened to Russia's late Andrei Sakharov, a figure of great stature. In mid-March he was back again, and this time a visit to the Foreign Office was arranged. On the eve of the meeting, Wei gave an interview to the *Daily Telegraph* in which he described Cook's new policy towards China as a 'wrong-headed gamble'. His trip coincided with controversy surrounding the refusal of HarperCollins, part of Rupert Murdoch's empire, to publish a book by Patten sharply criticizing the Chinese government. Wei called Cook a 'coward' and said China had shown over the years that it responds only to international pressure rather than 'dialogue'. In a caustic put-down, he said of Cook: 'He obviously isn't as involved in fighting human rights as he makes himself out to be. If you make empty promises on human rights, that indicates that the ethical policy is no more than a political slogan.'[14]

Wei said as much to Cook himself during a less than warm discussion. The situation was then compounded when a planned photo-call, an accepted ritual of just about every such meeting, failed to materialize. Wei had left the building at 11.45 a.m. but there were no photographers present. 'This was a deliberate attempt to stop Mr Wei standing side by side with Mr Cook because they cannot justify their policy to China's leading democratic activist,' said Wei's interpreter. The Foreign Office pleaded cock-up over conspiracy. Wei turned up at 11 a.m. as indicated on his letter of invitation; Cook had midday in his diary, but rearranged his schedule at the last minute. They finished their meeting early, and Wei left before midday, which was when the photographers had been summoned to take pictures of him with the Foreign Secretary on his arrival. If it was a cock-up, it was a desperately bad time for one.

Blair was forced to defend Cook over the Wei furore, telling the Commons during Prime Minister's questions that the UN resolution was 'not the right way to proceed'. Cook put it like this:

The media, and because of that, some of the public, seem to have an image of foreign policy that is either kow-tow or row. In other words, you either completely submit all your principles as you enter the minister's room, or you have a blazing row and get thrown out at the end of it. What I believe we have shown is that it is possible to have a middle way, to have a positive discussion about where you can co-operate in commercial terms to your mutual economic benefit, but that does not mean to say you cannot then raise issues of concern, that touch upon those values of civil liberty and good governance, democracy, which are so much part of our own political programme.[15]

Although the end was consistent, so the argument went, the means would vary. Sometimes it was softly softly; sometimes it was more upfront. 'It's not about emotions, hobby horses, but pursuing specific goals,' officials were told. They coined a slogan: 'Make a difference, not a point.'

Israel presented entirely different problems. The Middle East peace talks had collapsed since the arrival in office of the hard-line Likud Prime Minister, Benjamin Netanyahu. The Europeans had hitherto played little role in the region, something the British presidency sought to change. Cook had planned to go in mid-April, but Blair suddenly bagged that slot. The Foreign Secretary's visit was rearranged for mid-March, with the most important middle day of the three coinciding by chance with the budget back home. The preparations were rushed forward, the programme condensed. One of the main features of the trip was to be a visit to Jebel Abu Ghneim, where in 1997 Israel began building a large housing project it called Har Homa. The construction activity, in a part of Jerusalem which Palestinians consider to be their future capital, plunged the peace talks into further crisis. Netanyahu's refusal to implement parts of the Oslo Accords had provoked even the Americans into expressions of increasing frustration.

Cook gave notice of his intentions in a keynote address in London on 5 March, using as his pretext the celebrations to mark the fiftieth anniversary of the Anglo-Arab Association. The speech, given in the Locarno Room and cleared by Downing Street, represented an attempt to improve relations between Britain and the Arab world, which Cook believed had become 'unstuck'. Cook set out a new strategy to include the EU in efforts to reinvigorate the Middle East peace process. He offered more practical assistance to boost the Palestinian economy and fight terrorism; he vowed a stronger European input to 'complement' US efforts to revive the talks; and he called for six immediate measures to restore confidence. These included a 'substantial, credible and urgent' redeployment of Israeli troops from the West Bank, the reopening of the Gaza airport and a freeze on

Jewish settlements. At the same time, Palestinians would be encouraged to step up the fight against Islamic and other radical groups responsible for terrorist attacks.

His three-day visit to the region was meant to kick-start the process heralded in his speech. By going to Har Homa, where he would meet Faisal Husseini, the Palestinian representative in Jerusalem, he intended to underscore Britain's and the EU's objections to 'illegal' Jewish settlement construction in territories occupied by Israel since the 1967 war, including East Jerusalem. However, on the eve of the visit, Israel denounced Cook's itinerary as a 'provocation'. As a concession, the meeting with Husseini was dropped; instead, Israel would send two government officials to accompany the visiting delegation. The government also objected to a planned dinner with Ehud Barak, leader of Israel's opposition Labour Party. That too was dropped, and replaced by a dinner with Netanyahu.

As soon as he arrived in Israel, Cook went to Gaza. On his return to Jerusalem he was accompanied by Israeli officials to a spot close to Har Homa, where he was given a 'briefing'. Then, under hailstones and running the gauntlet of protesters, Cook made a short tour of the piece of land. After this, as he was preparing to get back in his car, he was presented to Salah Ta'amri, a former PLO guerrilla commander, now chairman of the land committee of the Palestinian Legislative Council, who had come to meet him. The sight of Cook trying to hold up his EU umbrella as he was jostled by Israeli settlers gave a poor impression on television back home. In Israel, the reception had already assumed an ugly mood. Graffiti was daubed on the British consulate in west Jerusalem accusing Cook of anti-semitism. The usual diplomatic courtesies were discarded by the host government. 'Too many Cooks spoil the broth,' remarked Netanyahu mockingly.[16] Netanyahu cut short their meeting later that day and cancelled the dinner. Cook made light of it: 'It is a mercy to have been spared another full-course meal. On reflection, it would have been wiser for the Prime Minister to have recognized that the international community has a legitimate interest in the peace process.'

The British were furious with the Palestinian authorities for ambushing Cook, when Husseini invited him to lay a wreath at a memorial for Deir Yassin, the scene of a massacre of Palestinians by a Jewish militia in 1948. The Palestinians were furious that he had reneged on an agreement to meet Husseini at a spot of their choosing. The Israelis were furious that Cook had not gone to Yad Vashem, the Holocaust memorial. British officials believe Netanyahu deliberately engineered the row as a show of strength to extremists in his coalition. The British deputy head of mission had gone to the Israeli foreign ministry to finalize details of the visit, and had been told that no offence would be taken if, on so brief a trip, it was decided not to visit Yad

Vashem. It was also noted that Cook had spent three hours there on his previous visit in September 1996. To demonstrate his pro-Jewish credentials, it was pointed out that in autumn 1997 Cook had visited the site of the Warsaw Ghetto, and that on 2 December that year had opened the London Conference on Nazi Gold, charged with getting to the bottom of the scandal of the misappropriation by the Nazis of gold belonging to their Jewish victims. In fact, the itinerary had been intended as a compromise. Cook had been urged by Palestinians to do what other foreign ministers do and visit Orient House, their headquarters in East Jerusalem. He declined, but agreed instead to meet Husseini at Har Homa, exactly as Derek Fatchett had done the previous summer, without so much as a murmur of discontent from the Israelis.

Whatever the rights and wrongs of the episode, it looked bad. Comparisons were made with David Mellor who, as a visiting junior Foreign Office minister, had berated an Israeli colonel in the Gaza Strip in 1988. The analogy was drawn of an American going to Belfast and seemingly siding with nationalists against unionists. Initial press coverage back home was disastrous. Cook was portrayed as gaffe-prone and insensitive, his blunt talking counterproductive among a political elite that makes a habit of taking offence. Most galling were comparisons of his political acumen on that particular day with that of Gordon Brown, whose budget was seen as a brilliant mix of the radical and the reassuring. A leader in *The Times* was particularly damaging to Cook. At the top was written: 'The artful radical. Brown takes the best of Labour high-roads.' Below it was the headline: 'Diplomatic disaster. Cook has not helped British foreign policy or the peace process.'[17]

It was perhaps inevitable that when, a month later, Blair made his own trip to the region, it was portrayed as repairing relations between the UK and Israel. Blair, fresh from his success in securing a deal in Northern Ireland, invited Yasser Arafat and Netanyahu to talks in London. Netanyahu was asked during his joint press conference with Blair what the difference was between the two recent British visitors. 'It is a fact that Mr Cook visited Israel before, and you see that he prepared an excellent visit,' was the barbed reply.

Yet Cook was adamant that what he did was right, and that many people who follow developments in the region understood what he was trying to do. He received supportive telegrams from other EU foreign ministers, and some of the more considered newspaper analyses praised him for breaking taboos. Many members of the parliamentary party sent him messages praising his courage, telling him that in time others would come to appreciate his actions. Once again, though, it was the first impression that stuck in the popular mind.

None of this was a surprise for Cook and his entourage, who now had become used to the deluge of media attacks. All the woes of January and beyond had led him to turn in on himself. There was a sense among his supporters that his personal difficulties had, for the first time, made him entirely beholden to Blair. He could no longer be the left's man in Cabinet, hamstrung as he was by the fear that any suggestion of stepping out of line would give Blair ample excuse to demote him in a reshuffle. The revelations by Margaret Cook, followed by the Anne Bullen saga, had harmed him on four fronts: he had seen his personal integrity challenged; he had been distracted from foreign affairs; his professional judgement had been called into question; and his ability to fight the soft left's corner in Cabinet had been damaged.

He had been virtually silent on domestic policy. Even in the deliberations on constitutional reform – an area in which he had formerly been a pivotal presence – he was little more than a bit-part player. Indeed, when he was asked at the Foreign Office Christmas party in 1997 his views on the composition of Lord Jenkins' electoral commission, which was looking into an alternative voting system for the Commons, he had to admit he did not know which names had been chosen or even that the announcement was going to be made that day. The issue of trade union recognition was no longer one for him; his last intervention in that debate had been the veiled warning about trade union links made at the previous autumn's party conference. Nor was the whole welfare debate – at least in public: he had been absent on official business from the vote on cutting benefit for lone parents. He no longer challenged the strictly defined bounds of departmental responsibility. Keynes had been well and truly dumped. Gordon Brown's hegemony on economic affairs was accepted. 'We've been waiting for Robin for fifteen years,' said one MP who counted himself as an early friend. 'But he's retreated from just about everything he stood for.' Another put it a different way. 'Robin puts stakes in the sand and is forced to move them.'

Nowhere was the constraint more clearly shown than at the Scottish party conference in March. Cook used a Friday night fringe meeting to the Blairite Scottish Labour Forum to set out his vision of a more pluralist political system, in which parties would cooperate more maturely on the minutiae of policy. He was talking about the Liberal Democrats; but his remarks were interpreted in the following Monday's *Scotsman* as a call for an alliance with the SNP, in defiance of party policy, something that was far from his mind. When it came to the main speech to conference the following day, Cook was still frantically going through his text minutes before, deciding to ditch domestic references and confine himself to foreign policy. Meanwhile, Brown was once again having it both ways. His speech was trailed, in inimitable fashion, by Whelan as warning of a tough budget offering no handouts, a line designed to go down well with Conservative newspapers. The actual speech was all about eradicating poverty, and a call to arms on the basis of everything that was positive about Scotland's socialist traditions. Just to mark his ground over Cook's forlorn ambitions to the first ministership, Brown lavished praise on Donald Dewar, 'whose name is almost synonymous with the parliament he played such a part in creating'. But this was no time to complain. Cook's advisers were even coordinating speeches with Brown's. A dinner was planned for the two couples – Cook and Regan, with Brown and his close friend Sarah Macaulay – to take place within weeks. It did not happen and, unsurprisingly, the truce did not last.

As for Cook's relations with Blair, it was time to return favours, to make more open declarations of loyalty. The Prime Minister had become embroiled in some controversy over his close relationship with Rupert Murdoch, demonstrated most clearly by his lobbying during a telephone call to Romano Prodi, the Italian Prime Minister, for help in Murdoch's proposed £4 billion acquisition of the country's leading commercial television network. 'The idea that Mr Blair intervened or had an axe to grind or was acting as any kind of lobbyist is indeed not true. His relationship with Mr Murdoch is no different to the relationship this government has with any other newspaper editors and proprietors. There is no special access for Mr Murdoch,' Cook told *The World This Weekend* on 29 March. For someone who had argued strongly for closer controls on media cross-ownership, and had attacked Murdoch specifically for predatory pricing, the apparent conversion was surprising.

Yet Cook could handle criticism of policy. What rankled with him most was that more column inches continued to be devoted to his private life than to his job. His every movement, his every utterance was closely scrutinized. His efforts to buy a house in Edinburgh's New Town were followed in the local press, which noted carefully that since the 'yes' referendum many a des. res. had risen in price beyond the reach of a man who had handed over virtually all his assets (house and contents) to his former wife. Just before Christmas 1997 Cook and Regan thought they had found the right place, only to be outbid at the last moment.

Margaret filed for divorce at Edinburgh Sheriff's Court on 29 January, adding herself and Robin to the tally of 190,000 couples petitioning for divorce each year. When her papers went through on 13 March she phoned Peter and Chris. 'I had really hoped it would come about much sooner. It's quite a relief. I feel quite liberated,' she said.[18] Just to rub salt into the wound, she wrote a column for the following weekend's *Sunday Times* looking forward to the odd 'dangerous liaison' of her own as a newly reinvented single woman. Her mother Joyce had just been in touch to celebrate the news, suggesting that her former husband might already be regretting his move: 'He's been in trouble since the moment he left you.'

Cook consistently refused to retaliate and looked back at the events of August with regret at the way it happened and sorrow at the way his ex-wife pursued her public vendetta. He realized that he should have plucked up the courage to end his marriage earlier once his relationship with Regan became serious – in other words at a time of his, rather than the media's, choosing. He confided in friends his share of responsibility for allowing his marriage to decay. As for his handling of the various crises, one of his closest friends had simple advice for critics: 'Live through it yourself and see if you could have done it any better.'

Chris and Peter did not try to stop their mother writing articles, and even tried to deny that there was any malevolent motive behind them. For them, it was as if everything Margaret had said to anyone in the media, not just to Linda McDougall, had been distorted, and that in fact she had meant no harm. As for their father's relationship with the newspapers, they saw him as pure victim. 'Before the August events they could never find anything to get him with,' says Peter. Both sons remained staunchly loyal to both parents. Chris was given a twenty-fifth birthday party to remember at Chevening, when he and twenty friends from Edinburgh and Aberdeen were given a free rein over the place for a weekend. Robin and Gaynor joined them on the Saturday morning, but only after Chris had been thrown into the lake of the grand mansion. Three weeks later Cook went with his son to Kempton Park as part of his own birthday celebrations. With his birthday falling close to Gaynor's, the couple decided on a joint party for about three dozen friends at Carlton Gardens. The guest list was a strange mix of the personal and political, of friends and contacts. Friends of Gaynor, including her ex-husband Stephen, mixed with the likes of Lord (Swraj) Paul, the Indian-born steel magnate, Lord (Michael) Levy, Blair's top fundraiser and leading light in the Jewish community; the only Cabinet presence was Chris Smith, although Frank Dobson and Jack Straw were invited but had had to decline. Elizabeth Smith, widow of John, was there, as were Colin Fisher, Cook's old advertising friend, Jim Devine, Anna Healy with her husband, Barbara and Ken Follett, as well as his ministerial team of Derek Fatchett, Doug Henderson, Liz Symons and Ken Purchase.

Although no formal meeting was held or explicit strategy devised, Cook sought the advice of his four closest allies, Devine, Mathieson, Fatchett and Purchase, on drawing a line under the first year of his life in government. Marriage to Regan would, they believed, neutralize future attacks on his personal life. To manage this crucial event – mindful of the events of January, when he and his team had tried with spectacular lack of success to manage public relations on their own – Cook allowed himself to be taken under the wing of Campbell and Mandelson. The Strategic Communications Unit, a new team in Downing Street charged with coordinating the 'message' across Whitehall, was also brought in to help on speeches. An interview was arranged with Philip Webster, political editor of *The Times*, to coincide with the halfway point of the UK's EU presidency. Cook surprised Webster by dropping in towards the end of their chat a reference to his plans to get married in April, two months earlier than planned. Webster was prevailed upon to keep the story under wraps until publication date on 30 March, by which time the story had been leaked to the *Mail on Sunday*, with a more precise date of 19 April. Cook phoned Webster on a Scottish golf course to apologize for the scuppered scoop. Webster asked him instead for an exclusive photograph of the couple, pointing out that the most recent available picture was of the two scurrying away scowling at Edinburgh airport in January. Cook agreed to a new one. The famous photo of them against the backdrop of the ornate Chevening gardens was arranged in a hurry, and was widely derided in the press as a pastiche of the original Charles and Di engagement shots nearly two decades earlier. It was also interpreted as a snub to Margaret, who had spent only one weekend at Chevening. Devine had in fact advised against such a setting for the photograph, suggesting something more down-to-earth such as an old people's home in the constituency.

Within days the plans appeared to be going awry. Cook's aides feared a media scrum at Chevening, and another piece by Margaret designed to undermine the occasion: so the following weekend the decision was taken to bring the wedding forward. On Tuesday morning, 7 April, Mathieson was dispatched to Tunbridge Wells, to buy a special licence for 5 p.m. that Thursday, 9 April. Only a small circle knew, among them Blair, Campbell, Mandelson and Cook's immediate entourage. That same Tuesday Cook told Fatchett and Purchase after Foreign Office questions in the Commons. Other ministers did not know. Of the civil servants, only the permanent secretary Sir John Kerr, Cook's private office and Nigel Sheinwald of the Foreign Office's news department were made aware, on the Wednesday. Lynn Rossiter was asked to clear his diary for the next few days. On the eve of the wedding, they agreed with the registrar to bring forward the ceremony to early morning. The only people who knew about the change of time were Cook, his bride, her close friend Mary Warner, Jim Devine and David Mathieson. The five of them went down to Chevening and stayed the night there, in a state of high excitement and anxiety.

At the crack of dawn they assembled. So secret was the operation that they even gave Special Branch the slip. The furtive group drove off just before 8 a.m. along a back route, only to find themselves confronted on their way out of the estate by a closed cattle gate. Devine, in his kilt, was detailed to get out in the pouring rain, open it, and shut it behind them. Had they told the security officers, they in turn would have phoned Kent police and almost inevitably the story would have got out. Cook was relieved at the absence of photographers outside Tunbridge Wells register office, a nondescript building between the fire station and the undertaker. The building had been opened at eight, the earliest time allowed and an hour before the official opening time. Building works and a skip full of rubble outside the door helped spoil any lurking photo-opportunity. The only special arrangement made was that the builders had been asked to stop drilling for a few minutes. Inside the room where the marriage was to be celebrated, the only concession to aesthetics was a couple of arrangements of dried flowers to offset the rows of metal-framed chairs stacked high against the wall. Mozart's *Eine kleine Nachtmusik* was played on a mini compact disc. As they left, Cook punched the air. He had finally beaten the press at their own game. 'This was the only time Robin was in control of the story,' said a friend. 'That mattered to him.' Yet the press still tried to have the last laugh, deriding his choice of an 'anorak' for the ceremony. Cook insisted it was a 'car coat' which he took with him because of the unseasonably cold temperatures. Of such stuff are modern images made.

Campbell's original idea had been not even to confirm the marriage had taken place. But within hours it had become common knowledge inside the Foreign Office. By the time it had become public, Sir John Kerr had announced to his top civil servants at their morning meeting: 'You might like to know the Foreign Secretary remarried this morning.' Cook issued a statement around midday saying he hoped his marriage 'will show that the true story of my private life is that it's a very content and fulfilled life with the woman I want to make as happy as she makes me'. Blair, who was in Belfast for the dénouement of the peace talks, congratulated them, adding that he 'completely understands why he has got married today, thereby avoiding a media circus. He is a hugely talented and able Foreign Secretary.' The first foreign dignitary to congratulate him was the Chinese ambassador, who enclosed a proverb in his card: 'May we stay happy together until our hair grows snow white.'

Cook had told his sons and his mother on the day before of his rearranged plans. Chris and Peter had been expected on the original date but could not get time off work for the new one; they said they understood why he was doing it and were looking forward to joining their father and Gaynor on the nineteenth for a private party at Chevening. Margaret was initially speechless on being told by the *Mirror* of the event that had just taken place; she made some play of the boys and mother-in-law not going, but her reaction was reasonably discreet. Nevertheless, Cook's friends never knew where or when she would strike next. 'It's like having a nuclear bomb on your doorstep,' said one of them. By contrast, Stephen Regan had turned down a number of potentially lucrative offers from papers to tell his side of the story. In fact, so friendly had he and his new partner become with Robin and Gaynor as a couple that plans were afoot for Cook to write a foreword to an anthology of poems about horses he was putting together.

The private party was an occasion for celebration. But it also allowed Cook's friends to take stock, and digest what had happened over the past nine months. Cook's closest friend now was John McCririck, the racing pundit. He and his wife Jenny were the only people who had remained close to both Robin and Margaret. One of the curious aspects of Cook's life is that many of the people he speaks of as good friends cannot remember the last meaningful conversation they had had with him. That oddity had most effect in politics. If only he had spent more time making friends, he might not have got into such difficulty. But McCririck – whatever his politics – had become a true Cook loyalist. What particularly riled him was the hypocrisy of journalists. 'Nearly 50 per cent of all marriages break up, many in acrimonious circumstances. So why is it so different for Robin? Who are these people casting stones? Are they so perfect themselves?' As for the media magnates, 'What right do they have to tell Cook when they might deign to lay off him? They're hardly paragons of virtue themselves.' And as for foreign politicians, how many marriages had Netanyahu been through? Or Gerhard Schröder, the likely next German Chancellor? Or, indeed, Nelson Mandela? These issues only seemed to matter in Britain. Another friend of Cook put it like this: 'Politics in the Anglo–Saxon world is now too driven by a media-sensitive presentation and not sufficiently driven by the problems that we're supposed to be addressing. It's very different from the continent, where European countries are blessed with papers that still treat politics as a serious issue for adults.'

There were times during this torrid year, as in trying periods earlier in his career, when Cook had thought long and hard about what he was doing in King Charles Street. Foreign affairs was a treadmill, the holders of its highest office judged by their ability to execute policy. So much of it had been set in stone so long ago. For all their anxiety about the advent of Cook in May 1997, many mandarins there believed that, after a long hiatus, they finally had a master with unrivalled clout in Downing Street, someone like Jim Callaghan under Harold Wilson. What frustrated Cook was the lack of outcomes in foreign affairs. This, he confided in a guest at his office's Christmas party, 'would have been a great job in the nineteenth century'. As for politics itself, the game had become unrecognizable. He told a small group in March that if he had his time again, he would become a teacher or doctor; if he had known how much politics would change, he would never have gone into it.

Yet however much he disparaged the emphasis on spin and presentation, he concluded he had to put up with it. The relaunch advocated by some of his friends in the New Year took place shortly after Easter. Three speeches were arranged for consecutive days. First came a joint report with Clare Short on progress to date on human rights, which emphasized specific achievements in certain countries, rather than the more sweeping promises of the original mission statement. For all the dashed expectations, at least he had forced the issue to the top of the agenda.

On 23 April, at the annual Lord Mayor's banquet, Cook extolled the achievements of his first year in foreign policy. To many in the press, the debacles of India and Israel would stick in the mind. (Cook differentiates between the two – the former which did contain mistakes and the latter which, he insists, did not.) But more to the point were the quiet successes of putting relations with other EU countries on an even keel, establishing an axis with the US State Department stronger than any for a long time, conducting a well-managed Hong Kong handover and its aftermath, and a tougher approach to Bosnia. It was, after all, no mean feat to address the assembly of the Bosnian Serbs in Banja Luka — a sign of their willingness to engage in more normal politics. What about the Nazi gold conference? What about EU enlargement? As for China, the release in April of Wang Dan – one of its most prominent dissidents – provided the first piece of evidence that closer dialogue was paying dividends. Cook also drew attention to the improvements in Britain's position in international fora under the new government. The UK's position in Europe was no longer one of complaining from the sidelines.

But who was listening? Attention that night, predictably, was elsewhere. Next morning, the front pages of virtually all the papers, including the broadsheets, had photographs of Cook in white tie accompanied by new wife with new haircut and ballgown. Cook was pleased at the coverage and believed it could mark a turning point, although he did not disguise his sadness that he had been forced to think in those terms.

Sandwiched between the two speeches was an address to the Social Market Foundation. It was Cook's most important platform for some time, giving him a rare opportunity to enter the domestic arena. He had been asked by Blair to help spread the gospel of the Third Way, to explain the philosophical underpinning of New Labour. Jack Straw had begun the process several months before. This was intended as the most considered explanation to date of what the Blairite 'project' was about. The Strategic Communications Unit played a major part in putting the speech together. It was looked at by others in Downing Street, the Cabinet Office and the Treasury. (Brown told his closest aides he thought it 'vacuous'.) For Cook, it was an attempt to get beyond soundbites, to show the country (and perhaps himself) that the government was guided by radical values.

'The Third Way', he said, 'is a political project as distinct from the individualist politics of neo-liberalism as it is distinct from the corporatist ethos of old-fashioned social democracy. The Third Way is squarely within the Enlightenment tradition. It shares the belief of that tradition that humanity has the capacity to shape their society and the duty to use that capacity to improve society.' Don't look back: that was the message to his friends on the left, as he pointed to six principles to chart their path:

1   strong communities as foundations of freedom and opportunities;
2   inclusive societies to produce prosperous economies;
3   open politics through constitutional change;
4   responsibility and rights as equal elements of citizenship;
5   globalization leading to interdependent nations; and
6   the need for policy to modernize as society changes.

'Some years ago,' he continued, 'the end of the Cold War was hailed as the End of History. We have had an awful lot of history since that claim. What we can say with great confidence is that the complexity of modern society and the rapid developments in technology have brought about the End of-Isms.'

Here, then, was the final discarding of socialism and Keynesianism by its most loyal proponent at the top of the Labour party over the previous decade. Here was someone who had said three years before: 'I am an unreconstructed Keynesian. I firmly believe that if you want to make sure you achieve steady, stable and sustainable growth then you have to have management of markets by the government in a way that was so successfully carried out in the first three decades after the war.'[19] For all his private, and not so private, reservations about the early Blair years, Cook found himself now ready and willing to fit himself inside the New Labour template. 'The final question which I wish to address is: are we radical as a government? My emphatic answer is yes. Indeed, I have never been one of those who believed that degrees of radicalism could only be measured by its depth of unpopularity. Tony Blair's achievement has been to build a politics of the centre-left which is both radical and popular.'

Blair's other achievement was to have got his most intellectually powerful and potentially most difficult long-time man of the left exactly where he wanted him: the loyal lieutenant working hard at his brief and his brief alone.

After a troubled first year in government, this was a time for retrench-ment. Cook was no longer indispensable to Blair. His judgement had, for the first time in a distinguished career, let him down. His cachet among the left of the party had decreased, and with it his influence on the leadership. There were many people out there – in the press, in his own department, and in his own party – who were determined to keep it that way.

16

Arms and the Man

'The job comes as a great shock to them, just the sheer amount of travelling, for example, and the enormous range of subject matter. A Foreign Secretary can be concerned at one moment about drugs in Thailand, the next moment about civil war in Sierra Leone, and on it goes. I mean, it is an extraordinarily disparate and wide agenda.'[1]

Sir John Coles, Cook's first permanent secretary, was trying to explain the perils of the job. The Civil Service is well attuned to the task of filtering documents – determining who should see what. At the Foreign Office the flow of telegrams is incessant, with diplomats on the ground reporting to their desk officers the latest developments; that information is then passed on to regional departments, then on to larger directorates. From there it is determined what should go to which minister's private office, where officials arrange the red boxes in order of priority. Cook had made clear to his officials that he wanted to see less routine paperwork than his predecessors. He wanted to keep a firmer hand on the development of policy on issues he deemed to be Britain's top priorities. Other tasks he would delegate to his officials and junior ministers.

The Labour government had taken some interest in Sierra Leone, a small west African state rich in minerals but torn asunder by years of civil war. The elections that brought Ahmed Tejan Kabbah to power as president in March 1996 were, on the assessment of international observers, democratic. But on 25 May 1997 – less than a month after the British elections – Kabbah was ousted in a coup by Johnny Paul Koroma, a Sandhurst graduate turned mutinous army officer. Koroma unleashed an orgy of unspeakable violence. The UK and other industrialized nations were determined to do what they could to help Kabbah back into power.

For Cook, success in this particular venture – so remote and obscure that it did not figure at all in the mainstream of British political life – was crucial to the newly trumpeted ethical dimension of foreign policy. But there was a problem. Kabbah, who had fled to Conakry, capital of neighbouring Guinea, had to rely largely on Nigeria – the regional superpower – to help him get back into power. Nigeria itself had been expelled from the Commonwealth for abuse of human rights. It was going to be a delicate balancing act between means and ends.

On 28 April 1998, around seven in the evening, Cook's car swept past the electric gates into 1 Carlton Gardens. It had been another long day. He had just been chairing another of those interminable meetings of European ministers, this time in Luxembourg. He wanted to get home, put his feet up and relax with his new wife – who had seen precious little of him since their marriage and who resented his bringing work home with him as often as he did. Two of his political advisers, Andrew Hood and David Mathieson, were waiting for him at the front door. This was the only time he could fit in a regular office meeting, and he wanted to get through it quickly. The main item on the agenda was Turkey, ahead of a planned visit there. But his advisers had come with bad news. The trio went up in the lift to his flat and straight into Cook's study. Hood told him that a fax had arrived in his in-tray from a firm of solicitors acting on behalf of Sandline International, a small British company. The letter said that Customs and Excise had launched an investigation into a shipment of arms by Sandline to Sierra Leone in contravention of a United Nations embargo. The company said it believed it had done nothing wrong, because its plans had been approved by Foreign Office officials.

Sandline had been set up by Tim Spicer who, after twenty years as a Guards officer during which he had served in Northern Ireland, the Gulf and the Falklands, had established the company to offer 'special forces rapid reaction' around the world. Registered in the Bahamas, but with its offices in Chelsea, Sandline was one of a growing number of security firms employing former special forces and intelligence officers – men whose roles had been emasculated since the collapse of Communism. Spicer and his team of quasi-mercenaries helped crush a rebellion in Papua New Guinea in 1997; but that episode ended messily and Spicer was charged with illegal possession of arms. It was this venture which brought Sandline and Spicer to the attention of the Foreign Office.

Hood warned that the story of Sandline's latest foray was almost bound to appear in the press. Before seeing his boss, Hood had been to see John Grant, Cook's principal private secretary. He then wrote a minute to Ann Grant, the head of the Equatorial Africa department. He was advised to choose his words carefully, as memos were likely to be used as evidence in the inquiry. He told Grant he was 'slightly concerned that this has the makings of a sequel to Matrix Churchill' – the flawed case against the Midlands company accused of sending arms to Iraq. Hood then went to see Grant, and her deputy directly responsible for Sierra Leone, Craig Murray, to get himself up to speed.

As Hood ran through the details Cook scratched his head, then took a deep breath. After a year of battering by the media, he had started to rebuild his image; but these allegations, he knew, were potentially embarrassing. He asked for a secretary to go to the residence first thing the next morning, where he dictated a minute to Sir John Kerr, his current permanent secretary. He dictated three points: there would be full cooperation with the customs inquiry; whatever customs decided, he would order an investigation independent of the Foreign Office; and he wanted it known that he would be as open as possible, although he needed advice about what he could and could not say publicly in order not to prejudice the inquiry. On no account would he sign any Public Interest Immunity Certificates – the gagging orders used liberally by the previous administration in its attempt to prevent the truth from being known about government connivance in illegal arms sales to Iraq.

Cook asked to see all the relevant papers on the issue. The following day, 30 April, he telephoned Blair and told the Prime Minister to expect trouble over this apparently obscure issue. Sure enough, Cook's advisers found out on 1 May that the *Sunday Times* was planning to 'break' the story. They prepared a statement in advance after consulting Downing Street officials – Cook and Blair were in Birmingham hosting a dinner for heads of government of the Group of Eight. On Sunday 3 May, as expected, the story was on the front page of the paper, the headline proclaiming: 'Cook snared in arms for coup inquiry'. The paper alleged that Spicer had secretly discussed his mission to export 30 tons of weapons, mainly AK-47 rifles, from Bulgaria to Sierra Leone with Foreign Office officials. The arms arrived in Freetown in February, but were immediately seized by advancing Nigerian forces.

Spicer's involvement had begun seven months earlier. After fleeing to Conakry, Kabbah tried to organize a fighting force that would bring him back to power. He had enough men, but they were not adequately trained and they lacked munitions. His main interlocutors were the Nigerians, but he also pursued other avenues. He was contacted in early July by Rakesh Saxena, a businessman on bail in Canada after being arrested for travelling on the passport of a dead Yugoslav. Saxena and Kabbah struck a deal under which Saxena would provide $10 million in three tranches to equip and train Kamajor tribesmen; in return, Kabbah would protect Saxena's diamond interests on his return to power. Saxena contacted Spicer asking him to prepare an appraisal. Spicer flew to Vancouver; they both went on to Conakry and struck the deal.[2]

The other key figure in this complex web was Peter Penfold, Britain's High Commissioner to Sierra Leone. An old Africa hand, Penfold had served through two coups in Uganda and a war in Nigeria. After a four-year respite as governor of the British Virgin Islands, he had returned to Africa in his mid-fifties. When Nigerian forces started a naval bombardment of Freetown, in an attempt to force the new military leaders to resign, Penfold became an instant folk hero by rescuing British and other western nationals from a burning hotel. He then shepherded them to Conakry. Cook showered him with praise. Penfold's close relations with Kabbah and his strong support for his ousted regime set him apart from the usual pattern of diplomat. He spent his time holed up in a Conakry hotel room doing what he could in the attempt to get his friend back to power. He did not write the usual formal dispatches to base, because there was no telephone or fax line secure enough. On his trips back to London he was keen to further Kabbah's cause. The Foreign Office let him get on with it.

As part of the campaign to support Kabbah, Britain agreed with other Commonwealth states to suspend Sierra Leone's existing government from the club. It was Kabbah, not Koroma, who was invited to the Edinburgh Commonwealth summit in September – on Tony Blair's personal instructions. A week before the summit, the Foreign Office organized a one-day conference on 'restoring Sierra Leone to democracy', at which Tony Lloyd, the minister responsible for Africa, shared a platform with Kabbah. Lloyd said Britain had taken a 'clear moral stand' and warned the junta to 'get out while the possibility of doing so peacefully remains'.

To maintain the pressure, the UN Security Council passed a resolution on 8 October demanding a return to constitutional order in Sierra Leone. Resolution 1132, sponsored by Britain, said in its sixth clause: 'All states shall prevent the sale or supply to Sierra Leone, by their nationals or from their territories, or using their flag vessels or aircraft, of petroleum and petroleum products and arms and related materiel of all types, including weapons and ammunition, military vehicles and equipment, paramilitary equipment and spare parts for the aforementioned, whether or not originating in their territory'. In short, an embargo was applied. The wording of the clause suggested that this ban applied both to the exiled government as well as to the junta in power. The resolution mandated Ecowas, the organization of west African states, and its military section, Ecomog, to monitor the embargo.

It was from that moment that trouble started to brew for the British government. Shortly before Christmas 1997 Kabbah contacted Spicer to ask for further help. According to Sandline, Spicer began a series of meetings to keep government officials and intelligence officers in the UK and US abreast of preparations to ship arms. On 19 January, Spicer went to see Craig Murray at the Equatorial Africa department. According to officials, Spicer put a hypothetical scenario to Murray. He said he had heard that someone was planning to run arms to Sierra Leone and wanted to know what the legal position would be. Murray asked a junior to fetch Security Council resolution 1132, which was then read to Spicer. 'They asked if the reference to Sierra Leone included everyone connected with Sierra Leone, and were advised that was the case,' said an official. Murray wrote a minute about the meeting that went to his boss, Ann Grant.

Enter Lord Avebury, formerly the Liberal MP Eric Lubbock, who combines a long-standing passion for west Africa with a new-found hobby of surfing the Internet. On 23 January, Avebury says, he was surprised to find himself invited to meet Ann Grant and other officials. Shortly after that meeting he found on the Net a report from the Toronto *Globe and Mail*, dated 31 July 1997, claiming the existence of a conspiracy involving mercenaries to overthrow the military junta in Sierra Leone. It named both Saxena and Spicer. On 5 February Avebury wrote to Grant, relating what he had found out about Sandline's involvement in the planned military action. He suggested it would contravene the UN resolution.

Grant informed Avebury that the Foreign Office was 'aware that a deal was in the offing for payment to be made for their services through the acquisition of mineral rights by a third party'. As for the allegation of sanctions busting, she said: 'We have referred the allegation to the appropriate authorities who will examine any evidence to substantiate it, and assess whether any crime may have been committed.'

On 18 February, the Restricted Enforcement Unit held a routine meeting. The committee was led by officials from the trade and industry department, with input from the Foreign Office, Ministry of Defence, Cabinet Office and intelligence organizations. So obscure and low-ranking is the unit that its existence was not well known within Whitehall. Its workload is heavy. Between the general election and that meeting, the REU had looked at 288 referrals from government departments of possible breaches of export licences. One such referral that day was the letter submitted by Avebury. It was one of sixty new intelligence items.

Four days later, on 22 February, Sandline's shipment of arms from Bulgaria reached Lungi airport, near Freetown. It got no further.

Elements of the story first appeared in public on 8 March, when the *Observer* alleged that Kabbah had in effect mortgaged diamond resources in return for arms, involving Sandline in contravention of the UN resolution. It took until 10 March for Foreign Office officials to refer the information to officers at the National Investigation Service at Customs House. At the same time, the Foreign Office minister Baroness Symons was answering a series of questions on Sierra Leone from Lord Avebury. She made no mention of the customs investigation. By coincidence, on that same day Kabbah swept back into Freetown, past huge crowds of cheering supporters. Mounting the podium at the national stadium, he declared: 'People have suffered too long.' Penfold hosted a party at his residence to celebrate Kabbah's restoration.

On 12 March Sierra Leone was the subject of a late-night adjournment debate in the Commons, called ostensibly to congratulate Kabbah on the restoration of democracy in the country. Tony Lloyd took the opportunity to deride the *Observer* piece as 'ill-informed and scurrilous'. At no time, he said, had Penfold 'had any meetings at which Sandline and President Kabbah were present together'. This line of attack had been prepared for him by his officials. They had been contacted by the *Observer* on the eve of publication to verify its report. In the event, the paper did not publish its claim of a triangular meeting. But no one – it transpired later – had thought of telling Lloyd that Penfold had met Spicer tête-à-tête. Nor, far more crucially, was Lloyd told that Customs and Excise had already begun preliminary enquiries into Sandline's activities.

Cook insists that he first heard of Sandline's involvement in Sierra Leone on 28 April. He told friends he could not recall a single intelligence report relating to Sierra Leone arriving on his desk. Following the imposition of the embargo, there were five intelligence reports in total on the general situation in Sierra Leone and west Africa, some of which may have contained brief mentions of Sandline. Of these, three went to the Ministry of Defence and two to the Foreign Office – which receives fifty thousand such reports a year. It was hardly surprising that ministers would not have regarded references to Sierra Leone as important. The order of priority for such reports is first, intelligence on matters affecting the security of Britain; second, matters affecting the economic well-being of Britain; and third, anything else.

The *Sunday Times* article should, and could, have been fended off – a background briefing here, a series of public rebuttals there. But events quickly ran out of control. The knives were being sharpened once again, by Cook's detractors inside the government as well as those outside.

The floodgates opened after an appearance before the foreign affairs select committee by Tony Lloyd on 5 May – two days after the *Sunday Times* piece had appeared and the first day of work following the May bank holiday. It should have been a straightforward meeting, but Donald Anderson, the committee's independently minded chairman, let it be known he would challenge Lloyd on Sierra Leone. Lloyd took the early train to London from his Manchester constituency that morning. He arrived at the committee room ludicrously under prepared. Nobody – from his private office, from the news department or from Cook's own office – had thought of briefing him about the latest details of the affair. Consequently Lloyd got a mauling from an unholy alliance of Labour left-wingers and Conservatives demanding to know which ministers and which officials knew what, and when. His performance was woeful. First he said he had not spoken to Cook ahead of his appearance before the committee; then he said he had, briefly, but had not discussed the meeting. 'I arrived on the six o'clock train from Manchester this morning. This is the first working day since the story appeared in the *Sunday Times*,' Lloyd said, adding: 'I am only aware of Sandline's activities in terms of what has been reported in the newspapers.'

Cook says the first he knew of the select committee's interrogation of Lloyd was when it hit the news that lunchtime. He had spent the holiday weekend working with Madeleine Albright in London, trying to get Yasser Arafat and Benjamin Netanyahu to talk to each other about peace in the Middle East.

On 6 May the shadow Foreign Secretary, Michael Howard – having had the first whiff of blood over the Anne Bullen saga in January – persuaded the Speaker to call Cook to make a statement to the Commons. Cook repeated denials that any Sandline activity had ministerial approval. But he admitted that papers about the customs investigation had gone to Lloyd's office in early April and had been shown to the minister 'for noting' in the middle of that month. 'However, he was not fully informed of the allegations by Sandline of Foreign Office contacts until Friday May 1.' But, by implication, he suggested that officials should not have kept ministers in the dark for as long as they did.

Cook restrained himself from saying anything more. He had been under strict instructions from Customs and Excise not to prejudice their preliminary inquiry. His problems were compounded when the letter originally sent to him the previous week, detailing alleged Foreign Office complicity, was made public on 9 May. Again, Cook felt he could not respond. He says he checked with Alastair Campbell and Peter Mandelson how much he should say, and they agreed on the line. He was then more than a little peeved to read suggestions in newspapers a few days later that he had been too pedantic in his approach. Cook assumed that this had come from Mandelson. But the criticism was not without foundation. It took the Foreign Secretary weeks to get in touch with Ann Grant and the others running the Africa operation. When pressed, he argued that any contact could be seen as being prejudicial to the inquiry – a legalistic justification that cut little ice among the more politically acute civil servants.

Cook was forced back to the dispatch box twice more in the next fortnight to deal with the problem. Lloyd was also questioned further, as was Sir John Kerr. Alastair Campbell worked on the assumption that even the most damaging stories had a shelf life of around a fortnight. But this one ran and ran, even though its details were convoluted in the extreme. It surely did not pass what he called the 'Dog and Duck' test. Was anybody in the pub talking about which ministers knew what about arms sales to an obscure African country? And even if they had known, the good side had won. Blair's aides concluded that the furore had much more to do with hostility to Cook than with getting to the bottom of a possible case of illegal arms sales.

The following Monday, 11 May, Blair stepped into the fray for the first time. Visiting a London college, he gave a classic 'doorstep', in which he answers selected questions to get a brief soundbite on to television news. Blair and Campbell had decided the night before to change tack. Somehow the big picture had been forgotten amid the welter of minutiae about who knew what when. After all, a ruthless dictator had been toppled. As Margaret Thatcher would have said, 'rejoice'. 'Don't let us forget', said Blair, 'that what was happening was that the UN and the UK were both trying to help the democratic regime restore its position from an illegal military coup. They were quite right in trying to do it.' Penfold, he went on, had 'done a superb job in dealing with the consequences of the military coup and working closely with the regime of President Kabbah. That is the background and people can see that a lot of the hoo-ha is overblown.' No one, he added, should be involved in 'deliberately' breaking the embargo.

Blair's rehearsed and deliberately chosen words were significant. They left some of Cook's friends confused, because they believed that, through an excess of zeal, Penfold might have had incautious conversations both with his good friend Kabbah and, later, with Spicer, and might have failed to keep his direct points of contact in London fully aware of those contacts. Penfold had certainly shown extraordinary bravery during the fighting in Freetown, and dedication to the cause of returning Kabbah to power while in Conakry, but – Cook's friends asked – was it helpful for Blair to portray him as a hero? They also wondered whether Blair was not jeopardizing the customs inquiry. The last thing Cook wanted was accusations that he had impeded an independent investigation.

So bemused was Kabbah at the importance attached in Britain to the Sandline allegations that he weighed in on behalf of Blair – or rather on behalf of his friend Penfold. In an open letter, Kabbah said he believed the UN embargo had not been directed against the 'legitimate government of Sierra Leone', described Penfold as 'a source of moral strength' and expressed 'profound gratitude' for the 'principled and ethical position' taken by the UK. 'My government's view on this is that there is no charge to answer.'

Once again, that should have been that. But once again, disaster struck. The normally unflappable Kerr was summoned before the foreign affairs select committee on 14 May. That encounter, which lasted an hour and forty minutes, could not have come closer to outright, and mutual, hostility between mandarin and politician. Kerr had assumed that the MPs would accept the need for propriety – namely, to avoid pre-empting the customs report on whether or not to prosecute Sandline. They refused to do that, and demanded answers. In response, much of the time he stonewalled. Unlike many civil servants sent into the lions' den, Kerr did not try to charm his questioners. Nor was his manner slippery. He was blunt. Sometimes he became angry. But at other points he appeared flummoxed.

Kerr confirmed that Spicer 'regularly rang the Foreign Office in order to report his view on what was going on in Sierra Leone and the Foreign Office quite liked it – didn't put the phone down on this guy because he had previous experience.' Spicer was certainly no pariah to the Africa hands. As to the original tip-off from Lord Avebury, Kerr could not recall accurately the sequence of events or when he first came to hear of it. Asked how far up the ladder the first warning about a possible breach had gone, he said: 'I don't know.' Intriguingly, he admitted he had not previously heard of the existence of the REU. The working levels in the Foreign Office see an awful lot of sanctions busting, he said. He had not told Cook about this particular case because 'it is not the sort of business I would immediately expect the Foreign Secretary to be bothered with. Probably in retrospect he thinks I should have told him. I don't know. It would be quite wrong to create a situation in which everyone wishing to cough in the Foreign Office had to have papers pushed up to the Foreign Secretary and back again.'

But the real drama came when Kerr left the committee with the impression that Lloyd had been briefed about the allegations concerning Sandline. This contradicted categorical assertions by both Cook and Lloyd. That morning, Cook had been preparing a statement to the Commons on the worsening nuclear crisis in India and Pakistan. Downstairs, Nigel Sheinwald had been monitoring Kerr's testimony. As soon as he realized what the permanent secretary had done, he rushed up to Cook's private office. Kerr, meanwhile, had gone over the road to St Margaret's church for a memorial service. On his return he was asked to see Cook in his office. Also present were John Grant, Tony Lloyd, David Mathieson, Andrew Hood and Sheinwald. Cook was furious. He did not say as much, but nor did he disguise his mood. 'John [Kerr] must have found it difficult to internalize the fact that his officials had failed to brief Tony Lloyd properly,' said a colleague of Cook. Kerr was trying to ride two horses at the same time. He was loyal to Cook, and yet he was angry at what he regarded as ministers' willingness to dump on their officials.

Kerr was instructed to send a letter immediately to Donald Anderson clarifying what he had meant. 'Following your committee's hearing this morning, I have checked my memory of the briefing pack prepared for Mr Lloyd's use in the debate on March 12. It mentions reports about a possible deal by President Kabbah for Sandline's services. But it does not mention arms shipments; and, as I thought, it does not say that one such report had already been passed to Customs and Excise.' Even his revised recollection was hardly a ringing endorsement of his ministers.

The strangest aspect of the episode was that none of Cook's advisers had thought of offering any advice to Kerr before his appearance in front of the committee. However ridiculous he might have thought some of the nit-picking, Kerr had not gone into that confrontation armed with the facts.

On 18 May John Morris, the Attorney-General, announced that, after a six-week inquiry, Sandline would not face prosecution. A statement by Customs and Excise said: 'Even though offences may have been committed, the circumstances leading up to the supply affect the fairness of the case to the extent that any prosecution could well fail and would certainly not be in the public interest.' Cook responded immediately by announcing an independent inquiry by Sir Thomas Legg, a QC and retired civil servant. Legg set about interviewing all the main players forthwith. The select committee, for its part, stepped up its parallel inquiry. It summoned Kerr again on 9 June. That session was even more acrimonious, with Kerr repeatedly insisting that he could not answer MPs' questions before Legg's inquiry was complete – until he was warned that he would be in contempt of Parliament if he failed to respond. So he did, disclosing that Liz Symons had been briefed about the customs investigation before answering questions in the Lords on 10 March. Lady Symons was forced to admit as much, though she denied knowingly misleading the upper house.

All this played straight into the hands of Cook's enemies. Newspapers were awash with stories, attributed to so-called Foreign Office insiders, of low morale, chaos and confusion. Cook's aides, and his all-too-small coterie of friends, suspected that the briefings from around Gordon Brown and Peter Mandelson had restarted. The brief truce initiated by Brown at the beginning of the year appeared to be over. Cook did not know why, but suspected that it was no longer in Brown's interests to be seen to be being generous. As for Mandelson, Cook's friends saw a long-term strategy taking shape to prepare the ground for his getting a senior post in the Foreign Office. But Schadenfreude was not universally shared by other government ministers. 'When you think of the kind of stuff in your red box you force yourself to go through with glazed eyes in the early hours of the morning,' said one, 'you think, "There but for the grace of God..."'

Blair and his aides were exasperated at Cook's inability to extricate himself from the morass, at the weakness of the political antennae of civil servants – especially in the Foreign Office – and at the press's fixation with doing down the Foreign Secretary. Blair had wanted Cook's wings clipped in government, but had not thought that his star would wane so far, so fast. Publicly, the Prime Minister defended his colleague at every turn. On Sierra Leone, he was staunch. 'The person in charge of that was the Foreign Secretary and he did it excellently,' Blair said. 'When people say they run an ethical foreign policy, I say Sierra Leone was an example of that.'[3]

But throughout the spring and summer little was done to prevent character assassinations of Cook taking place routinely in the media. Part of the reason was that Blair's aides did not want him to recover too strongly; also, they believed he had brought many of his woes on to himself. 'Robin seemed to be treated differently from other ministers who got into trouble,' said a close friend of Blair. 'It all seemed to come down to his private life. Many people at Westminster find it hard to forgive him. It's been an unfortunate backdrop.'

If anything, the Sandline furore hardened Cook's resolve. Unlike the problems over his private life, which caused him frequent bouts of self-doubt and remorse, this episode just made him angry. His only source of regret was his boast that successful Foreign Secretaries need not finish their paperwork. He was convinced he acted impeccably on being told at the end of April about the Sandline affair. He established an independent inquiry as soon as he could. His actions, he believed, were as far removed from those of the Tories during the arms-to-Iraq affair as was humanly possible. The issue had been taken 'grotesquely out of proportion', his friends said. Throughout the period, as Cook was bombarded with questions about which official had told what to whom on which day, he was having to deal with nuclear proliferation in the Indian subcontinent, Serb attacks on Kosovo, the Middle East conflict, the removal of President Suharto in Indonesia and the release of the British nurses held in Saudi Arabia, as well as the G8 summit and the six-month British presidency of the EU.

In any case, Cook was never convinced that he could have stopped the shipment of arms, as it originated in Bulgaria. It was never a matter of approving an export licence, or sending hapless customs officers to seize material. So – his argument ran – what did it matter whether a particular minister was told in March, April or May? The arms had gone in February. 'It's as if he's having his tea and a plane falls out of the air on him and he's blamed for the plane falling out of the air. He had no part in this, no responsibility for it. At no stage did he contribute to this either through a sin of commission or through any sin of omission,' said a close ally.

There was more than a hint of fatalism about this kind of talk. A year into government, Cook's private office and advisers had developed a bunker mentality. They believed they were the target of a campaign waged in the media with the help not just of Conservatives but also of several camps at high levels in the Labour hierarchy. They were 'convinced that Gordon Brown's zeal to trim the Foreign Office budget was spiteful, and that journalists who attacked Cook were being feted in the Treasury. And yet every time they tried to take the initiative, it seemed to backfire. Cook, by promising with his mission statement to do things differently, had created a rod for his own back.

The Legg Report on the Sandline affair was finally issued on 27 July. It confirmed Cook's view that ministers were not to blame and that the problem lay in a lack of communication between officials in London and the ever-eager High Commissioner, Peter Penfold. Although the Tories accused Cook of a cover-up, he and his ministers survived. His ally Tony Lloyd was retained by Blair in the reshuffle of the same day. There was even better news for Cook when Blair moved Joyce Quin to become Minister for Europe, the job he had always wanted her to have. Doug Henderson, Gordon Brown's man in the Foreign Office, was sent over to the Ministry of Defence.

For many Foreign Office staff, it was still a disappointing year. That department had long been regarded with suspicion by others in Whitehall. Margaret Thatcher's relations with her Foreign Secretaries had invariably been tense. The incumbents during John Major's tenure of the premiership had been paralysed by Conservative wrangling over Europe. This time, they had hoped, it would be different. Cook would recreate the Foreign Office as a strong power base. It was not to be.

Sandline and the other crises of his first year at the Foreign Office had embedded more deeply a contempt Cook had begun to feel long before for the way modern politics was being conducted. He had resigned himself to the fact that any remotely distinctive remark was likely to get him into trouble. Many civil servants in a department not known for self-deprecation were disappointed in him. They had hoped that their Secretary of State would recreate the Foreign Office as a strong power base. His woes had become theirs, and in frustration they were briefing voraciously against their boss. Year one in government had been a classic public relations failure for him. And there were more dark clouds ahead.

17

No Time to Wallow

Some stories, as they say in journalism, have 'legs'; others do not. If this one had been about Gordon Brown or even John Prescott, it would have passed virtually unnoticed. But when Glasgow's *Herald* and the *Daily Mail* suggested in their 1 October editions – in the middle of Labour's 1998 party conference – that Cook would look for a job outside Westminster after the next general election, the reports created a stir. He was said to be Europe-bound, either as a commissioner (President of the Commission was not out of the question, in his mind) or as the Council of Ministers' first foreign affairs supremo. The idea was that he would give up his seat at some point after the election to be in place in Brussels by 2005. It was all very speculative. Cook – as was catalogued in previous chapters – had been pondering his fate throughout his difficult first year. Was Scotland still on the cards? Europe? A peace-keeping role in the Balkans?

However, the problem with these reports is they reinforced a feeling that Cook was only keeping the seat warm until Blair decided on his replacement. Three key figures were said to be in the frame: Jack Straw, Mo Mowlam and Peter Mandelson. Straw was seen as the most likely because, apart from the odd mishap, he had scarcely put a foot wrong as Home Secretary, a job seen as a political graveyard. Mowlam's status as the darling of the party was reinforced at the party conference and, although her popularity was annoying some in Downing Street, there was a sense that if the new political arrangements could finally be settled for Ulster then she could return to London to a top job.

But it was the spectre of Mandelson which most concerned Cook. Blair's right-hand man was enjoying a meteoric rise. Within weeks of becoming Trade and Industry Secretary in July he was exercising powers which went well beyond his department. Europe was his hobby-horse. Travelling up to the annual conference of the CBI, Mandelson decided to try to shift policy on the single currency single-handedly. So, according to people in the Foreign Office, he changed a speech that had already been cleared with Downing Street, proclaiming to business leaders the conditions that would have to be met *when* rather than *if* the UK adopts the Euro. Blair was said to be cross, but so well had Mandelson settled into his job that little was said. Ministers made clear, however, that the line had not changed. Mandelson had also developed close relations with Bodo Hombach, who was playing a similar role for Germany's new Chancellor, Gerhard Schröder. Those two seemed to be running Anglo-German relations. What was most galling for Cook was to be shown cuttings of interviews Mandelson was giving to European newspapers opining on government policy. He was the prize catch of the London diplomatic circuit and was becoming well acquainted with Britain's top envoys abroad. And then there were the off-the-record briefings to friendly journalists, replete with snide comments. The *Independent on Sunday* on 29 November was the most brazen. It talked about how Cook was the only senior government member not interested in Europe, suggesting that he preferred to deal with 'macho crisis situations' like Iraq. Mandelson had, well before the election, planted the suggestion in newspapers of a separate Department for Europe with Cabinet status. That idea was resurfacing. All this left Cook furious. He tried to get his private office to monitor Mandelson's appearances in the foreign media and his appearances at international gatherings. But, given his vulnerability, he kept his anger to a small côterie.

Despite long professing a disdain for the modern-day obsession with presentation and spin, Cook had agreed over the summer to a new media strategy. Central to that was John Williams, a former *Daily Mirror* political editor, who had come in as deputy head of the News Department. In truth, he was running the show and not doing a bad job in turning things around. Compromises were made. Gaynor allowed herself to be put on public display, most noticeably when she accompanied the Royal party to Brunei and Malaysia in September. Stories on board the Royal flight were proferred, suggesting how well the Queen and her Foreign Secretary got on, sharing a common interest in horse racing. Cook also handled the embarrassing arrest of the Opposition leader, Anwar Ibrahim, with more aplomb than his previous state visit to India.

Williams was putting in place a new media strategy. Cook was encouraged to have dinners with newspapers proprietors, editors and commentators, something he had rarely found time for before. Trips to the House of Commons to vote (where he could fraternize with other MPs), meetings of the parliamentary Labour party, even sitting in on prime minister's question time were all put in his diary.

Cook's team tried harder than it had before to build bridges. In December it was agreed that he and Mandelson should have dinner soon after the New Year, but, just as Cook's anxieties were reaching a peak, disaster struck for Mandelson. On 23 December he was forced to resign after admitting he had taken an interest-free loan from Geoffrey Robinson, the Paymaster-General, to pay for his house. Robinson also went. Shortly after, the crisis claimed its third victim in Charlie Whelan. In the space of three weeks, just as his fortunes were reaching their lowest, Cook found that the two people who in the previous years had briefed most against him were gone.

Nevertheless, the dinner with Mandelson went ahead on 5 January, just the two of them in Cook's flat in Carlton Gardens. Mandelson was still in shock after his downfall. Cook was also hardly in the best of spirits: he was steeling himself for the first instalment of the serialization of his ex-wife's memoirs that weekend. Cook told him how he would try to handle it. Mandelson approved of the strategy. They talked also about Europe. They tried to get on. The original plan had been to go out to a London restaurant, but, given the inevitable publicity, they thought better of it. The three-course dinner with wine, prepared by outside caterers, was served with the usual flummery of waiters and butlers. But the food was nothing special. A few days later, though, Cook was shocked to see buried in his red box a bill. Mandelson had, a few days earlier, become just an ordinary citizen. So the host paid up, writing out a cheque, and with a wry smile placed it in his box.

On his way to the dinner, Cook had popped in for a drink at the Treasury with Gordon Brown. He just walked between the two departments, across King George Street. It was a risky strategy as television cameras were still there, waiting for pictures of the departing Whelan. Cook and Brown drank whiskey on their own in the Chancellor's office. It was the latest of several attempts at reconciliation, but, with Whelan gone, this appeared to have more chance of success. Indeed, shortly after, on 27 February, Brown was guest of honour at a dinner to mark Cook's twenty-five years in the Commons. The event took place in the unlikely surroundings of a function room at Livingston Football Club. Brown rose to the occasion, making a warm speech and signing bottles of whiskey. The event had been arranged by Jim Devine and Sue Nye, Brown's political secretary. (She had also persuaded Mandelson and Brown to meet at her house to try to bury their own hatchet. The reconciliation gathered further pace when, in May, the much-postponed dinner 'à quatre' finally took place, Brown accompanied by Sarah Macaulay and Cook by Gaynor.)

Christmas for Cook and Gaynor was dampened by fear of what his ex-wife had in store. He was desperate to prevent a repetition of the Ann Bullen fiasco and resolved that, whatever happened, he would not engage in a slanging match over her book. He tried to find out what was being planned for the first instalment of the serialization, presuming that she might name various ex-partners. What he did not reckon on were her allegations of heavy drinking.

The night it came out, John Williams was at home on 9 January. Cook was in Chevening. They spoke on the phone early that Saturday evening, and Williams agreed on a formula which would give him the title of 'a friend authorized to speak on Cook's behalf'.

They had expected the worst, but they were genuinely shocked at the extent of the vitriol. Williams said he would fax over the full text if Cook wanted, but he did not ask for it. Their conversations were deadpan.

Several MPs volunteered their services, including Harriet Harman. She phoned several newspapers to say that in her time as Cook's deputy in opposition she had not seen anything close to a drink problem. Frank Dobson, the following morning, phoned Cook and went straight on to *The World This Weekend* in his attempt to put the record straight. Cook had spoken the previous evening to Blair, who had just returned from Kuwait and who said on Sunday morning's *Breakfast with Frost*: 'We can either have the news agenda dominated by scandal and gossip and trivia, or we can have it dominated by things that really matter.' He described Cook as 'probably one of the most respected foreign ministers in the rest of Europe that Britain has had for years and years and years.' It was fortunate for Cook that on Monday, as the Commons returned from a Christmas recess which had seen crisis after crisis for the government, he could get straight back in with a statement to the House on developments in Yemen. Government whips saw to it that the Labour benches were full. Cook later remarked to friends: 'For the first time in my career I found myself the recipient of the sympathy vote.'

By the middle of the week the story had lost its momentum. There was a feeling that he was going to survive it. Subsequent instalments, although similarly poisonous, did not cause him particular trouble. There was a sense among Cook's friends that no one had come out of the events well. By trying to humiliate her former husband, Margaret had not done her own reputation any favours. But for him, it was still personally gruelling. He did not talk to her once during the period and could not bring himself to watch or hear her on the media. When it was her turn on *Breakfast with Frost*, he refused to watch. John McCririck telephoned him and sent him a video, but Cook played it only after being assured that Frost had given her a grilling. Gaynor, meanwhile, tried to shut herself off from it all. 'When you saw them together they looked like two victims,' said a friend. 'These were two battered people sticking together.'

There was no little *schadenfreude* when a few weeks later, in an interview with *Woman's Own*, Margaret all but admitted she had overstepped the mark. 'It's a dreadful thing to have done,' she said: 'There's part of me that says perhaps nobody deserves that – to have so much revealed about you, so much that's private and intimate.' As one friend of Cook put it: 'As soon as her book stepped into their bedroom, we felt she was going to lose public sympathy.' Cook was convinced that the more his ex-wife vented her fury in public, the more she demeaned herself. Throughout the saga he had tried to keep good relations with Christopher and Peter. The boys had been acutely embarrassed by the public discussion by their mother of their parents' sex life. The culmination of that was Margaret's assertion in *The Times* (31 May) that life in the bedroom with her new man, appropriately also named Robin, was considerably better than with her old Robin. 'She's got the house, a new partner, her horse, a small fortune, and still she's obsessed with trying to ruin me,' an exasperated Cook told friends, describing her book as 'self-revealing, self-indulgent and self-absorbed'.

Cook had not spoken to Margaret since a phone call in April 1998 shortly after their divorce papers had come through. He reminded her then – when he got wind that she was writing a book – of what he said was a promise she had made not to write about their marriage. Cook's friends say she told him she was writing a book, but would not reveal intimate secrets. A few days after that he received a vituperative letter. That, and the fact that in the book their telephone conversations after the separation had been relayed in great detail, convinced him to keep well away.

Cook's aides capitalized on the adverse reaction to Margaret in the media to try yet another relaunch. Helped by the absence of Mandelson and Whelan, they tried to use Mandelson's demise to pitch Cook as the only remaining disciple of Blair's commitment to constitutional reform. In fact, the subtext of everything Cook was by now supposed to stand for was that he was a true Blairite believer. His dependence on his master was total.

So much mental energy was being expended on that drama that Cook's aides failed to notice what was potentially an even more damaging one. That week a fax arrived at the private office. The address on the top belonged to Ernie Ross, MP. It was a draft of the final report of the Foreign Affairs Committee's investigation into the Sandline affair. It was taken off the fax machine and sat in the in-tray of Andrew Hood for a fortnight; he and others in the office were otherwise engaged. Eventually he read it. After all, it was not the first leak: they had received a copy of a report on human rights just before Christmas and another, on EU enlargement, in mid-January. Hood read it towards the end of the month, gave it to a few other advisers, and then they told Cook of the contents on 1 February. This was eight days before the report was due to be published.

The findings were, not surprisingly, much harder hitting than the Legg report the previous summer. It accused Sir John Kerr of having 'failed in his duty to ministers'. It said Foreign Office officials were guilty of 'at best political naivety, and at worst a *Yes Minister*-like contempt' for their duties. The Committee was angry that Kerr, the Permanent Secretary, and other officials had been reluctant to talk to them while the Legg inquiry was going on. Officials had also denied the MPs access to certain documents and refused permission to interview the head of MI6, Sir David Spedding. On the morning of 9 February the report was to be issued, and newspapers were already full of detailed rebuttals from the Foreign Office. *The Independent* that day had officials saying Cook would stand by Kerr and other officials. 'This inquiry does not appear to have uncovered new facts which would change the central findings of Legg. There was no connivance, no cover up. That's why he feels it would be unfair to officials to put them through the wringer again,' it quoted a Foreign Office source as saying.

Any thoughts that they had put the long-running saga behind them were shattered when, on 23 February, Ross admitted he had leaked the report and resigned from the Committee. Cook tried to play a straight bat. Forced to make a Commons statement the following day, he said: 'I am confident that neither I nor anyone else at the Foreign Office has committed any impropriety on the basis of the draft or broken any of the rules of procedure.' The Committee vowed to investigate the leak. The more powerful Standards and Privileges Committee, with the Speaker's blessing, said it would launch a formal inquiry. Cook looked in serious trouble, but speaking on the *Today* programme on 5 March during a visit to Russia he maintained he had 'nothing to apologize for'. He admitted receiving the three leaked reports, but added: 'Any use of that knowledge would have been an offence, but I made no use of it. There was no action taken upon it.'

There was, though, a further twist to Cook's long-standing feud with the Foreign Affairs Select Committee. On 16 March the *Guardian* reported a plot to smear him, alleging that he had commissioned officials to delve into the private life of Diane Abbott, his scourge over the Sierra Leone affair. She was startled when she received anonymously in her post a Foreign Office memo and four-page dossier. She did not know what to think of it and did not know whether Cook had anything to do with it. It was based on genuine confidential information held on her by the Home Office and details taken from a Filofax stolen from her ten years ago. The memo purported to say that Cook had asked for personal and political background on her culled from the security services. It accused her of having links with 'black extremists' and criminal drug gangs. Cook's friends were staggered.

They quickly denounced the dossier as a 'sinister attempt to set Mr Cook up. Whoever has done it has gone to a lot of trouble and had some degree of acumen, financial backing and access.' The episode reinforced a fear that persisted among some of Cook's friends that his detractors in the Foreign Office and elsewhere still had access to the security services.

As an institution, Cook's Foreign Office was still the butt of constant criticism. Downing Street wanted to know, for example, how the VIP welcome that under the Tory government had been accorded General Augusto Pinochet during his several private trips to the UK was continued without a second's thought under the incoming administration. The contrast between this preferential treatment and the extradition order served on him a few days later at the behest of a Spanish judge was, inevitably, blamed on the Foreign Office. Downing Street was also not particularly happy at feedback it had received from Washington over Cook's role in the air strikes on Iraq the previous December. Cook's otherwise close relations with Madeleine Albright were dented when, according to some officials, he suggested Washington was just a bit too gung ho, adding: 'You know, Madeleine, we're a new generation of politicians that doesn't believe in that kind of thing.'

But Cook received unqualified praise for resolving two seemingly intractable diplomatic problems. In September 1998, after secret negotiations with the Iranian Foreign Minister, Kamal Kharazzi, the Iranian government announced that it would do nothing to threaten the life of novelist Salman Rushdie. The *fatwah* was, in effect, over.

On 5 April 1999 Cook achieved arguably his biggest single diplomatic success. Abdul Basset al-Megrahi and Lamen Khalifa Fhimah, indicted for the bombing of Pan Am flight 103 over Lockerbie on 21 December 1988, in which 270 people died, arrived at Her Majesty's Prison Zeist to be committed for trial on charges of murder and conspiracy. Cook had originally floated the idea of a trial under Scottish judges but taking place in the Netherlands to Madeleine Abright when she visited him at Chevening over the Christmas holidays in 1997. In August the following year Britain and the US reversed their long-standing refusal to hold a trial outside their jurisdiction. A 100-acre strip of land was found at Camp Zeist, a disused US air base near Utrecht, and the whole area was temporarily redesignated as subject to Scottish law. Nevertheless, it took more than six months of cajoling of General Muammar Gaddafi – much of it by President Nelson Mandela – to persuade him to accept the deal.

As the two suspects were surrendered at Tripoli airport under UN supervision, Cook hailed it 'a creative and imaginative solution'. He won good press for his efforts, but not as good as he had hoped. Still, by then, he had a far bigger crisis on his hands.

Cook never had much time for what he would privately call fascist warlords. He would grimace when having to conduct diplomacy with many a leader in the Balkans. Slobodan Milosevic was one. The conflict in the former Yugoslavia was a constant headache for the Foreign Office, each crisis ebbing and flowing. By the start of 1999 the rebellion by the Kosovo Liberation Army was intensifying, as were the reprisals of the Yugoslav army and paramilitary police, mainly against civilians. It was when forty-five ethnic Albanians were gunned down in the village of Recak that the story returned to the front pages. Cook was instrumental in convening a meeting of the six-nation Contact Group – the USA, Russia, Britain, France, Germany and Italy – in London on 22 January to discuss developments.

At that point Western frustration was directed at both sides. In spite of Russian objections, Nato stepped up talk of air strikes. But given the amount of times it had cried wolf in previous conflicts, there was little reason to believe that this time the alliance meant business.

Both sides were summoned to negotiations at the château of Rambouillet, south of Paris, on 6 February. The plan they were being asked to work on called for much greater autonomy for the province, including its own government and police. Both sides would have to disarm almost completely, but Serbia would retain sovereignty, and Kosovo's status would be reviewed after three years. Cook went to Belgrade for one final go at Milosevic – a task he did not relish – and came back dismayed by the experience. He had met Milosevic many times before, but he found this mission particularly chilling. He saw the Serbian president as emotionally dead, a man who spoke and thought only in historical clichés. Intelligence reports that came through shortly after said Milosevic had spent the rest of the day drunk and depressed. (There was an irony that, during the war, Cook was relying on the security services as never before, those very agencies whose hegemony and secrecy he challenged so hard in his *New Statesmen* articles of the 1970s.) Crucially, according to the intelligence reports, no matter how blunt Cook was – and he was blunt – Milosevic remained convinced Nato was bluffing.

Even before the talks had begun, Madeleine Abright was warning darkly of air strikes. 'Force is the only language he [Milosevic] appears to understand,' she said. Her approach troubled the British and French, whose officials privately dubbed her 'Madame Bomber', but Cook was more circumspect. 'If we are to take military action, military action must be in support of a clear political demand and a clear political process. Neither side is going to win this war,' he said on the BBC *Today* programme. A British official suggested that Cook was trying to bridge the gung-ho approach of Albright and the extreme caution of Hubert Vedrine, the French Foreign Minister and co-host of the talks.

The deadline of 20 February came and went with the Serbs refusing to countenance the deployment of 28,000 Nato troops into Kosovo to monitor any deal. The talks were extended for another week, but it was around this time that Cook reluctantly resigned himself to the prospect of conflict. The talks then went on for another week, but, while there were signs that the Kosovar Albanians might sign up, Serb intransigence increased.

On 6 March the Kosovar Albanians asked for a week's grace to go home and consult their people. They agreed to report back for more talks in Paris on the 15th. They came back, and signed. Milosevic sent word that the Serbs would not. Five days later the 1,200 international monitors in Kosovo were withdrawn and Western embassies began to close. By this point Cook was convinced that military action was only a matter of time. The air strikes on Iraq the previous December had not been difficult to reconcile with his conscience, especially as they were always going to be limited. But, for a peace campaigner such as himself, being responsible for the first allied war in Europe since 1945 required considerable emotional and intellectual justification.

On Monday 22 March Blair gathered a small group of ministers and it was decided that the bombing would begin that week. The following day Blair, Cook and Brown left for Berlin, for a special EU summit to discuss Agenda 2000 – a new budget – knowing that this would be unlike any other summit. That night Javier Solana, the Nato Secretary General, gave formal authorization for air strikes, which began twenty-four hours later. Cook returned to London shortly after midnight to prepare a speech for an emergency Commons debate on the start of hostilities. The Left was split; a minority went down the diplomacy-at-all-costs route. The government knew that to maintain a broad consensus it would have to ensure that Milosevic was portrayed as a fascist leader of the 1930s. Cook told MPs there had been no alternative to air strikes. 'Not to have acted, when we knew the atrocities that were being committed, would have been to make ourselves complicit in their repression.'

Cook and George Robertson became the mainstays alongside Blair. Downing Street preferred, where possible, to use Robertson at press conferences and in media interviews – he was seen as more acceptable to the Americans – but such was the scale of the conflict that Cook found himself in the forefront of the public relations and diplomatic offensives. Blair, Robertson, Cook and General Sir Michael Guthrie, the chief of the Joint Defence Staff, either met or spoke by conference call every day. Cook also talked each day with his Western counterparts – Albright, Vedrine, Joschka Fischer of Germany and Italy's Lamberto Dini.

Sometimes Cook joined Robertson at the Ministry of Defence daily briefing. When he did so, the two would meet Guthrie and military and intelligence chiefs in the ministry's basement office at 8.30. Cook would go off to the MoD canteen with Williams and, over a bowl of cereal, they would go over his lines.

As the war progressed and the humanitarian disaster for the Kosovar Albanians unfolded, that was the line Blair ordered to be taken. The blanket moral justification for the war was used to offset criticism of strategy and tactics. Cook, like the others, could not explain why the allies had failed to appreciate the sheer tenacity (and brutality) of Milosevic's regime. The worse the killings and enforced refugee exodus became, the more embroiled the West became, but also the more Western politicians were able to play the ethical card.

For Cook, as for Blair and the other Nato protagonists, the mistaken attacks on civilian targets were deeply troubling. At one point Cook suggested to Albright that she urge the US military to tighten up procedures. But none of this altered his personal conviction that this was a moral war the closest parallel to which was the Spanish Civil War in the 1930s. Cook was adamant that despite all his anti-Vietnam and pro-CND demonstrations of his early career, he had never been a pacifist. 'I'm entirely comfortable fighting fascism in Serbia,' he would say.

While he was on the ropes, Cook had taken to disavowing his original mission statement, even to the point of denying his use of the term 'ethical foreign policy'. On that he was semantically correct, but he had early on in his term of office been happy to associate himself with the idea. Now it was set to return and was retrospectively given a new military interpretation – in effect, armed action was a legitimate means of imposing Western liberal values on those who violated democracy.

Cook knew he would not be thanked for Blair's conversion to a more distinct and controversial foreign policy. Throughout the conflict he remained wary, telling friends that, if it went badly, he would be the one to be sacrificed. He needed no reminding that the key decisions were being made in Downing Street with himself brought in as and when required. He kept his head down, worked assiduously and tried to avoid adverse publicity. This meant, to Gaynor's considerable annoyance, no time off. They had been supposed to go to Seville that Easter, but had to settle for Chevening instead. Similarly, he avoided the Grand National, although he did make sure he had no diplomatic phone calls to make so that he could watch the race on television.

Cook's second year in office was just as traumatic as his first, but, at the end of it all, he felt he was in a stronger position than at any point since his nightmare began with separation from Margaret in August 1997. During his darkest days and weeks Cook thought only of survival. Cook tried to build bridges, to make new allies, just to be thought of as reliable. His circle of friends in politics remained perilously small. He was deprived of one of his closest when Derek Fatchett – regarded as a particularly good foreign office minister – died suddenly of a heart attack. He was replaced by Geoff Hoon, very much a Blairite. On domestic policy Cook's influence continued to wane. Electoral reform for Westminster, of which he was a passionate supporter, was put on the back burner. His role in the Scottish elections was negligible, convincing him that, whatever he might have thought in the first year of the government, his chances of replacing Donald Dewar as first minister were minimal. Dewar's successor would almost certainly come from within the Scottish parliament.

The war had certainly given Cook a platform to display his diplomatic skills to a world audience, and he had come out of it reasonably well. The Left had been split, but Cook's anti-fascist militarism was certainly the majority view. Within government, the briefings against him continued. Less-than-flattering portrayals continued to seep out of Number 10, but none of them had the vehemence or the frequency of the earlier attacks. Asked whether the resignations of Mandelson and Whelan had anything to do with this, Cook would just smile and point out that he had outlasted them. He had long given up ambitions of usurping Gordon Brown at the Treasury or of ever getting Blair's job. What he wanted was to stay where he was for as long as he could. He still remembered the goal he had expressed to the Foreign Affairs Committee back in January 1998 to become the longest serving Foreign Secretary of modern times. It was entirely out of his hands, though. Blair had, in war as in peace, got Cook just where he wanted him, as his now ever-loyal executor of a foreign policy made in Downing Street.

Notes

Chapter 1

1 Royal High School, Edinburgh, *Schola Regia* (annual report), 1963.
2 John Whitworth, *Poor Butterflies*, London, Secker & Warburg, 1982, pp. 51–2.

Chapter 3

1 Letter to *Guardian* and *Scotsman*, 16 September 1997.

Chapter 4

1 *Hansard*, House of Commons, 29 October 1974.
2 *New Statesman*, 10 December 1976.
3 Andrew Marr, *The Battle for Scotland*, Penguin, 1992, p. 122.
4 *The Red Paper on Scotland*, Edinburgh University Students Publication Board, 1975.
5 Quoted in Marr, *The Battle for Scotland*, p. 157.

Chapter 5

1 *Hansard*, House of Commons, 22 July 1980.

2 *Herald*, 9 May 1996.
3 *Herald*, 20 May 1996.
4 Letter to the *Scotsman*, 10 November 1981.
5 *Tribune*, 11 June 1981.
6 *Financial Times*, 1 November 1983.
7 *Edinburgh Evening News*, 29 January 1985.
8 *Sunday Telegraph*, 30 March 1997.
9 *Guardian*, 21 January 1985.
10 *Scotsman*, 1 December 1984.
11 *Sunday Times*, 5 February 1989.
12 *Guardian*, 24 June 1987.

Chapter 6

1 *Scotsman*, 4 October 1988.
2 Colin Brown, *Fighting Talk: The Biography of John Prescott*, London, Simon & Schuster, 1997, p. 182.
3 *Guardian*, 8 February 1988.
4 *Scotsman*, 22 August 1988.
5 *Guardian*, 3 October 1990.
6 *Hansard*, House of Commons, 13 April 1988.
7 Paul Routledge, *Gordon Brown, the Biography*, London, Simon & Schuster, 1998, p. 328.

8 *Sunday Times*, 5 February 1989.

9 *Newsnight*, BBC2, 9 March 1995.

10 Nicholas Jones, *Soundbites and Spin Doctors: How Politicians Manipulate the Media – and Vice Versa*, London, Cassell, 1995, p. 68.

11 *Independent on Sunday*, 22 November 1992.

12 Bryan Gould, *Goodbye To All That*, London, Macmillan, 1995, pp. 225–6.

13 *The Wilderness Years*, BBC2, 18 December 1995.

14 Nicholas Jones, *Election 92*, London, BBC Books, 1992.

15 *The Wilderness Years*, BBC2, 18 December 1995.

Chapter 7

1 *Hansard*, House of Commons, 19 October 1992.

2 *Independent on Sunday*, 22 November 1992.

3 *Guardian*, 9 December 1993.

4 John Rentoul, *Tony Blair*, Little, Brown, London, 1995, p. 377.

Chapter 8

1 *The Times*, 10 October 1994.

2 *Scotsman*, 23 November 1995.

3 *Observer*, 19 November 1995.

4 *Herald*, 20 May 1996.

5 *Westminster Live*, BBC2, 16 May 1996.

6 *Hansard*, House of Commons, 15 February 1996.

7 Ibid., 26 February 1996.

8 *Herald*, 20 May 1996.

Chapter 9

1 *Herald*, 20 May 1996.

2 *Daily Telegraph*, 26 June 1996.

3 *Sunday Times*, 29 September 1996.

4 *Guardian*, 14 October 1996.

5 Ibid., 7 March 1997.

6 *On the Record*, BBC1, 27 October 1996.

7 *Financial Times*, 29 October 1996.

8 Nicholas Jones, *Campaign 1997: How the General Election Was Won and Lost*, London, Indigo, 1997.

9 *Independent*, 11 March 1997.

10 *This Morning*, ITV, 6 March 1997.

11 *Sunday Telegraph*, 30 March 1997.

12 *Scotsman*, 7 November 1997.

13 *Financial Times*, 19 April 1997.

14 *The Times*, 10 April 1997.

15 *Guardian*, 21 April 1997.

16 *Independent*, 22 April 1997.

Chapter 10

1 *How to be Foreign Secretary*, BBC2, 4 January 1998.

2 Ibid.

3 *Guardian*, 28 June 1997.

4 *Financial Times*, 8 May 1997.

5 *Independent*, 10 May 1997.

6 *How to be Foreign Secretary*, BBC2, 4 January 1998.

Chapter 11

1 *Financial Times*, 14 February 1997.

2 *The Military Balance 1997/98*, London, International Institute for Strategic Studies, 1997.

3 *Guidelines for Assessing Arms Export Licence Applications*, London, Saferworld, 15 June 1997.

4 Parliamentary written answer, *Hansard*, House of Commons, 28 July 1997.

5 *How to be Foreign Secretary*, BBC2, 4 January 1998.

6 *Financial Times*, 2 August 1997.

7 'Taking the High Road', *Analysis*, BBC Radio 4, 2 October 1997.

8 *How to be Foreign Secretary*, BBC2, 4 January 1998.

Chapter 12

1 *Observer*, 26 April 1998.

Chapter 13

1 *Independent on Sunday*, 31 August 1997.
2 *Financial Times*, 16 September 1997.
3 *Independent*, 30 August 1997.
4 *Financial Times*, 3 October 1997.
5 *Independent*, 11 September 1997.
6 *Daily Mail*, 18 October 1997.
7 *The Times*, 27 September 1997.
8 *Hansard*, House of Commons, 28 October 1997.
9 *Daily Telegraph*, 14 November 1997.
10 *Financial Times*, 17 December 1997.

Chapter 14

1 *Scotsman*, 24 November 1995.
2 *Guardian*, 28 June 1997.
3 *Scotland on Sunday*, 4 January 1998.
4 *Daily Telegraph*, 12 January 1998.
5 *Independent on Sunday*, 1 February 1998.
6 *Daily Mail*, 29 January 1998.
7 *Herald*, 11 October 1997.
8 *Hansard*, House of Commons, 28 January 1998.
9 *Sunday Telegraph*, 1 February 1998.
10 *Hansard*, House of Commons, 4 February 1998.

Chapter 15

1 *New Statesman*, 6 March 1998.
2 *Hansard*, House of Commons, 17 February 1998.
3 *Daily Telegraph*, 1 October 1997.
4 *Edinburgh Evening News*, 21 February 1998.
5 Joint press release, Saferworld/Basics/Oxfam/ Amnesty International, 13 February 1998.
6 *Independent*, 17 February 1998; *The Times*, 17 February 1998.
7 Ministry of Defence press release, 5 March 1998.
8 *Financial Times*, 11 November 1997.
9 *New Statesman*, 6 March 1998.
10 *Guardian*, 1 April 1998.
11 *The Times*, 30 March 1998.
12 *New Statesman*, 6 March 1998.
13 Ibid.
14 *Daily Telegraph*, 11 March 1998.
15 'Taking the High Road', *Analysis*, BBC Radio 4, 2 October 1997.
16 *The Times*, 18 March 1998.
17 Ibid.
18 Ibid.
19 *Newsnight*, BBC2, 9 March 1995.

Chapter 16

1 *How to be Foreign Secretary*, BBC2, 4 January 1998.
2 *Sunday Times*, 3 May 1998.
3 *GMTV*, 17 May 1998.

Bibliography

Paul Anderson and Nyta Mann, *Safety First*, London, Granta, 1997

Colin Brown, *Fighting Talk: The Biography of John Prescott*, London, Simon & Schuster, 1997

Gordon Brown, *The Red Paper on Scotland*, Edinburgh, Edinburgh University Student Publications Board, 1975

Gordon Brown and Robin Cook, *Scotland: The Real Divide*, Edinburgh, Mainstream, 1983

Gordon Brown and James Naughtie, *John Smith: Life and Soul of the Party*, Edinburgh, Mainstream, 1994

David Butler and Dennis Kavanagh, *The British General Election of 1983*, London, Macmillan, 1984

Margaret Cook, *A Slight and Delicate Creature*, London, Weidenfeld, 1999

Derek Draper, *Blair's 100 Days*, London, Faber, 1997

Michael Foot, *Aneurin Bevan*, repr. London, Victor Gollancz, 1997

Bryan Gould, *Goodbye To All That*, London, Macmillan, 1995

Robert Harris, *The Making of Neil Kinnock*, London, Faber, 1984

Peter Hennessy, *The Hidden Wiring: Unearthing the British Constitution*, London, Victor Gollancz, 1995

Peter Hennessy, *Whitehall*, London, Fontana, 1990

Colin Hughes and Patrick Wintour, *Labour Rebuilt: The New Model Party*, London, Fourth Estate, 1990

Will Hutton, *The State We're In*, London, Jonathan Cape, 1995

Mervyn Jones, *Michael Foot*, London, Victor Gollancz, 1994

Nicholas Jones, *Election '92*, London, BBC Books, 1992

Nicholas Jones, *Soundbites and Spin Doctors: How Politicians Manipulate the Media – and Vice Versa*, London, Cassell, 1995

Nicholas Jones, *Campaign 1997: How the General Election was Won and Lost*, London, Indigo, 1997

Nicholas Jones, *Sultans of Spin: The Media and the New Labour Government*, London, Victor Gollancz, 1999

Gerald Kaufman, *How to be a Minister*, London, Faber, repr. 1997

David Leigh and Ed Vulliamy, *Sleaze: The Corruption of Parliament*, London, Fourth Estate, 1997

Linda McDougall, *Westminster Women*, London, Vintage, 1998

Andy McSmith, *Faces of Labour: The Inside Story*, London, Verso, 1996

Andy McSmith, *John Smith: A Life, 1938–1994*, London, Mandarin, 1994

Andrew Marr, *The Battle for Scotland*, London, Penguin, 1992

Andrew Marr, *Ruling Britannia: The Failure and Future of British Democracy*, London, Michael Joseph, 1995

Ben Pimlott, *Harold Wilson*, London, HarperCollins, 1992

John Rentoul, *Tony Blair*, London, Little, Brown, 1995

Paul Routledge, *Gordon Brown: The Biography*, London, Simon & Schuster, 1998

Jon Sopel, *Tony Blair: The Moderniser*, London, Michael Joseph, 1995

Index